Springer Series: FOCUS ON WOMEN

Violet Franks, Ph.D., Series Editor
Confronting the major psychological, medical, and social issues of today and tomorrow. *Focus on Women* provides a wide range of books on the changing concerns of women.

Judith Frankel, PhD, is a developmental psychologist who has been teaching at the University of Cincinnati, College of Education, since 1969. She received her PhD degree from Ohio State University in 1958 and wrote her dissertation on the effects of maternal employment on preschool children's behavior.

Dr. Frankel studied family therapy for 3 years under Dr. Marian Lindblad Goldberg, at the Department of Psychiatry of the University of Cincinnati, and uses that knowledge in her teaching and research. Her particular interest is adult relationships and the relationships of all family members to each other and the family system.

THE EMPLOYED MOTHER AND THE FAMILY CONTEXT

Judith Frankel, PhD
Editor

 Springer Publishing Company • New York

Springer Publishing Company, Inc.
536 Broadway
New York, NY 10012-3955

93 94 95 96 97 / 5 4 3 2 1

Library of Congress Cataloging-in-Publication Data

The Employed mother and the family context / Judith Frankel, editor.
        p.   cm. – – (Focus on women series ; v. 14)
     Includes bibliographical references and index.
     ISBN 0–8261–7950–9
     1. Working mothers – – United States.   2. Work and family – – United
States.   I. Frankel, Judith.   II. Series: Springer series, focus on
women ; v. 14.
HQ759.48.E48   1993
306.87 – – dc20   92–44886
                                                                                             CIP

Printed in the United States of America

To Bob, my inspiration

Contents

Contributors

Nancy E. Barbour, Ph.D.
Kent State University

Mary Benin, Ph.D.
Arizona State University

Felecia M. Briscoe, M.A.
University of Cincinnati

Donald L. Bubenzer, Ph.D.
Kent State University

Yinong Chong, M.A.
Arizona State University

Scott Coltrane, Ph.D.
University of California,
Riverside

Claire Etaugh, Ph.D.
Bradley University

Louise F. Fitzgerald, Ph.D.
University of Illinois,
Urbana-Champaign

Nancy L. Galambos, Ph.D.
University of Victoria

Jennifer L. Kerpelman, M.S.
Auburn University

Susan McCarty, M.A.
Great Oaks Joint Vocational
School District

Vonnie C. McLoyd, Ph.D.
University of Michigan

Patricia O'Reilly, Ph.D.
University of Cincinnati

Maureen Perry-Jenkins, Ph.D.
University of Illinois,
Urbana-Champaign

Joe F. Pittman, Ph.D.
Auburn University

Rhonda A. Richardson, Ph.D.
Kent State University

Heather A. Sears, M.A.
University of Victoria

Dolores A. Stegelin, Ph.D.
University of Cincinnati

Elsa O. Valdez, Ph.D.
Loyola Marymount University

Lauren M. Weitzman, Ph.D.
Virginia Commonwealth
University

Foreword

Writing the foreword to *The Employed Mother and the Family Context* has felt a little like attending a family reunion! While I was a graduate student at the University of Cincinnati I had the opportunity to take a course with Judith Frankel on family relations. It was through participating in this course that I became familiar with the research on employed mothers. Judith's mentoring of me and my career in women's career development led me to collaborate with her on research on employed mothers. I translated her mentoring skills to my own mentoring of graduate students, especially Ruth Anderson-Kulman, with whom I published an article on employed mothers and day care in 1986. To this day, in teaching courses on the psychology of women, gender, and power in the workplace—in which I use my book *The Psychology of Women* (Paludi, 1992)—and an introduction to women's studies, I incorporate the information I learned from Judith's work on employed women and the family. I am pleased to have an opportunity to thank her publicly in this foreword for introducing me to this field of study. And I am happy to have the opportunity to review the material again.

Judith's mentoring also contributed to my involvement in professional networks of researchers studying employed mothers and the family context. I was thus able to meet other contributors to this volume, especially Claire Etaugh, Louise Fitzgerald, Lauren Weitzman, Nancy Barbou, Rhonda Richardson, and Patricia O'Reilly. The work of these colleagues has contributed to my own research, teaching, and advocacy in women's career development. From reading this volume I also have an opportunity to meet new "family" members: Susan McCarty, Heather Sears, Nancy Galambos, Joe Pittman, Jennifer Kerpelman, Elsa Valdez, Scott Coltrane, Vonnie McLoyd, Mary Benin, Maureen Perry-Jenkins,

Donald Bubenzer, Yinong Chong, Dolores Stegelin, and Felecia Briscoe. It is a pleasure to have all of this work collected in one volume.

The issues raised in *The Employed Mother and the Family Context* relate to the powerful motherhood mandate that exists in a variety of cultures. According to this mandate, articulated by Nancy Felipe Russo (1976), women should bear children and be primarily responsible for their care. Psychologists made popular this belief in their insistence on mothers remaining at home with their children to ensure children's optimal development. The majority of women with children, however, work outside the home. The most recent rate of maternal employment for two-parent families with school-age children is 71% (Hoffman, 1989). In 1987, 53% of women with children aged 1 year and under were in the labor force. This rate is more than double the rate of 24% in 1970 (U.S. Bureau of Labor Statistics, 1987). Black women with school-age children are more likely to be employed than white or Hispanic women with children (National Commission, 1986).

What is made clear by the contributors to this volume is that employed mothers constitute a heterogeneous group of women who differ on several variables: age, relationship status (e.g., single, divorced, widowed, in lesbian relationships, married), stage in the family life cycle (e.g., number and ages of children), and a variety of socioeconomic factors. The reasons for women working outside the home are related primarily to financial needs and personal self-actualization (Scarr, Phillips, & McCartney, 1989). As a result of the decline in family income from 1973 to 1988, families must have two incomes to support them at a level previously achieved by one wage earner. Single, widowed, and divorced women with children *must* work to avoid poverty.

Employed women with children have also reported wanting to work for the social support, adult companionship, and social networks offered by workplaces (Repetti, Matthews, & Waldron, 1989). Lois Hoffman (1989) described employment for mothers as a morale boost and a buffer against stress from family roles. In addition, research on the impact of maternal employment on children has generally found no negative effects on the children of employed mothers (Hoffman, 1989). Maternal employment appears to have a positive influence on adolescents, particularly daughters. They are more likely to be self-confident, to achieve better grades in school, and to pursue careers themselves.

By 1995 women will comprise two thirds of all new employees (Johnston, 1987). Eighty percent of women in their childbearing years are expected to have children during their career path. Despite this statistic, as well as the research that indicates the positive effects of maternal employment and quality day care on children, the United States is still ambivalent about employed mothers and day care. As Sandra Scarr, Deborah Phillips, and Kathleen McCartney (1989) stated:

> . . . the lack of high-quality, affordable child care has more impact on working mothers than on any others. Not only is there a critical shortage of high-quality child care in this country, but there also is such ambivalence about providing child care that we have a shameful national dilemma: More than 50% of American mothers of infants and preschool children are now in the labor force and require child care services, but there is no coherent national policy on parental leaves or on child care services for working parents (p. 1404).

This "national dilemma" is unique to the United States. Women in France have a job-protected leave of 6 weeks before childbirth. Women in Italy have a 6-month job-protected leave, paid at a flat rate that is equal to the average income for women. They also have available to them an unpaid job-protected leave for 1 year following this 6-month period. In Sweden parents have the right to a leave following the birth of children that is paid at 90% of one parent's salary for 9 months. This is followed by a fixed minimum benefit for an additional 3 months. Parents also have the option of taking an unpaid but job-protected leave until their child is 18 months old. They may also work a 6-hour day until their child is 8 years old. In addition, Spain, Italy, France, and all of the Eastern European countries have more than half of the infants, toddlers, and preschool children in subsidized child care because their mothers are employed. As is reflected in the chapters in this volume, in the United States, policies on child care and maternal leave reflect myths about *all* women's "personalities" and career goals as well as what is involved in caring for infants.

What are the social policy applications of this research on employed mothers and day care? On a societal level, child care costs can be subsidized by society. In addition, areas of conflict endorsed by employed mothers indicate that managing the household, home cleaning, and taking care of sick children are major sources of stress (Anderson-Kulman & Paludi, 1986). Other problems include issues with time management, stress, and fatigue. The lack of time appears to be most accentuated in areas that are self-related: community activities, reading, hobbies, physical fitness. Consequently, women must not do it alone. Women need help from other women and from men. Family chores and child-rearing responsibilities are not "women's work." Traditional occupational policies reflect the separation of family and work life and the societal expectation that mothers remain at home to care for their children. There is thus an incompatibility between the workplace and family demands as well as the relative lack of provisions to ease women's integration of these roles. These conditions may be expected to produce greater potential stress and conflict among employed mothers, who hold the primary responsibility for child rearing and child care. Many businesses have adopted family-oriented policies such as job sharing, flexible work hours, and employer-sponsored day care as an employee benefit. These organizations have found positive ramifications for the businesses as well as for parents, including lower absenteeism, higher morale, positive publicity, lower rate of turnover, child care hours that conform to work hours, and access to quality infant and child care (Anderson-Kulman & Paludi, 1986).

Finally, women's salaries need to be addressed. In the United States, employed women earn less than 70% of men's wages. Black women earn less money than do women or men of any other ethnic group. Black women earn substantially less than do black men (Betz, 1993; Smith, 1983; U.S. Bureau of Labor Statistics, 1987). Like white women, black women are concentrated in low-paying, stereotypic "feminine" jobs such as domestic and service jobs (U.S. Bureau of Labor Statistics, 1987). The average employed woman must work nearly 8-1/2 days to earn as much as the average employed man earns in 5 days! Disparity between women's and men's incomes still exists when job category, education, and experience are taken into account. This salary disparity is in large part due to the cultural belief that men should earn more than women because men are the primary "breadwinners" of the family.

The Employed Mother and the Family Context is a much-needed volume for students in undergraduate and graduate training programs as well as for researchers and advocates. I congratulate the contributors to this volume for sharing their research and perspectives.

MICHELE A. PALUDI, PhD
Coordinator, Women's Studies Program
Professor of Psychology
Hunter College, City University of New York

References

Anderson-Kulman, R., & Paludi, M. A. (1986). Working mothers and the family context: Predicting positive coping. *Journal of Vocational Behavior, 28,* 241–253.

Betz, N. (1993). Career development. In F. L. Denmark & M. A. Paludi (Eds.), *Handbook on the psychology of women.* Westport, CT: Greenwood.

Hoffman, L. W. (1989). Effects of maternal employment in the two-parent family. *American Psychologist, 44,* 283–292.

Johnston, W. B. (1987). *Workforce 2000: Work and workers for the 21st century.* Indianapolis, IN: Hudson Institute.

Paludi, M. A. (1992). *The psychology of women.* Dubuque, IA: Wm. C. Brown.

Repetti, R. L., Matthews, K. A., & Waldron, I. (1989). Effects of paid employment on women's mental and physical health. *American Psychologist, 44,* 1394–1401.

Russo, N. F. (1976). The motherhood mandate. *Journal of Social Issues, 32,* 143–153.

Scarr, S., Phillips, D., & McCartney, K. (1989). Working mothers and their families. *American Psychologist, 44,* 1402–1409.

Smith, E. (1983). Issues in racial minorities' career behavior. In W. Walsh & S. Osipow (Eds.), *Handbook of vocational psychology.* Hillsdale, NJ: Erlbaum.

Preface

This book is a treat from me to myself. It is a coming of full circle for me. It revisits the topic of my dissertation—but against a very different backdrop. Today maternal employment is not only accepted, it is expected; not so in 1958 when I wrote my dissertation on working mothers. At that time the topic was a new one, of little academic interest. There was limited literature to be searched, few studies to be dealt with, and not much popular interest. Even the term "working mother," which made sense in 1958, sounds out of place today. Mothers have always worked. How could there be a "nonworking mother"? By its very definition motherhood is labor-intensive, with little time off for good behavior. If mothers worked in the home, however, they were considered nonworking mothers. Although some folks today still think that mothers not employed outside the home watch soaps all day, most people are aware of the working status of *all* mothers. I am therefore more comfortable calling mothers who work for pay outside the home "employed mothers."

There were mothers working outside the home for many years, whatever label we used to describe them. In the past, and the not-so-distant past at that, it was assumed that employed mothers held jobs out of either economic necessity or personal perversity. I know. When strangers—and occasionally even those closer to me—found out that I planned to follow a career *and* rear children, their first thought was one of pity that my husband could not support me. When they discovered that he could, their next comment had to do with "selfishness" in some form on my part and a lack of appropriate priorities. Then when they discovered that he valued my employment and shared in the child rearing and housekeeping, he was enshrined as a saint. I often heard remarks such as "Your husband lets you work?" "Your husband helps with the children and house?"

"What a remarkable man!" Indeed he was, but for being ahead of his time, for recognizing that he was not the gatekeeper of my personal decisions, for recognizing that he was the father of our children in the fullest sense of the word, for recognizing that we shared responsibility for domestic tasks, and for recognizing that he was not mother's helper at home and I his helpmate in the outside world.

The fact that I was challenged on my choice of combining career and home made sense in the 1958 social milieu. So did my choice of dissertation topic, "The Security Status of Young Children Whose Mothers Are Employed." I found that maternal employment does not have a direct negative effect on the child, on the mother or father, or on anyone in the family. There were many factors to be considered, and maternal employment was not a causative variable of joy or misery in and of itself. Well, that was very nice to know. Nicer still was the support given by other studies in the ensuing years, studies that showed that what was important for the child was a contented mother, rather than an employed or nonemployed mother.

Times have changed since 1958. In the 1990s more mothers are employed than are not. The progression of attitudes toward maternal employment is a fascinating one and raises all kinds of questions, which are addressed in this book. How has this revolution in family roles, in behavior, and in expectations about maternal employment unfolded? What are the outcomes? My husband's behavior in 1958 was exceptional; is it still exceptional today? Is there really a revolution in family roles, or have women just been given the go-ahead to add a new role to their already busy lives? Is there support—from business, government, extended family, and friends—that allows new definitions of family roles to be adaptive and fulfilling? Do women today have employment choices that are satisfying and functional for them and all other family members?

This book, then, is a natural extension of my dissertation. I salute my family, friends, and colleagues for making the journey from then to now such a wonderful and fulfilling one.

Acknowledgments

I want to express my appreciation to Dr. Beth Neman, Dr. Maita Levine, Dr. Rita Hoppert, and Dr. Michele Paludi for all their assistance in helping with the conception and revising of this book.

I also thank my children, Karen, Desha, and Lois, for being so supportive of their employed mother throughout the years.

■ 1
Introduction

Judith Frankel

In the past 20 years, one of the most dynamic social changes in the history of the United States has taken place. Although there have always been employed mothers, today a greater proportion of mothers are employed. The Department of Labor projects that by 1995 roughly two thirds of all new labor force entrants will be women, and 80% of those in their childbearing years are expected to have children during their work lives. It is estimated that this increased involvement of mothers in the labor force will continue into the 21st century, until the participation of women in the labor force equals that of men (Johnson, 1987).

Earlier in this century, it was assumed that mothers worked because of financial need. Indeed, many did so and continue to do so to the present day. It was also assumed that employment was not a choice for mothers who had economic security, an assumption that clearly does not hold today. The vast numbers of mothers entering and remaining in the workplace demonstrate the power of the role of employment in mothers' lives today.

Life-styles have changed drastically for American families as a result of this dramatic shift in *maternal* roles. No longer is it the norm for mothers of infants, toddlers, and school-age children to spend their days at home taking care of their children. The traditional role of mothering is changing, and in its place is the beginning of a new "tradition" of American motherhood.

The purpose of this book is to examine this new tradition and to see what its impact on the family has been. We now have over 20 years of experience with the new tradition. This book reviews and summarizes how the changes have taken place and what their effects have been. In doing so, we clarify what is real and what is mythic about maternal employment. We examine where different life experiences and circumstances of employed mothers lead them. We see what can be done to help families function more effectively when the mother is employed and what public policy can do to strengthen and support families of employed mothers.

This examination of the parameters and consequences of maternal employment is done in the context of the family. Maternal employment has had a revolutionary effect on the workplace and the social arena, but for purposes of this book, its effect on the family as a unit and on each member of the family is the focus.

The perspective taken in all of the chapters is a feminist perspective. As described by Michele Paludi in the Foreword, this perspective celebrates the diversity of womens' experiences as mothers, especially those of ethnic and minority women.

The book is divided into four sections. The first presents a general approach to the topic and describes the parameters of the new tradition mentioned above. The first chapter, by Weitzman and Fitzgerald, examines the demographics of maternal employment for diverse groups of women. They emphasize the employment increase in the past 40 years, especially for mothers of young children; describe the changing work patterns that are emerging; and address the challenges that face families of employed mothers today.

These challenges are the underpinnings of the decision-making practices that women follow when making maternal/employment decisions, as is seen in the following chapter, by McCarty and myself. It is apparent that the decision to be an employed mother is a popular option, but it is ringed with problems that must be addressed, not only within the family but in the societal sphere as well.

These generalizations emerge as a refrain throughout the rest of the book. In the chapters that follow, these constant refrains are heard: the dramatic increase in employment of mothers of young children; the changing shape of women's career patterns; the positive outcomes of maternal employment if demanding challenges facing families of employed mothers are met; and above all, the necessity for society to provide structural support for child care for families of employed mothers.

Part 2 discusses the impact of maternal employment on the various members, dispelling some prevalent myths. In the opening chapter, Sears and Galambos conclude that it is the quality of the roles of the employed mother, along with the nature of the job and the work environment, that predict her well-being. They suggest that, for married mothers, the benefits of employment (such as increased self-esteem) outweigh the costs of role strain, especially if the children are of school age. The picture they draw for single mothers is less positive. The lives of single mothers are complicated by the burdens they face as a result of both their child care responsibilities with little or no community support and the structure of the labor market that results in their being concentrated in low-paying jobs with little chance for advancement.

Etaugh finds that maternal employment often has positive effects on the child's behavior when the mother is satisfied with her role and there is familial and community support for the child's care. The specific effects for children of different ages is discussed, often supporting desirable outcomes and contradicting popular mythology about children of employed mothers. For example, studies find that there is better social adjustment for infants and preschoolers of both sexes when the mother is employed.

In Pittman and Kerpelman's chapter we find that men's attitudes toward employed mothers have changes from fear that their wives' employment will threaten their masculinity to an expectation that their wives will be employed. However, their low level of participation in family work remains. The authors investigate some previously little-examined variables that may help produce a viable explanation of this continuing lack of participation.

Part 3 deals with the diversity of experiences different segments of employed mothers face. Although each group has its own unique concerns and traditions, a common thread runs throughout these differing experiences, requiring domestic management on limited resources for all of the groups discussed. Steglin and I report on working-class families where mothers' employment is financially mandated and particularly dependent on economic conditions. In this literature, which deals primarily with middle-class dual-career families, we expand the vision of family to include more than the usually discussed nuclear family.

This extension is continued in the chapter by Barbour, Richardson, and Bubenzer on adolescent mothers and vocational potential. Instead of painting the usual gloomy picture of adolescent mothers, these authors offer a possibility of positive outcomes under conditions that they identify and examine.

Valdez and Coltrane report on families of Chicana employed mothers and find that they too have much in common with most other families of employed mothers. The report of a qualitative study of a group of Chicana employed mothers helps us to feel the texture of their lives more clearly.

Mothers in African-American families have always been employed in America, from the days of slavery to the present. They have developed ways of dealing with this situation that have led to coping strategies and familial strengths, as discussed in the chapter by McLoyd. These chapters demonstrate that maternal employment is a growing phenomenon and that families face many challenges today in making it a positive one.

Part 4 addresses issues raised by the preceding chapters. It suggests ways that the role the employed mother plays as the "new traditional woman" in the context of her family can be supported by institutional and societal developments. Benin and Chong's chapter supports the agreement reached in all of the preceding chapters and calls for more effective, widespread, quality day care. However, it does so by providing a meaningful framework and understanding of the development of the present situation that allows us to proceed with solutions to the serious problem of providing quality day care for all children.

The next chapter, by Perry-Jenkins, suggests a different way of looking at family roles, one that focuses on the symbolic meaning both men and women give to work. She recognizes husbands' and wives' roles are dynamic and interactive and that it is necessary to look at the congruence between ideas that husbands and wives hold about roles they enact and the responsibilities of those roles.

The last chapter, by O'Reilly and Briscoe, summarizes what public policy is doing to help strengthen families of employed mothers. The paucity of governmental policy helping to make maternal employment a positive option for families is frightening in the face of the dramatic need for such governmental action. Therefore, O'Reilly and Briscoe urge strengthening legislation to outlaw sex discrimination, including sexual harassment and inequality of male/female work conditions and payment, and endorse the provision of quality day care supported by community and governmental sources. The days of mother as the only caretaker of the family are over. O'Reilly and Briscoe inform us that now is the time to develop a new perspective on family roles and dynamics.

It is the hope of all of the contributors to this book that by our chapters we have succeeded in defusing myths that surround the topic of the employed mother. The new tradition of the employed mother is a strong and viable one that must be recognized by the agents of power in the community. It must be understood that the old traditional image of the nuclear family, with the mother remaining at home all day taking care of home, hearth, and children, is true only for a minority of families. For the majority of families, then, the new tradition demands dramatic change in the way family members perceive their roles and calls for community action to develop supports and resources for their continuing good health.

REFERENCE

Johnson, W. B. (1987). *Workforce 2000; Work and workers for the 21st century.* Indianapolis, IN: Hudson Institute.

■ Part 1
General Perspectives

■ 2
Employed Mothers: Diverse Life-Styles and Labor Force Profiles

Lauren M. Weitzman and Louise F. Fitzgerald

> The woman who begrudges her own children a few years of her undivided attention perhaps cannot be suppressed, but she need not be admired. Her example is pernicious, her ethics immoral, her selfishness destructive for the nation. (Martin in Hughes, 1925)

The dramatic increase in maternal employment has been labeled the most significant labor force development of the last half century (U. S. Department of Labor, 1983). In record-breaking numbers, mothers are entering the labor market, combining their occupational and maternal roles in a manner almost unthinkable only 50 years ago. This development has enhanced the lives of many American women, bringing them enhanced autonomy, independence and the increased sense of self-worth that accompany them. At the same time, it has presented special challenges and concerns, both for women themselves and for society at large.

This chapter explores the implications of this phenomenon from both an individual and societal perspective. We begin by examining current social attitudes towards maternal employment, noting that such attitudes are changing much more slowly than the actual behavior itself. We situate our discussion within a broader consideration of the occupational experiences of American women as a whole; before turning to an examination of the changing demographics of employed mothers. Recognizing the diversity of women's experiences, (e.g., single heads of households, members of dual-earner families, the various racial-ethnic groups) the third section of the chapter examines differential patterns in the working lives of various groups of women, concluding with a discussion of the special issues and challenges associated with enhancing the quality of the lives of mothers who work outside the home.

SOCIETAL ATTITUDES AND THE OCCUPATIONAL CLIMATE FOR EMPLOYED MOTHERS

When examining the experiences of employed mothers, it is instructive to consider first the quality of working life for women in general. Despite the enormous social change of the last several decades, the nature of women's labor force experiences and career development remains much more complex than that of men (e.g., Betz & Fitzgerald, 1987; Osipow, 1983), and the understanding of women's work lives still requires attention to variables rarely salient to the men's career behavior. Most of these variables are closely related to the maternal role; for example, the presence and number of children remains a powerful predictor of the level and nature of women's work force participation, although it is essentially unrelated to that of men. And as we will show, the presence and number of children continues to influence factors such as earnings and occupational attainment, although gradually losing its influence on actual labor force participation as employment becomes increasingly normative for adult women.

The special challenges and problems faced by employed women, including multiple role conflict and role overload, reflect deeply rooted cultural values mandating that individual women retain almost total responsibility for the care and rearing of children, despite their employment status, financial necessity, or personal preference. This value system finds its most systemic reflection in U.S. social policy, a policy that continues to resist consideration of any national child care initiatives. Thus, although today's young women face what amounts to a "cultural imperative" to combine work and family (Rand & Miller, 1972), structural supports for such a life pattern are almost nonexistent.

The complex of attitudes reflecting our cultural expectations of maternal responsibilities has been aptly labeled the *motherhood mandate* (Russo, 1979), defined as "[requiring] that a woman have at least two children (historically as many as possible and preferably sons), and raise them 'well.' She can . . . become educated, work, and be active in public life, as long as she first fulfills this obligation" (pp. 8–9). Russo indicates that this mandate is largely incompatible with other social roles, but the rise in maternal labor force participation suggests that women are no longer influenced by social conceptions of appropriate maternal behavior, behavior that often conflicts with the expectations of the workplace.

Recent research examining the influence of the motherhood mandate on perceptions of employed mothers demonstrates that they are perceived as independent, competitive, and dedicated to their careers as well as less sensitive to the needs of others (Etaugh & Study, 1989). Conversely, "stay-at-home" mothers are seen as expressive and nurturing, sensitive to the needs of others, affectionate and unselfish. Illustrating a common gender difference, women evaluate employed mothers more favorably than do men. Such research suggests that the continuing rise in maternal employment exists in uneasy tension with our nostalgic cultural insistence on the fiction of "mom and apple pie"; thus, the roles of worker and mother are seen as more or less mutually exclusive, and success in one is often thought to preclude success in the other. Such attitudes also influence beliefs about the desirability of exclusive maternal care of children (e.g., Hock et al., 1984; Greenberg, Goldberg, Crawford, & Granger, 1988), the attitudes of a woman's partner or husband toward participation in childrearing activities (e.g., Gilbert & Rachlin, 1987), and attitudes toward pregnant women at work (e.g., Blasko et al., 1989). Women are faced not only with reconciling behavior with the attitude of those with whom they must live and work, but must also struggle with their own internalized beliefs about the inappropriateness of maternal employment, no matter how desperately they and their families may need the financial support.

In contrast to such beliefs stands the body of evidence demonstrating that the general effect of employment for women is strongly positive. Reviewing the psychological and physical adjustment of working mothers, Nye (1974) concluded nearly twenty years ago that employed mothers are physically healthier and enjoy a more positive self-image when compared to housewives; working women have been found to have a greater power in the marital relationship and a larger degree of influence on fertility and childrearing decisions (Bahr, 1974). In addition, the worker role may serve as a buffer for the stress experienced in other roles (Barnett & Baruch, 1985). Contrary to popular belief, there is no evidence that maternal employment has a detrimental effect on children, and in fact, considerable research has shown positive effects (particularly for girls) on their intellectual and social development. Despite such data, working mothers are held responsible in the opinion of the general public for a wide variety of social ills (Betz & Fitzgerald, 1987; Faludi, 1991), a pattern that contributes not insignificantly to the role conflict and stresses experienced by those who must or wish to work outside the home.

PATTERNS OF WOMEN'S LABOR FORCE PARTICIPATION

As is frequently pointed out, the overall increase in women's labor force participation has not been accompanied by an integration of women into all areas of the work force. The majority of women continue to be segregated into relatively few fields, fields characterized by low status and low pay. In 1988, almost half (46%) of all women workers were employed in administrative support and service positions (Rix, 1990), a figure that has remained relatively constant over the past 10 years.

Despite this overall tendency toward occupational segregation, women are making some inroads into occupations traditionally dominated by men. For example, the numbers of women in the sciences have more than tripled since 1976 (Rix, 1990), although they are still more likely to be found among social scientists and psychologists than among physical and chemical scientists. Similarly, women are entering management positions in large numbers, yet relatively few move beyond the "glass ceiling" into higher-level positions (Morrison & Von Glinow, 1990).

As might be expected, women's earnings reflect this occupational segregation. In fact, when the economic compensation of women workers is discussed, it is inevitably in terms of the "wage gap." In 1984, the median annual salary of full-time women workers was 63.7% of men's, a figure that is almost identical to that found in 1955 (63.9%) (Blau & Ferber, 1987). An examination of the annual salaries for women and men in various occupations illustrates the dramatic nature of the wage gap. In 1984, male lawyers aged 25 to 34 earned $27,563, compared to the $20,573 earned by female lawyers in the same age bracket. Male bus drivers earned $15,611; female bus drivers, only $9,903. Male retail sales clerks earned $13,002, nearly double the $7,479 earned by female sales clerks (Hewlett, 1986). In 1983, the salaries of women in executive, administrative, and managerial occupations were barely 60% of those earned by their male colleagues (Dipboye, 1987). Such figures suggest that the wage gap exists across a wide range of occupational categories and overdetermines the traditional effects of educational attainment, with female college graduates earning less on the average ($25,544 in 1987) than a man with only a high school education ($27,293) (Rix, 1990).

Against this picture of the working woman in America, we turn now to an examination of the economic and social condition of working (i.e., employed) mothers. Despite the dictates of the motherhood mandate, we will see that, far from being a deviant group, such women are quickly becoming the social norm.

LABOR FORCE PARTICIPATION AND
COMPENSATION OF WORKING MOTHERS

Paralleling the general increase in women's employment, the labor force participation of working mothers has more than tripled since 1950. For married mothers with children, this rate has risen from 18.4% in 1950 to 61.6% in 1990, an increase of more than 300%. This increase is especially notable for women with infant and preschool children. In the 15 years between 1970 and 1985, the labor force participation rates of women with children less than 1 year old almost doubled; there was a 77% increase in the rates for women with children 2 years old and a 60% increase for mothers of 3-year-olds (Hayghe, 1986).

Although the presence of children continues to influence the nature and level of a woman's occupational status, it appears to be losing its influence on actual labor force participation itself. Shank (1988) cites figures to support this contention. For example, 67% of all mothers worked in 1987, compared to 79% of women with no children under the age of 18. Fifty-five percent of women with children under the age of 3 were labor force participants. Noting that the magnitude of differences among these figures are relatively small, Hayghe (1986) suggests that social changes are weakening the traditional correlation between a mother's labor force participation and the age of her youngest child. In 1970, the highest participation rates were for mothers with children 14 years old (57%), a figure twice that of mothers of infants, who had the lowest participation rate (24%). In contrast, participation rates in 1985 were much less differentiated.

Related to these changes are statistics indicating that women are continuing to work throughout the great proportion of their pregnancies. O'Connell (1990), reporting on a Census Bureau study of 9,000 women who had their first child between 1981 and 1985, found that 78% of those women who worked during pregnancy worked in the last trimester; 47% were at work less than 1 month before the birth. In addition, one third of the participants returned to work 3 months after the births of their children. Two factors were found to be associated with a rapid return to work: the number of months before birth that the mother stopped working and the opportunity to obtain maternity leave benefits from one's employer.

Participation

This general increase in maternal labor force participation appears against the backdrop of significant changes in the work patterns of women more generally. For the first time, the traditional "M-shape" characterizing female work patterns (e.g., a decrease in labor force participation during childbearing years) is being replaced by the "inverted-U" shape that has traditionally been the norm for men, suggesting continuous work involvement during the adult years (Shank, 1988). For example, the labor force participation rates for women in traditional childbearing years (ages 25–34) rose from 34% in 1950 to nearly 73% in 1988 (Rix, 1990). Thus, women are no longer casual participants in the work force; rather their work patterns are characterized by full-time, year-round employment. They return to work sooner after childbirth and tend to work continuously during pregnancy (e.g., O'Connell, Betz & Kurth, 1989; Shank, 1988).

Employed mothers also demonstrate work patterns characterized by full-time, year-round employment. Hayghe (1986) reported that in 1985 two thirds of mothers with children under the age of 3 were employed full-time. Similar patterns are found for mothers of children aged 3 to 5 (67%), as well as for mothers of school-age children (ages 6–17; 70%). Not surprisingly, divorced mothers are even more likely to work full-time than are their married counterparts (U.S. Department of Labor, 1989). Fully 88% of divorced women with children worked full-time in 1988. When the labor force participation rates of teenage mothers are examined, however, a much lower figure is found (37.1% in 1988), suggesting the employment difficulties faced by women who become mothers at an early age. Whether or not mothers work full-time, they tend to have jobs throughout the year. For example, in 1983, two out of three employed mothers worked more than 30 weeks (Hayghe, 1984). Such figures document the increased labor force commitment of contemporary mothers of all sorts, illustrating once again the persistent discrepancy between cultural fictions and contemporary reality.

Compensation

Although women as a group are disproportionately underpaid, this problem is exacerbated for employed mothers (National Report on Work and Family, 1989). For example, the average earnings in 1987 for married women with children under 6 years were $12,160. Such women earned less than married women with older children ($13,070); in contrast, mothers with no children below the age of 18 earned $14,260. The overall earnings of married women with young children were the lowest of all married workers between 1981 and 1987, reflecting not only the general wage gap but also the effect of age and education on the dismal economic circumstances of this group.

In addition to such factors, the earning power of employed mothers is also influenced by racial-ethnic status. In 1984, married black women with young children earned more than did their white counterparts

(Hayghe, 1986). Such increased earnings, however, do not translate into higher total family income for blacks because of the significant difference in earning power between black husbands and white husbands. This pattern points to the heterogeneity of the group generally designated "employed mothers" and underscores that their experiences vary widely as a result of factors such as racial-ethnic and marital status, education, socioeconomic condition, and so forth. Understanding the experiences of mothers in the work force requires attention to such factors, and it is to this diversity that we now turn.

EMPLOYED MOTHERS: A DIVERSE GROUP

The heterogeneity of employed mothers is associated with factors such as age at first birth, racial-ethnic origin, and marital status. In this section we examine these influences in an effort to counteract the stereotype that all employed mothers are similar and that the most notable thing about them is simply the fact that they are employed at all (Smith, 1981). Differences related to family type and marital status will be considered first, followed by an examination of racial-ethnic and life-style differences.

Marital Status and Family Type

As the foregoing discussion makes clear, the traditional family with a male breadwinner and female housewife is rapidly becoming a thing of the past and, in fact, accounted for only 13% of all families in 1987 (Rix, 1990). Accordingly, there has been a marked increase in dual-earner families (23.6% of all families with children in 1987) as well as in women-maintained households, including divorced, separated, widowed, or never married women (Johnson & Waldman, 1983). As such figures make clear, it is no longer reasonable to speak of a "typical" family (Hayghe, 1990).

The U. S. Department of Labor (1989) provides a general perspective on the many types of families that exist. The majority of mothers are in married-couple families (75.5%); smaller percentages are divorced (9.4%), single or never married (8.1%), married with an absent spouse (5.4%), or widowed (1.6%). The marital status of women is related to their employment status, with divorced mothers and mothers in married-couple families most likely to be employed (75.1% and 61.5% in 1988, respectively). The mothers least likely to be employed are those married with an absent spouse, widowed, or never married (only 46% of these mothers were employed in 1988).

Noting the influence of family type and marital status, the following section will consider employed mothers in three different family structures: *married-couple families, women-maintained families,* and *teenage moth-ers.* As labor force participation rates and earnings have been discussed above, this section focuses more specifically on variables related to the quality of these women's daily lives and their psychological well-being.

Married-Couple Families

The rise in dual-earner families has led to an increase in the attention paid to the special difficulties faced by women in such families, although most of the research in this area suffers from strong heterosexist bias. As with families more generally, married-couple families are not a homogeneous group, and considering them as such results in a picture that is not only partial but distorted. Differences in social class, career orientation, sexual orientation, and so forth are associated with life experiences that differ from one another in important ways.

One of the most important distinctions was noted by Gilbert and Rachlin (1987), who distinguish *dual-earner* from *dual-career* families. In dual-earner families, both spouses are employed, but only one—generally the husband—pursues a *career*, the other viewing employment as a *job* (i.e., work taken on for economic purposes or work more likely to be interrupted). Alternatively, both spouses may consider their occupational involvement to be a job. Dual-career families, on the other hand, are a special case of the dual-earner family; here, both spouses maintain a strong commitment to their careers (which are characterized by substantial training and work commitment) in addition to maintaining a family life together.

Dual-Earner Mothers. The "modal mother" described by O'Connell (1990) is an example of the dual-earner pattern. O'Connell describes this modal mother as the "average" working mother who has participated in the labor force since the 1960s. She is white, she married a high school graduate, and she had her first child between 22 and 24 years of age. This type of mother is similar to the general profile of women who work by choice (U.S. Department of Labor, 1983). Such women tend to be married to men who are also full-time workers, to have children of at least school age, to be high school graduates, and to be employed in pink-collar occupations (e.g., clerical or sales). Mothers in dual-earner families may face less psychological conflict between their work and parenting roles than do dual-career mothers, especially if they value their occupational involvement to a lesser degree than their maternal role.

Although this profile highlights mainly the experiences of white women, it should be pointed out that it also describes the lives of many women of color. The earnings of such women contribute substantially to their family income, resulting in a financial situation very different from that of women maintaining households on their own. As discussed previously, however, black married mothers are still at a disadvantage when total family income is considered.

Dual-Career Mothers. The experiences of mothers in dual-career families have received considerable publicity and research attention, ranging from the idealized glamour of the "Superwoman" stereotype to the recommendation of "mommy tracks" (Schwartz, 1989) for employed mothers in managerial positions. The research efforts in this field are important and have illuminated many of the challenges involved in simultaneously managing the roles of career and family. The results of these studies, however, are representative only of the small portion of working mothers who tend to be well-educated and of middle-class status. Such limitations should be borne in mind in the following discussion.

Gilbert (1985) defines three types of dual-career families, varying according to the distribution of household and child-rearing responsibilities. The first of these, the *traditional* dual-career family, is characterized by a woman partner who maintains full responsibility for family work in addition to her career obligations. This situation is thought to lead to considerable role conflict and overload, as the woman works a "second shift" at home (Hochschild, 1989) in addition to her job-related duties. The second type of dual-career family is the *participant* type. Here, parenting is shared by both partners, but the woman still maintains primary responsibility for household chores. As might be expected, the degree to which the male partner contributes to child rearing is determined by the importance he places on these tasks and on the flexibility his work role affords him. Finally, *role-sharing* marriages are those in which both spouses are equally and actively involved in both parenting and household responsibilities. This type of dual-career family is the ideal situation for many women; unfortunately, it is not a common pattern. Although there has been considerable popular and media attention devoted to the supposed increase in participant and role-sharing marriages, there is little evidence that such arrangements characterize more than a tiny fraction of the population. Obstacles to creating a role-sharing dual-career family lie in the structure of the employment situations of both men and women, as well as in individual attitudes related to gender roles and parenting.

In addition to negotiating household and child-rearing responsibilities, dual-career families are faced with decisions about the timing of starting a family. It is becoming more common for women to delay the birth of a first child, and this is especially true of white, college-educated women. Many of these mothers work during pregnancy, making it likely that they will return to work relatively soon after the birth. They also tend to receive maternity benefits from their employers. O'Connell (1990) suggests that female executives are likely to be characterized by this demographic profile, estimating that 70% of women who fall into this category will return to work within 6 months after the birth of a child. This projection is contrary to the concerns raised by employers, who believe that once a woman has a child, she is likely to interrupt her career for extended periods of time.

As might be expected, mothers in dual-career families experience both stressors and benefits from their rich but hectic life-style. Stressors identified by Gilbert and Rachlin (1987) include the decision on whether or when to parent, child care decisions, the necessity of developing coping strategies for combining occupational and family roles, and occupational mobility and job placement issues. However, such a life-style provides sources of satisfaction and fulfillment as well; these include the opportunity for spousal support and shared values and the creation of a family structure that minimizes traditional gender-role differences, providing alternative models for children in the family.

As was the case for dual earners, the focus of the research on dual-career families is often on white mothers, rendering invisible the experiences of women of color. As black and Hispanic women continue to upgrade their educational attainment, they are becoming involved in dual-career families in increasing numbers. Little is known about these women and their families, and the relative influence of racial and ethnic factors in the dual-career pattern remains to be determined.

Women-Maintained Families

In contrast to the life-styles of women in married-couple families, the experience of those who have primary economic responsibility for their families is much more difficult. In 1983, 9.8 million families were supported solely by women who were divorced, separated, widowed, or never married (Johnson & Waldman, 1983), and in fact, living in a woman-headed household is one of the strongest predictors of living below the poverty line. Three fifths of these women-maintained families include children under the age of 18. Despite the stereotype of the "welfare mother," these women retain strong ties to the labor market, although they often experience considerable difficulty finding a job, especially when they have preschool children (Johnson & Waldman, 1983). Thus, the unemployment rates for these women are higher than those for women in married-couple families.

Johnson and Waldman (1983) report that single mothers, like most working mothers, work primarily in administrative support and clerical positions. In addition, single mothers tend to remain in lower-paying and less-skilled jobs within broad occupational categories. Divorced women are more likely than other single mothers to be in managerial and professional occupations (most likely because of their higher levels of education). Relative to working wives, a larger proportion of women who maintain families have not completed high school (23% vs. 15% in 1983), although they have been obtaining more education in recent years (Johnson & Waldman, 1983).

As always, racial-ethnic status and the disadvantages it often codes exert their influence on the experiences of woman-maintained families. In 1983, 6.8 million women maintaining families were white (including 800,000 who were Hispanic), and 2.8 million were black (Johnson & Waldman, 1983). Black women with families tend to have more children under 18 and less education than do their white counterparts. In addition, both black and Hispanic women who are single heads of families have lower median earnings, lower labor force participation rates, and higher unemployment than do their white counterparts. Black and Hispanic women-headed families are also less likely to have more than one wage earner, compared to white families, in which adolescents of working age and nonspousal relatives are more likely to be employed.

Minority women who maintain families tend to be clustered in occupations reflecting their educational background (Johnson & Waldman, 1983), resulting in large proportions being employed in service and operative jobs. This occupational distribution in turn influences their earnings: the annual median income of black and Hispanic women-maintained families in 1983 ($7,489 and $7,611, respectively) fell far below that of comparable white women ($13,145) (Johnson & Waldman, 1983). And the median income for all three groups is much lower than that of married-couple families. As mentioned previously, this situation results in a much greater proportion of women-maintained families who live in poverty.

The profiles of employed mothers who have sole economic responsibility for their families present a bleak picture. A vicious circle appears to exist, with low educational attainment resulting in low-paying employment situations, which in turn increases the probability that such families will live in poverty. In addition, the markedly lower salaries paid to even well-educated women, the well-documented difficulty of securing child support payments following divorce, and similar factors ensure that even previously middle-class women will have difficulty keeping their families out of poverty. The aspirations of the children in these families are, in turn, limited and stunted by the circumstances of their youth. Women of color experience the double disadvantage of their combined status as women and as members of minority groups.

It is difficult to imagine the stressful conditions under which these women exist. They do not have the luxury to choose whether or not to work, and they retain full responsibility for the care of their children in addition to their work obligations. They are among the most underpaid and disadvantaged members of the work force, and their difficulties are exacerbated by an almost complete lack of adequate, affordable child care and of the income to obtain what services do exist. In the most cruel irony of all, they are blamed for delinquency, drug abuse, and adolescent crime, as newspapers blare forth headlines describing the empirical link between such social problems and the phenomenon of "women-headed families." Politicians urge them to return to the home for the good of their children, ignoring the fact that if they did so they (and their children) would soon have no homes to return to. Such women are faced with tremendous obstacles and minimal support in a society that persists in maintaining the fiction of a "typical" family, consisting of an employed father and stay-at-home mother. Although many of these women have devised creative solutions to the problems they face, they and their children remain at risk for a difficult and stressful existence.

The Teenage Mother

Possibly the most disadvantaged group of women are those who begin motherhood while still in their teen years. The U.S. Department of Labor (1989) reports that in 1988 there were over half a million teenage mothers (between the ages of 16 and 19) in the United States. The great majority of these young women were unmarried (68% in 1988), and most had not completed high school. Thus, to the difficulties described above can be added the exacerbated effects of low educational attainment.

The prospects for these young women in the labor market are almost uniformly bleak. The profile of the teenage mother is that of a young black women who has her first birth outside a marital relationship (O'Connell, 1990); she has less than a high school education and is unlikely to be employed at the time of her pregnancy. To give some sense of the scope of the problem, we note that fully 92% of first births to black teenagers in 1985 were to unmarried women, the majority of whom had not finished high school.

The tremendous cost of this life pattern, to the women themselves, their children, and society in general, has stimulated some efforts to improve the lives and prospects of those who have been called the "children who have children." Such efforts, generally linked to programs allowing pregnant teenagers to complete their high school education and providing medical care to them and their children, have shown some promise. In fact, McAdoo (1987) reports that single black mothers who never married but remained within their extended family and completed high school obtained better jobs and earned higher salaries than did teenage women who married after becoming pregnant but later became single mothers. Despite the positive effects of such programs, the generally depressing economic picture of the early 1990s, with its concomitant cuts in social programming, suggest not only that more comprehensive efforts are unlikely but that those that do exist may be cut back or eliminated. The human cost, as well as the ultimate social implications of such policy decisions could well be enormous.

Racial-Ethnic and Life-style Influences

As we have emphasized, employed mothers come from all strata of society and represent all forms of ethnic, racial, and life-style diversity. This section will highlight the discussion, begun previously, of the influence of racial-ethnic and life-style differences on the lives of employed mothers. We identify two general themes: that the use of even broad groupings obscures the diversity that exists among these women, thus reifying the notion that they represent some identifiable, possibly deviant group, and that the disadvantaged labor force position of many of them is exacerbated by their minority status. Although minority women are constantly discussed in the context of their disadvantages, we also seek to highlight the strengths of these women, who face the struggle of living within a society with racist, sexist, and homophobic attitudes, and to recognize the unique contributions that they make as members of the labor force and society more generally.

African-American Mothers

Popular culture and stereotypes often depict the African-American mother as a strong matriarch who is likely to be single-handedly heading a large and diverse household. Although many such families are indeed maintained by black women, there are, as we have seen, even larger numbers of African-American mothers living in married-couple families. The extended family network exists as a major source of support for these mothers, especially with respect to child care. In fact, a "kin help exchange" child care arrangement, whereby relatives in one's extended family share child care responsibilities (McAdoo, 1981), is often used by African-American mothers and may provide these women a resource generally unavailable to their white counterparts.

On the other hand, African-American mothers without such extended family support face great financial and personal burdens. Malveaux and Wallace (1987) have labeled the greater propensity for African-American women to be single heads of households as a third disadvantage in addition to the "double-jeopardy" of being female and nonwhite (Beale, 1970). Divorced black mothers are only half as likely as their white counterparts to receive alimony and much less likely to be awarded property settlements (McAdoo, 1990).

This doubling or tripling of factors related to gender and race often results in extremely limited opportunities for African-American women, which in turn has devastating consequences for their children. Within clerical occupations, women of color receive less economic compensation for their work than do white women, and those in management have fewer opportunities for promotion and decision making than their white colleagues have (Morrison & Von Glinow, 1990). Although data on this point are sparse, Defour (1990) has speculated that black women are even more likely to be sexually harassed than are other women, adding an additional source of work-related stress to their lives. In particular, women of color in the trades and blue-collar occupations are even more vulnerable to such harassment, not only because of their racial-ethnic status but also because of their more extreme economic disadvantage.

It is important to recognize that even within these constraints, African-American mothers maintain strong ties to the labor force. With the exception of mothers of preschoolers (whose 20% unemployment rate places them among the most disadvantaged group), they are more likely to work full-time than are either their Hispanic or White counterparts; in addition, as a group, they maintain a sense of optimism and remain committed to the possibility of improved life circumstances for their children. McAdoo (1990) notes a survey conducted by the NAACP Legal Defense Fund that reports that more than half of single African-American mothers, though living in poverty, expressed hope for their children's futures.

Hispanic Mothers

Hispanics are part of one of the fastest-growing segments of the U.S. population. In 1988, 8% of the U.S. population was Hispanic, and women made up 51% of that total (U.S. Bureau of the Census, 1988). It is important to recognize that these women represent a diverse group, including women of Mexican, Puerto Rican, Central and South American, and Cuban origin, and that this diversity manifests itself in their labor force experiences.

Increasing numbers of Hispanic immigrants consist of women with children, reflecting the growing proportion of Hispanic women-maintained families in the United States (Bonilla-Santiago, 1990). As is the case for all woman-headed households, these families are at great risk for living below the poverty level, and in fact, relatively large numbers of all Hispanic families are at risk for poverty, with variation by subgroup. In 1987, Puerto Rican families were most at risk (constituting 38% of the Hispanic families living in poverty), followed by families of Mexican and "other" Hispanic origin (26% each) and Central and South American families

(19%). Families of Cuban descent are least likely to be poor (14%) (Bonilla-Santiago, 1990).

The experiences of Hispanic mothers in the labor market resemble the overall pattern for Hispanic women more generally. A 1988 survey by the National Council of La Raza documented the marginal work force position of these women, noting that they are likely to be highly concentrated in operative occupations and that their earnings reflect this occupational segregation. The median annual earnings for Hispanic women in 1987 were $8,554. Unique obstacles for this group often include a language barrier, more traditional gender-role expectations, and lower levels of educational attainment (Bonilla-Santiago, 1990).

Like African-American mothers, Hispanic mothers are likely to value education for their children and to maintain strong ties to their extended family (Natera, 1988). Despite the difficulties they often face, the proportion of Hispanic women in the U.S. labor force continues to grow, contributing to the diverse nature of the large segment of the population known simply as "working mothers."

Asian- and Pacific-American Mothers

Like Hispanic women, Asian- and Pacific-American mothers represent a diverse and varied group, including women with Chinese, Japanese, Korean, Filipino, and Asian Indian origins. Many originally immigrated to the United States to work with their husbands or as Asian brides for American men (Lott, 1990), and according to the 1980 census, they constitute 52% of the Asian/Pacific-American population.

In contrast to other racial-ethnic groups many of these women have attained high levels of education. Lott (1990) attributes this to restrictive U.S. immigration policies favoring persons who have college educations, but it should also be noted that Asian families traditionally encouraged educational persistence and attainment; thus, many Asian women posses the support and motivation necessary to become upwardly mobile. On the other hand, certain subgroups of this population (e.g., women of Vietnamese, Chinese, or Korean origin) have completed no more than an eighth-grade education, illustrating once again the dangers of generalizing on the basis of stereotypes or broad ethnic groupings. The 1980 census showed an overall labor force participation rate of 58% for all Asian- and Pacific-American women, ranging from a high of 68% for Filipino women to the lowest figure, 47%, for women of Asian Indian and Samoan extraction (Lott, 1990). If experience is any guide, these figures will be considerably higher when data from the 1990 census become available.

Asian/Pacific-American families appear likely to contain multiple wage earners, suggesting that mothers in these families must work out of economic necessity. Lott (1990) notes that the small businesses often operated by Asian-American families provide a major source of income, yet female family members often work in these businesses without pay. In addition to this somewhat unique situation, Asian- and Pacific-American women share with other minority women the tendency to be segregated into lower-paying, traditionally female occupations and are less likely to receive earnings that are commensurate with their educational attainment. Asian women also experience discrimination when they are employed in managerial positions (Morrison & Von Glinow, 1990). Without in any way denying the success and accomplishments achieved by highly educated and upwardly mobile Asian/Pacific-American women, it should be noted that many continue to suffer from the same disadvantages typically associated with nonwhite status in this country.

Native American Mothers

Native Americans are relatively invisible as a separate racial-ethnic grouping, most likely because of their small numbers and the ways in which they have been traditionally treated by the U.S. government. Considerable diversity exists among even this tiny group, however, depending on factors such as tribal background, regional distribution, and living in urban versus rural environments. Poverty rates are especially high among American Indian women (Snipp, 1990), and as is the trend for all minority groups, there is a greater likelihood of women-maintained families and the economic disadvantages that this status codes.

Like other American women, American Indian women are increasing their labor force participation, nearly half being employed in 1980. Even women in the traditional childbearing years are likely to be in the labor force, with those in their 30s most likely to work outside the home (Snipp, 1990). Although native American women as a group have relatively higher fertility rates than do black or white women, those who are employed tend to have fewer children than those who are not (a trend that is common for all women). Snipp (1990) interprets these data to suggest that the kin networks typical of many native American communities may not facilitate maternal labor force participation in the same way as for other groups such as Hispanics or blacks.

As with other women, increased levels of educational attainment result in stronger attachment to the labor force for native American women. Interestingly, in married-couple families, native American wives are more likely to work when their husbands make relatively high salaries. Aside from these few facts, little is known about this group of women. The relative isolation of the many who live on reservations and the traditional neglect of the native American population by government and researchers alike render them virtually invisible, both in official statistics and in the public consciousness. What little is known about the condition of the native American population more generally suggests that this invisibility obscures conditions of enormous poverty, relatively little education, and high levels of unemployment. If traditional relationships hold, women and children are likely to be the most disadvantaged of all members of this population, making native American mothers possibly the most poorly situated of all of the groups discussed here.

Lesbian Mothers

Lesbian mothers are even more likely to be invisible than women of color because of both heterosexist cultural assumptions and the prevalence of homophobic attitudes ensuring that most such women must conceal their life-style. Federal statistics on lesbian labor force participation do not exist, and only recently have the special concerns of lesbian women in the workplace been discussed. The choice of a lesbian life-style has important implications for a woman's career development, however; compared to heterosexual women, lesbians are likely to have stronger commitments to work and career, as well as a greater recognition of the need to support themselves financially. In choosing not to have a male partner, lesbians are unable to rely on a source of economic security that has traditionally been available to married heterosexual women (Hetherington & Orzek, 1989).

It appears inaccurate to assume, as many do, that lesbian women are not family-oriented; many are mothers living with their children, thus facing the increased responsibilities and stresses inherent in single-parent families. Often, they must struggle to obtain custody from a legal system that does not consider them suitable parents. For those with partners, however, relationships are often characterized by greater role flexibility and a more egalitarian sharing of tasks than is traditional in heterosexual marriages, a situation that may facilitate the balancing of multiple role responsibilities. Thus, lesbian mothers exhibit particular strengths yet also face unique challenges as a result of their life-style. They represent yet another group of women whose labor force participation and experience on the job is worthy of increased attention.

SPECIAL ISSUES AND CHALLENGES

This final part of the chapter briefly considers social policy issues relevant to improving the quality of life for employed mothers. The three areas we believe are most important are *pay equity, maternal and parental leave poli-*

cies, and *child care*. Each of these issues is closely tied to our discussion of the often arduous lives of mothers who work outside the home. As we will show, it remains an unfortunate reality that policies in the United States, supposedly the richest and most progressive nation in the world, lag woefully behind those of other industrialized nations and fail to reflect the striking evidence that working mothers are a growing and integral component of the American labor force. Our society's failure to come to terms with the fundamental changes in women's social and economic roles continues to plague policy decisions, resulting in heavy burdens for both women and families, although practical solutions are beyond neither our vision nor our grasp. Some of these solutions are discussed below.

Pay Equity and Comparable Worth

The explanations usually offered for the documented wage gap between men and women tend to focus on occupational segregation or the greater tendency for women to stop working for some part of their lives (e.g., Blau & Ferber, 1987; Dipboye, 1987; Hewlett, 1986). The first of these explanations relates to the issue of pay equity and comparable worth. As discussed previously, occupational segregation results in dramatic differences between the types of employment women attain (compared to man), as well as in the economic compensation they receive. Affirmative action strategies seek to decrease this segregation, with the expectation that a closing of the wage gap will follow. Affirmative action policies range from special recruitment and training procedures to preferential treatment for persons who possess basic job qualifications and are members of underrepresented groups (Rhode, 1990). Such efforts can also be expanded to desegregating vocational education and improving women's math and science skills. These strategies have provided an important initial entree for women into traditionally male-dominated fields, although they continue to generate philosophical, political, and practical opposition.

Comparable-worth procedures (i.e., the practice of paying equally for jobs of similar skills and difficulty even though their actual content may differ) have been suggested as another solution to improve pay equity. This strategy also attempts to reduce the proportion of the wage gap created by occupational segregation. Assessing comparable worth entails a systematic evaluation of the levels of knowledge, skill, and ability that are required for particular jobs and development of a compensation system that cuts across occupational fields (Fitzgerald & Betz, 1983).

Although the technical procedures for implementing comparable-worth evaluations have been available for some time and there has been some legal precedent for their use, this solution to the wage gap has met with considerable resistance (Hewlett, 1986), and its future remains un-clear. The National Committee on Pay Equity has reported that as of 1988, 48 states have begun preliminary research into this issue. Twenty-three states have started to examine potential job classification and compensa-tion systems; only *six* states, however, have actually implemented pay eq-uity plans, and seven states have taken no action at all on this issue (Rix, 1990). An extensive analysis of the technical, social, and philosophical con-siderations involved in the evaluation of comparable-worth procedures are beyond the scope of this chapter; we argue, however, that the imple-mentation of procedures that maximize pay equity are central to improv-ing the lives of employed mothers. We have presented considerable evidence that demonstrates the economic disadvantage of most mothers who work. Without governmental intervention, this situation is likely to remain unchanged.

Maternal and Parental Leave Policies

The second explanation for the wage gap (i.e., that women tend to "stop out" of the labor force for varying periods) is closely linked to the interac-tion between traditional notions of women's childbearing responsibilities and the lack of adequate provisions for maternity leave and child care. Many women experience some job interruption after the birth of their chil-dren; such interruptions influence a woman's ability to maintain seniority on the job and contribute to the risk of being unable to compete with younger colleagues who remain at work and maintain their job-related skills.

Maternity leave benefits in the United States are seriously inade-quate, thus hindering the progress of the increasingly large portion of working mothers currently in the labor force. The only federal provision for maternity leave falls under the 1978 Pregnancy Disability Amendment to Title VII of the Civil Rights Act, which makes it illegal to fire a worker solely because she is pregnant. The mandatory provision of temporary disability insurance for a pregnant worker is determined by individual states, with only *five* states currently providing such compensation (Hewlett, 1986)!

Aside from this small provision for maternity leave, there exists no federal maternal or parental leave policy in the United States, which is thus the *only* industrial nation without statutory maternity leave, a situ-ation that does not appear to be changing. The president recently vetoed a fairly conservative family leave policy that would have guaranteed the se-curity of women's (and men's) jobs when they had to take time off for fam-ily responsibilities. In sharp contrast, 117 countries provide leave from employment for childbirth, job protection while on leave, and the provision of a cash benefit that replaces all or most of a woman's earnings (Hewlet, 1986). Clearly, the current perception in the United States that child rearing is a "private" matter works to the strong disadvantage of the majority of American women who both work and raise families and perpetuates the stereotype that a women's "place" is at home, not in the work force.

Such social policies take a tremendous economic toll on individual women, as well as on the children and families that depend on them. The National Report on Work and Family (1988) reported that women without parental leave benefits lost $607 million over a 3-year period, compared to women with such benefits, as estimated by the cost of loss of seniority, increased unemployment, and the return to lower-paying jobs. Ironically, Census Bureau data have documented that women who receive maternal leave are likely to return to work sooner than women who do not: during 1981 to 1984, 71% of women receiving such leave returned to work within 6 months, compared to only 43% without maternal leave (National Report on Work and Family, 1989). Thus, such leave benefits can actually decrease the time a mother interrupts her employment. Although social policy must always seek a balance of (often conflicting) interests and visions of the social good, we submit that legal provision for some form of parental leave is an absolute necessity for ensuring the full integration of women into the labor force and for alleviating the economic burdens under which employed mothers currently labor. Such a policy is both economically sound and socially responsible, and to do less is to perpetuate a policy that is not in the best interest of women, children, or society at large.

Child Care

Possibly even more critical than the issue of maternal leave is that of child care. Employed mothers must make provisions for the care of their children while they are at work, and the choices available to them are limited by the lack of affordable, high-quality child care as well as by their personal resources. A 1982 *Current Population Report* notes that 23% of employed mothers depend on fathers to care for children or cared for them themselves at the workplace. Of course, fathers cannot care for children when they themselves are working, thus suggesting that this is not a long-term solution for the majority of mothers and no solution at all for single mothers. And it is the rare woman whose job or employer is such that she can herself care for her child on the job. Many employed mothers depend on relatives to care for children, particularly grandparents, and black women are more likely to use such arrangements, reflecting their greater access to extended-family kinship networks. Although extended-family care may be among the most desirable solutions, the reality is that it is simply not available to the great majority of mothers who work and thus cannot serve as any real solution to this problem.

According to the *Current Population Report* (U.S. Bureau of the Census, 1982), group care services are utilized by 15% of women with children under 5 years old. The women who made these arrangements were more likely to be well educated, to work full-time, and to have the higher family incomes necessary to afford them; and women who were married, with a husband present, utilized group care more than did those from other types of families. Multiple child care arrangements are becoming increasingly more common and represent creative attempts to provide care for children in the face of limited opportunities. Seventeen percent of mothers studied in the 1982 report used more than one type of child care. White women were more likely to do so than were black women, and this type of arrangement is often associated with having the primary source of care provided by the father. Although such statistics have likely changed considerably since the 1980 census on which these are based, it is still true that no comprehensive solution to the child care issue is in sight, and government and employers alike continue to treat it as a private rather than a societal issue.

The lack of adequate, affordable child care provisions creates critical problems for women workers and their children. Not only are individual women left with the responsibility of finding and paying for child care, but many women are simply not able to work when such services are not available. Bloom and Steen (1990) provide evidence suggesting that an increased supply of child care would bring many more women workers into the labor force (especially those with lower levels of education), would allow women already working to work more hours, and would increase the skill level and economic benefits of women employees. It is impossible to overemphasize the fact that, compared to other nations, the child care policies of the United States are woefully inadequate and do not reflect the current realities of American families (e.g., Kamerman, 1980). The strong pronatalist attitudes of recent administrations, combined with an unwillingness to provide even the most minimal of family supports, produces social policy that is not only inconsistent and unworkable but functions at the immediate expense of American women and their children and to the long-term detriment of society more generally. Further, given the link between the lack of adequate child care and women's decisions to drop out of the work force, such policies contribute to the poverty and hardships endured by millions of the most vulnerable of families.

SUMMARY

This chapter has attempted to provide a realistic picture of current demographic trends for employed mothers and to identify the most prominent policy issues raised by the return of late-20th-century American women to the work force. The 1990 census will no doubt reinforce our conclusion that working mothers are a prominent, valuable labor market resource; it will also most likely document the continued problems produced by American society's determined embrace of the "motherhood mandate" (Russo, 1979). This chapter documents our hope that working mothers will begin to receive the basic economic and personal benefits that are their due and that their lives and the lives of their children may be improved. As a society that professes to value both families and children, we can do no less.

REFERENCES

Bahr, S. J. (1974). Effects on power and division of labor in the family. In L. W. Hoffman & F. I. Nye (Eds.), *Working mothers* (pp. 167–185). San Francisco: Jossey-Bass.

Barnett, R. C., & Baruch, G. K. (1985). Women's involvement in multiple roles and psychological distress. *Journal of Personality and Social Psychology, 49*, 135–145.

Beale, F. (1970). Double jeopardy: To be black and female. In T. Cade (Ed.), *The black woman: An anthology* (pp. 90–100). New York: New American Library.

Betz, N. E., & Fitzgerald, L. F. (1987). *The career psychology of women*. Orlando, FL: Academic Press.

Blau, F. D., & Ferber, M. A. (1987). Occupations and earnings of women workers. In K. S. Koziara, M. H. Moskow, & L. D. Tanner (Eds.), *Working women: Past, present and future* (pp. 37–68). Washington, DC: Industrial Relations Research Association.

Bloom, D. E., & Steen, T. P. (1990). The labor force implications of expanding the child care industry. *Population Research and Policy Review, 9*, 25–44.

Bonilla-Santiago, G. (1990). A portrait of Hispanic women in the United States. In S. E. Rix (Ed.), *The American woman: 1990–91* (pp. 249–257). New York: W. H. Norton.

Defour, D. C. (1990). The interface of racism and sexism on college campuses. In M. A. Paludi, *Ivory tower: sexual harassment on campus* (pp. 45–52). Albany, NY: S. U. N. Y. Press.

Dipboye, R. L. (1987). Problems and progress of women in management. In K. S. Koziara, M. H. Moskow, & L. D. Tanner (Eds.), *Working women: Past, present and future* (pp. 118–153). Washington, DC: Industrial Relations Research Association.

Etaugh, C., & Study, G. G. (1989). Perceptions of mothers: Effects of employment status, marital status, and age of child. *Sex Roles, 20*, 59–70.

Faludi, S. (1991). *Backlash: The undeclared war against American women.* New York: Crown.

Fitzgerald, L. F., & Betz, N. E. (1983). Issues in the vocational psychology of women. In W. B. Walsh (Ed.), *Handbook of vocational psychology* (Vol. 1). Hillsdale, NJ: Erlbaum.

Gilbert, L. A. (1985). *Men in dual-career families: Current realities and future prospects.* Hillsdale, NJ: Lawrence Erlbaum.

Gilbert, L. A., & Rachlin, V. (1987). Mental health and psychological functioning of dual-career families. *The Counseling Psychologist, 15,* 7–49.

Greenberger, E., Goldberg, W. A., Crawford, T. J., & Granger, J. (1988). Beliefs about the consequences of maternal employment for children. *Psychology of Women Quarterly, 12,* 35–59.

Hayghe, H. (1984). Working mothers reach record numbers in 1984. *Monthly Labor Review, 107,* 31–34.

Hayghe, H. (1986). Rise in mothers' labor force activity include those with infants. *Monthly Labor Review, 109,* 43–45.

Hayghe, H. V. (1990). Family members in the work force. *Monthly Labor Review, 113,* 14–19.

Hetherington, C., & Orzek, A. (1989). Career counseling and life planning with lesbian women. *Journal of Counseling and Development, 68,* 52–55.

Hewlett, S. A. (1986). *A lesser life: The myth of women's liberation in America.* New York: Warner Books.

Hochschild, A. (1989). *The second shift.* New York: Viking.

Hock, E., Gnezda, M. T., & McBride, S. L. (1984). Mothers of infants: Attitudes toward employment and motherhood following birth of the first child. *Journal of Marriage and the Family, 46,* 425–431.

Johnson, B. J., & Waldman, E. (1983). Most women who maintain families receive poor labor market returns. *Monthly Labor Review, 106,* 30–34.

Kamerman, S. B. (1980). Child care and family benefits: Policies of six industrialized countries. *Mounthly Labor Review, 103,* 23–28.

Lott, J. T. (1990). A portrait of Asian and Pacific American women. In S. E. Rix (Ed.), *The American woman: 1990–91* (pp. 258–264). New York: W. W. Norton.

Malveaux, J., & Wallace, P. (1987). Minority women in the workplace. In K. S. Koziara, M. H. Moskow, & L. D. Tanner (Eds.), *Working women: past, present, future* (pp. 169–196). Washington, DC: Bureau of National Affairs.

McAdoo, H. (1987). Family changes within African-American families. *Smith College School for Social Work Journal, 5,* 19–22.

McAdoo, H. P. (1981). Stress and support networks of working single black mothers. In Mathews, E. L. (Ed.), *Black working women: Debunking the myths, a multidisciplinary approach* (pp. 169–196). Berkeley, CA: University of California Women's Center.

McAdoo, H. P. (1990). A portrait of African American families in the United States. In S. E. Rix (Ed.), *The American woman: 1990–91* (pp. 71–93). New York: W. W. Norton.

Morrison, A. M., & Von Glinow, M. A. (1990). women and minorities in management. *American Psychologist, 45,* 200–208.

Natera, M. (1988). *Hispana perspective.* Los Angeles: California State Department of Education, Career-Vocational Preparation Division.

National Council of La Raza. (1988). *Hispanics in the work force: Part 2. Hispanic women.* Washington, DC: Policy Analysis Center.

The National Report on Work and Family. (1988). *Parental leave would save women $607 million a year.* Washington, DC: Buraff Publications.

The National Report on Work and Family. (1989). *Women with maternity leave likely to resume work sooner.* Washington, DC: Buraff Publications.

Nye, F. I. (1974). Emerging and declining family roles. *Journal of Marriage and the Family, 36,* 238–245.

O'Connell, L., Betz, M., & Kurth, S. (1989). Plans for balancing work and family life: Do women pursuing nontraditional and traditional occupations differ? *Sex Roles, 20,* 35–45.

O'Connell, M. O. (1990). Maternity leave arrangements: 1961–85. In U.S. Bureau of the Census, Work and family patterns of American women. *Current population reports,* Ser. P-23, No. 165. Washington, DC: U.S. Government Printing Office.

Osipow, S. H. (1983). *Theories of career developments* (3rd ed.). New York: Prentice-Hall.

Rand, L. M., & Miller, A. L. (1972). A developmental cross-sectioning of women's careers and marriage attitudes and life plans. *Journal of Vocational Behavior, 2,* 317–331.

Rhode, D. L. (1990). Gender equality and employment policy. In S. E. Rix (Ed.), *The American woman: 1990–91* (pp. 170–200). New York: W. W. Norton.

Rix, S. E. (Ed.) (1990). *The American Women: 1990–91.* New York: W. W. Norton.

Russo, N. F. (1979). Overview: Sex roles, fertility, and the motherhood mandate. *Psychology of Women Quarterly, 4,* 7–15.

Schwartz, F. N. (1989, January–February). Management women and the new facts of life. *Harvard Business Review,* pp. 65–76.

Shank, S. E. (1988). Women and the labor market: The link grows stronger. *Monthly Labor Review, 111,* 3–8.

Smith, E. J. (1981). The working mother: A critique of the research. *Journal of Vocational Behavior, 19,* 191–211.

Snipp, C. M. (1990). A portrait of American Indian women and their labor force experiences. In S. E. Rix (Ed.), *The American woman: 1990–91* (pp. 265–272). New York: W. W. Norton.

U.S. Bureau of the Census. (1982). Child care arrangements of working mothers: June 1982. *Current population reports,* Ser. P-23, No. 129. Washington, DC: U.S. Government Printing Office.

U.S. Bureau of the Census. (1988). The Hispanic population in the United States, March 1988. *Current population reports,* Ser. P-20, No. 431. Washington, DC: U.S. Government Printing Office.

U.S. Department of Labor. (1983). *Time of change: 1983 handbook on women workers.* Washington, DC: U.S. Government Printing Office.

U.S. Department of Labor. (1989). *Working mothers and their children.* Washington, DC: Bureau of Labor Statistics.

■ 3
Women's Employment and Childbearing Decisions

Judith Frankel and Susan McCarty

There is no one pattern of work involvement for all women today. Women have options, choices available to them that will lead them down different employment paths. Women today can choose to follow the male model of uninterrupted employment throughout their lives by avoiding marriage and/or having children, and in fact it is projected that 20% to 25% of baby boomers will do so (Bloom & Russell, 1984). They can spend a significant portion of their lives rearing children and working as housewives and mothers without paid employment, as do 25% to 35% of mothers (Children's Defense Fund, 1987). They can combine the two options: continuous employment and rearing children simultaneously.

One of the most profound and dynamic social changes in the history of our country has taken place in American families in the years since 1970. Fifty-two percent of married women with children less than 1 year old now work outside the home. This is more than double the rate of maternal employment for mothers of infants in 1970 (Hayghe, 1986). More women are choosing to be employed throughout their childbearing years than in the past. It is estimated that by 1995 more than three quarters of all school-age children and two thirds of preschool children will have mothers in the labor force (Children's Defense Fund, 1987).

Women are also moving into male-dominated professions (Beller, 1984) at a faster rate than ever before. If male-dominated fields generally require greater investment and commitment to continuous full-time work, are the women entering these professions adopting male career models? The historically female pattern of interrupting work when children are very young seems to be changing to a male model of virtually uninterrupted work.

It is this singularly contemporary choice the authors are especially concerned with. But to understand why so many women make this decision, as well as the consequences of this choice, this chapter examines initially the reasons some women choose the options of remaining child-free and employed or rearing children while unemployed.

EMPLOYED AND CHILD-FREE

Choosing not to have children is a viable alternative for many women. This choice has become increasingly popular among the women born during the baby boom following World War II. For some women, employment is so primary they choose not to marry at all. Because employment can enable women to pursue self-fulfillment and economic independence, it might lessen women's motivation to marry in the first place. Although being currently employed increases or has no effect on marriage rates, Goldscheider and Waite (1986) showed that future work plans of young women decrease marriage probabilities over the short term. A number of factors other than employment history also influence a woman's decision to commit herself to being child-free and employed.

Career Orientation

When societal disapproval against women in the workplace began to dissipate, those women who cherished the opportunity to express their achievement needs through careers flourished. They chose to be employed. If they perceived that their employment would be threatened by a joint maternal role, they often chose to forgo the latter role in favor of the more salient one for them, that of career woman. When society began to accept this role as a valid one for women, more women made this choice. Nevertheless, large pockets of resistance to this choice remain, and child-free women still often have to defend their childlessness to family and friends.

Women who pursue high levels of education and professional careers are likely to be highly committed to their careers and are less likely to marry and become parents (Bloom & Russell, 1984; Rudkin, 1986). If and when they do marry and have a child, they would be most likely to remain involved in their careers, as we will see later in this chapter.

Women who are highly motivated toward careers and choose not to marry or have children may do so because they perceive the dual role as disadvantageous to their careers and thus to their personal satisfaction.

Costs of Child Rearing

For women who are employed and plan to continue their employment, having children has certain costs associated with it, both direct economic costs and what Nock (1987) calls "opportunity costs." When considering maternity, an employed woman must take into account whether she can take leave to have her baby, whether the leave will be paid, if health insurance will continue throughout the leave, and if her job will be there for her when she is ready to return to work. There is presently no policy mandating uniform employer support for any of these variables, and thus some women are reluctant to have children.

Direct Costs

Many women postpone or give up motherhood because they are convinced that the direct monetary cost, or outright expense, of having children is an expensive proposition and rising. Nevertheless, the expense of child rearing has remained relatively constant. The percentage of annual disposable income allocated for the cost of raising a child did not increase over the 20 years from 1961 to 1981 (Espenshade, 1984). The family cost per child (in terms of percentage of annual disposable income) remained relatively unchanged during this same period as well. So, despite the impression of bearing and raising children as a costly proposition, the evidence indicates that there has been little if any increase in the cost to a family (Nock, 1987).

For many families, the income needed to rear a child is seen as more profitably spent in other personal areas. The major reason given in Veevers's 1980 study of couples who chose to be child-free was that a child-free life-style suited them best. Most of the life-styles referred to required use of much discretionary income, as well as time to enjoy the fruits of their labor without the need to care for children.

Opportunity Costs

Actual or potential "opportunity costs" are the opportunities a woman gives up or feels that she may have to give up to have children (Nock, 1987). An employed woman might anticipate that having children would prohibit her from pursuing a career that requires many hours on the job, a fluctuating schedule, or travel that might be especially difficult to manage along with the demands of a family. Butz and Ward (1979) point out that as the wages an employed woman contributes to the family income increase, her perceived opportunity cost to the family of having children will rise. This concern would be an especially important factor when having children causes an interruption in employment or missed opportunities for advancement in one's career.

But women perceive high opportunity costs beyond the actual interruption of their labor force participation. Women are aware that combining employment and maternity may give them less time at home, less time with their spouses, less time to enjoy leisure pursuits, and less time generally for themselves. This perceived role strain resulting from the additional responsibilities a child brings to a woman is a potential cost. For some women this cost is high enough to limit themselves to either career or motherhood.

The present authors believe that decisions concerning childbearing include considerations of time, money, and particularly life-style; however, Nock (1987) feels that most couples making decisions about childbearing are not fully aware of the time and money changes that having a child brings. He believes that these factors play a small role in the decision making. Instead, he sees the symbolic meaning of children as playing a more decisive role.

Symbolic Meaning of Children

How men and women look at the meaning and value of children will determine whether they choose to have them. Children are generally less likely to be seen as an asset to the family than they were in society's recent agrarian past. Because we have a more independent, individualistic outlook in the 1990s, we do not value having children for the purpose of their taking care of us in our old age or providing workers for the family farm.

Much recent research implies that children are now often seen more as a burden on a family than as a joy and enhancement to it. Nock (1987) suggested that this view may be due to a shift in the symbolic meaning of child rearing within our culture. He appears to feel that this shift is most demonstrable in those women who, he contends, endorse male–female equality and "are more like 'consumers' of children—deciding carefully when, how many, and increasingly, what type of child they will have" (p. 374). He asserts that lower fertility among women who endorse male–female equality is a predictable outcome of this symbolic meaning of childbearing. Children have a very different symbolic meaning for these women than they do for women who retain a traditional view, who do not see men and women as equal, and who expect motherhood to be a central and defining aspect of their adult lives. Although the present authors do not necessarily hold with his analysis, we recognize the importance of the symbolic meaning of children to childbearing/employment decisions and will address the issue again later.

REARING CHILDREN AS FULL-TIME CAREER

Despite the current emphasis on women's careers, a number of women continue to follow what has been called the traditional pattern for women; they remain at home full-time while rearing their children.

This option is not readily available to poor mothers who must work for monetary reasons. Because of financial need, employment would seem more likely to be mandated for single mothers as a group. Marital status has been shown to be a powerful predictor of maternal employment (Tienda & Glass, 1985) across groups of black, Hispanic, and white mothers.

Mothers who are financially able to make the choice to remain unemployed while rearing their children do so for many complex reasons.

Beliefs about Maternal Care

One of the most important reasons a mother decides not to seek employment is her belief in "exclusive maternal care." Women who are full-time homemakers have a significantly greater distrust of nonmaternal care (Hock, 1978; Morgan & Hock, 1984). They believe that a mother can meet her child's needs better than anyone else and that a child is happier with its mother than with baby-sitters or teachers. These mothers feel needed at home because they think their children cannot be cared for adequately by others.

In 1989, Mason and Kuhlthau conducted research that sought to determine what ideals parents of preschoolers hold about child care situations. Most women in the sample felt that parents are the ideal daytime caregivers for children. One third of respondents said that when mothers are not available for child care because of employment, the father would be the ideal caretaker. There was a surprisingly widespread preference for parental care, given the high rates of maternal employment in the sample.

The cultural norm that children must be cared for exclusively by their mothers has weakened in the past two decades (Mason & Yu, 1988). Nevertheless, the evidence shows that women who choose to be employed outside the home have a great deal of cognitive dissonance to deal with if they are attempting to live out their ideals regarding the best care for their children. Those women who remain at home during the child-rearing years avoid this dissonance.

Role Strain

Role conflict, or role strain, theories assume that because individuals have finite energies, the demands of multiple social roles will produce conflict between competing roles or overload from overwork (Goode, 1960). Women who hold this position will then choose between child-rearing and employment roles rather than assume both. Those women who decide that having children is a primary value for them will leave the workplace to rear their children in order to avoid role strain.

For some of these mothers the choice has negative consequences. New mothers who stay home but who were highly involved in paid work before the birth are more irritable, depressed, and have lower self-esteem (Pistrang, 1984).

Problems with Day Care

Mothers who chose to remain at home while caring for their children may do so because of anticipated problems with obtaining substitute care that will meet the social, emotional, and physical needs of their children. And in fact, research by Belsky and Rovine (1988) suggests that maternal employment in the first year of life is associated with increased insecure maternal attachment relationships. More will be said about problems of day care later in this chapter.

Age and Number of Children

The age of a woman's child and the number of other preschool children in the family have also been shown to influence a mother's employment decisions (Morgan & Hock, 1984; Tienda & Glass, 1985). Although there are psychological factors (such as career orientation) that exceed these in importance, it does seem that, to some extent, the more children there are to be cared for in a family, the more likely it is that the mother will decide to stay home to take care of them. The high cost of child care outside the home may also be a factor as the number of children in a family increases. It may also be that women more oriented toward homemaking and traditional roles are more likely to decide to have larger families in the first place.

Mothers who are not employed during their child's infancy are less likely to have been employed before the pregnancy and are more likely to have negative attitudes about maternal employment, regardless of the income level of the family. Keep in mind that it is the mothers of infants who experience the greatest homemaker workload at home. Hartmann (1981) found that an employed mother of an infant spends 50 hours a week on housework, including 20 hours on child care. Her employed husband spends a total of 20 hours a week on all home-related chores, including do-it-yourself repairs, car maintenance, painting, and child care. Under these conditions, we can see why some women opt to remain out of the workplace and devote their efforts to their home responsibilities.

COMBINING HOMEMAKING WITH EMPLOYMENT

Despite the reasons that so many women choose either to forgo children for career or to forgo career for children, being employed, married, and experiencing motherhood simultaneously is the preferred life-style for most women today. Projections from the Department of Labor are that by 1995, roughly two thirds of all new labor force entrants will be women (Johnson, 1987), and 80% of those in their childbearing years are expected to have children during their work lives.

Economic Necessity

One of the most commonly cited explanations for the dramatic increase in the labor force participation of mothers is economic need. To avoid poverty, most divorced, single, and widowed mothers simply must be employed. Divorced women with children, who remarry, usually continue their employment after remarriage as well, regardless of their new family income.

Some scholars point out, however, that the sift in perceived financial need is as likely to be a precipitating factor in maternal employment decisions as is a shift in "real" need (Eggebeen, 1988; Fox & Hesse-Biber, 1984).

Eggebeen and Hawkins (1990) assert that the meaning of economic necessity as a reason for married mothers entering the labor force has changed significantly during the past 30 years. Economic necessity used to mean that the mother's income was needed to provide basic necessities. Now economic necessity can mean that the family seeks a preferred standard of living, higher than what one salary alone can provide. They found that whereas 67% of all employed mothers in 1960 worked to provide basic necessities, only 37% did so in 1980. These authors seem convinced that although women cite economic necessity as a factor in employment decisions, the real changes in levels of maternal employment have come about either because of women working to provide a higher standard of living for their families and themselves or for noneconomic reasons.

Hoffman (1989) points out that researchers found evidence of a gradually declining effect of husband's income on labor force participation of mothers up through the mid-1970s. This position supports the notion that mothers are more likely to be employed in the 1990s regardless of their family income level. Noneconomic factors, such as self-fulfillment, self-worth, and achievement needs related to career commitment, may be increasing in importance.

Personal Satisfaction

Women today are encouraged to fulfill their potential as human beings. For many of them, that includes both mothering and achieving in the workplace. Under positive conditions, women can "have it all" and be most content. For those who see life as richest when employed *and* rearing children, the choice of a dual role, mother/worker, is most satisfying.

Women will choose the combined role when they are pleased with the quality of their jobs, with their husbands' attitudes toward their employment (Baruch & Barnett, 1987), and with the availability of stable child care arrangements (Goldberg & Esterbrooks, 1988).

Career Orientation

For many women, work outside the home is not just a job but a career. During the 1970s, researchers Fogarty, Rappoport, and Rappoport (1971) and Hock (1978) pointed to the importance of a career to mothers. And in the 1980s, Morgan and Hock (1984) found that career orientation was an important factor in mothers' employment decisions. Career orientation—the amount of expressed interest in a career— was the factor most predictive of the level of employment of all of the variables they studied. It accounted for 46% to 62% of the variance in maternal employment over the 6-year period of their study.

According to Avioli (1985), prior work experience and the plan to be employed in the future are the most salient factors discriminating between employed mothers and nonemployed mothers.

Higher education is a factor in increasing maternal labor force participation because it creates access to attractive jobs and sometimes professional careers, which are less easily given up when children are born. It seems sensible to assume that the more attractive and interesting the job opportunities are for women, the more likely they will pursue employment.

However, the attributes that we think of as comprising career commitment are also present in workers at jobs other than professional levels. Surveys by Hiller and Dyehouse (1987) of working-class mothers with jobs as waitresses, factory workers, and domestics showed that these women are quite committed to their jobs and satisfied with their diverse roles. They would not leave their jobs even if they did not need the money. This finding was supported by DeChick (1988), who concluded that most employed mothers would not leave their paid employment if the family did not need the money.

Role Enhancement

Some women see performing more than one role—being an employee and a mother, for example—as a way of enhancing their lives. Researchers (Marks, 1977; Sieber, 1974; Thoits, 1983) have proposed that multiple roles provide multiple sources of social support, skills that transfer from one role to another, and an increased sense of meaning and purpose. The employment role can enhance a woman's self-esteem, help her realize important goals and experience greater measures of financial autonomy and independence. Motherhood can validate her life, giving meaning and purpose as well as the joys inherent in rearing children. The interplay of both roles multiplies the satisfaction received by each separately.

Fulfilling Social Needs

Women's need to participate in a social support system outside the family may also be a factor in maternal employment decisions. Employment offers the opportunity for a larger social network, which can be beneficial to mental health. In fact, because employed women are less likely to feel socially isolated, they are less likely to suffer from depression (Repetti, Matthews, & Waldron, 1989).

Availability of Good Day Care

The presence and availability of good-quality day care and the parents' perception that their child will be positively affected by their experience in day care may be a factor affecting maternal employment decisions. Many parents no longer believe it necessary for infants and children to have the full-time care of their mothers. This concept is perhaps part of a changing cultural value about what children need or do not need.

Demand for day care is high, and the need for more quality day care is critical. Problems with day care will be discussed later in the chapter.

Employment Options

Mothers are more likely to work when they can find employment with flexible options. Part-time employment is often cited as being ideal for the family during the early years of motherhood, providing women with an outlet for personal achievement while reserving adequate time to devote to family needs. Several studies have determined that women prefer part-time employment over nonemployment during their active mothering years. Bollman et al. (Bollman, Schumm, Bugaighis, & Jurich, 1988) demonstrate that actual and ideal maternal roles (as assessed by mother, father, and an adolescent family member) were closest when mothers were actually employed part-time.

However, disadvantages of part-time employment, such as relatively low pay, few benefits, and less chance for career development, often make the consideration of part-time work an unaffordable luxury. Mothers chose to work part-time regardless of these disadvantages. A saving grace for them is the fact that the number of hours a mother is employed is not clearly related to maternal employment satisfaction. On the other hand, when the number of hours worked exceeds full time, negative effects on family life have been documented. This problem will be discussed later in the chapter.

Homemaking

Help with homemaking is another reason women may choose to work outside the home. There is some evidence that fathers are increasing their involvement in providing child care and housework in dual-earner families (Darling-Fisher & Tiedje, 1990; Hoffman, 1986).

Women are encouraged to work outside the home even though husband involvement in housework may not be adequate. It is certainly not equally divided between the husband and wife if both are employed (Bernardo, Shehan, & Leslie, 1987; Hiller & Philliber, 1986). It appears that as a woman's own earnings increase, the amount of time she spends on housework decreases. This is not because her husband does more of the housework but rather because she can afford to hire another person—usually a poor, minority woman—to do the housework for her (Bernardo et al., 1987).

DISCUSSION

Women today *do* exercise their options to (1) be employed without having children, (2) to rear children while not employed, or (3) to be employed and rear children at the same time. The majority are choosing the latter course, and this decision leads to some serious problems. If women are to make even more viable and meaningful choices about employment and motherhood, these problems must be addressed. Solutions should take into account all members of the family and should attend to the needs of mother, father, and children.

Problems in the Day Care Industry

One of the best predictors of positive outcomes for children in day care is the quality of caregiver/child interactions. High-quality day care may be defined as

- Care with caregiver/child interactions that are positive and re-sponsive.
- Small groups.
- An appropriate ratio of well—trained adult caregivers to children.

Such day care appears to have positive effects on children's intellectual development (Breitmayer & Ramey, 1986). Unfortunately, quality day care situations have *not* been able to keep up with the dramatic increase of children requiring such care.

In the past decade, the quality of day care has declined. Child care staff wages, when adjusted for inflation, have decreased more than 20% (Whitebrook, Howes, & Phillips, 1989). Child care teaching staffs earn less than half as much as comparably educated women and less than one third as much as comparably educated men in the civilian labor force (Whitebrook et al., 1989). Direct federal funding for child care programs actually decreased by 18% in real dollars between 1980 and 1986 (Kahn & Kamerman, 1987).

Fewer children are actually reaching day care centers. Given the lack of an official government policy mandating a child care system, parents are left on their own to seek out child care where they can find it. According to Nelson (1988), only 6% of parents use licensed providers. Ninety-four percent of the children are cared for in private homes by unlicensed providers, usually neighbors, and, shockingly, Hewlet (1986) finds that about 23% of working parents using unlicensed care must regularly leave their children without any adult supervision at all.

Children are going to day care at younger and younger ages as more women are employed during the child's first year of life (Kamerman, 1986). This trend, taken in conjunction with the general decline in the quality of day care and the fact that licensed centers are reluctant to take infants, is a cause for real concern. Recent longitudinal research shows that during infancy the teacher's influence on the child is even more important than that of the family (Howe, 1990).

Howe's (1990) study emphasizes the critical importance of high-quality day care, with enough stable, trained caregivers to interact positively with infants. Quality care is thus a national concern; therefore, we must seek solutions to this problem in the national rather than only in the personal sphere.

Work Hours

American workers are working longer hours than previously, and employed mothers share in the general trend. The U.S. Census Bureau (1990) reports that 23.9% of women working as executives, managers, or administrators put in 49 or more hours a week in 1989. Twenty percent of women, working as salespeople, professionals, journalists, bureaucrats, secretaries, clerks, or self-employed, spent 49 or more hours per week on the job last year. Ten years ago only 18% of all people with full-time jobs, men and women, worked so much.

In 1970, only 2.2% of women worked at more than one job. Today 5.9% of women workers hold more than one job. Although the numbers of women who have more than one job are still relatively small, it is important to note that there has been almost a threefold increase in their numbers, an additional indication that women have increased their activity in the job market in the past 20 years.

Although much research shows that children are not harmed by their mothers' working (Zaslow, Pederson, Suwalsky, & Rabinovich, 1983), a number of recent studies indicate that when mothers work more than 40 hour a week, they and their families experienced negative effects.

These negative effects were noted for children at all ages. For example, Owen and Cox (1988) found that infants' mothers who worked more than 40 hours a week were more anxious and dissatisfied. Kindergarten-age children, boys in particular, of mothers who worked longer hours were found more likely to suffer separation anxiety (Goldberg & Easterbrooks, 1988). And Guidubaldi and Nastasi (1987) found that school-age children of mothers who worked long hours scored more negatively on an adjustment scale both at first testing and 2 years later.

Long hours of employment seem to have destructive consequences for the family. It thus is time for industry to rethink the long hours now needed to be successful on the job.

Homemaking and Parenting Concerns

A major challenge for families of the 1990s is combining parenting with employment, and a secondary challenge is to find time and energy to engage in homemaking. Because homemaking remains a time-consuming task in the 1990s (Ogden, 1986), the questions of who is going to do housework and how he or she will do it are of critical importance.

Presently, women bear the main burden for housework, whether they are employed outside the home or not. They believe that it is their responsibility to do so. Men do housework to help out their wives (Gunter & Gunter, 1990).

It is quite clear that the role of homemaker is a demanding one for any woman, particularly one employed outside the home. Full-time homemakers spend an average of 50–60 hours a week on housework. Employed homemakers spend 30–40 hours a week on housework. these amounts vary according to the changing demands on the household, such as the presence of infants and young children who require much of the homemaker's time for caretaking (Cowan, 1983).

How the household work is divided and how equitable that division is perceived to be are closely related to a woman's satisfaction in her maternal/employment roles. A recent survey of 1,300 readers of *Redbook Magazine* determined that 64% of working women who said their husbands "seldom or never [do] a fair share of the housework" showed high rates of marital dissatisfaction, whereas only 10% who said their husbands do a "fair share most of the time" showed similar dissatisfaction (Belle, 1990).

Being responsible for the majority of housework, without any realistic assistance from family members or paid help, contributes to the role strain felt by employed mothers, who, instead of feeling that they "have it all," must surely feel at times that they must "do it all." Surely, it is time to reevaluate the responsibility for housework within the family. It is also time to reevaluate the responsibility for parenting within the family. The shift in the symbolic meaning of childbearing for women, discussed earlier in the chapter, has far-reaching implications for the family. In the past, men did not see children as giving core meaning to their lives but shared women's perceptions that parenting was the focus of a woman's life. Now that women are reexamining the meaning of children in their lives, it becomes imperative that men do the same. Then, decisions around maternal employment will fit the expectations of both parents.

Only when the roadblocks that this chapter has highlighted are eliminated will women be able to make wise and freely chosen maternal/employment decisions in the best interests of themselves and their families.

REFERENCES

Avioli, P. S. (1985). The labor-force participation of married mothers of infants. *Journal of Marriage and the Family, 47,* 739–745.

Baruch, G. K., & Barnett, R. C. (1987). Role quality and psychological well-being. In F. Crosby (Ed.), *Spouse, parent, worker* (pp. 63–84). New Haven, CT: Yale University Press.

Belle, D. (1990, June). Rate your stress life. *Redbook Magazine,* pp. 83–90.

Beller, A. H. (1984). Trends in occupational segregation by race and sex. In B. F.

Reskin (Ed.), *Sex segregation in the workplace: Trends, explanations, remedies* (pp. 11–26). Washington, DC: National Academy Press.

Belsky, J., & Rovine, M. (1988). Non-maternal care in the first year of life and attachment security. *Child Development, 59,* 157–167.

Bernardo, D. H., Shehan, C. L., & Leslie, G. R. (1987). A residue of tradition: Jobs, careers, and spouse's time in housework. *Journal of Marriage and the Family, 49,* 381–390.

Bloom, E., & Russell, J. (1984). What are the determinants of delayed childbearing and voluntary childlessness in the United States? *Demography, 21,* 591–611.

Bollman, R., Schumm, W. R., Bugaighis, M. A., & Jurich, A. (1988). Family members' perceptions of actual and ideal maternal roles as a function of maternal employment. *Perceptual and Motor Skills, 67,* 185–186.

Breitmayer, B. J., & Ramey, C. T. (1986). Biological nonoptimality and quality of postnatal environment as codeterminants of intellectual development. *Child Development, 57,* 1151–1165.

Butz, W. P., & Ward, M. P. (1979). The emergence of countercyclical U.S. fertility. *American Economics Review, 69,* 318–328.

Children's Defense Fund. (1987). *A children's defense budget.* Washington, DC: Author.

Cowan, R. S. (1983). *More work for mother: The ironies of household technology from open hearth to microwave.* New York: Basic Books.

Darling-Fischer, C. S., & Tiedje, L. B. (1990). The impact of maternal employment characteristics on father's participation in child care. *Family Relations, 39,* 20–26.

DeChick, J. (1988, July 19). Most mothers want a job, too. *USA Today,* p. D1.

Eggebeen, D. J. (1988). Determinants of maternal employment for white preschool children: 1960–1980. *Journal of Marriage and the Family, 50,* 149–159.

Eggebeen, D. J., & Hawkins, A. J. (1990). Economic need and wives' employment. *Journal of Family Issues, 11*(1), 48–66.

Espenshade, T. J. (1984). *Investing in children: New estimates of parental expenditures.* Washington, DC: Urban Institute.

Fogarty, M. P., Rappoport, R., & Rappoport, R. W. (1971). *Sex, career, and family.* Beverly Hills, CA: Sage.

Fox, M. F., & Hesse-Biber, S. (1984). *Women at work.* Palo Alto, CA: Mayfield.

Goldberg, W. A., & Easterbrooks, M. A. (1988). Maternal employment when children are toddlers and kindergartners. In A. E. Gottfried & A. W. Gottfried (Eds.), *Maternal employment and children's development: Longitudinal research* (pp. 121–154). New York: Plenum.

Goldscheider, F. K., & Waite, L. J. (1986). Sex differences in the entry into marriage. *American Journal of Sociology, 92,* 91–109.

Goode, W. J. (1960). A theory of role strain. *American Sociological Reviews, 25,* 483–496.

Guidubaldi, J., & Nastasi, B. K. (1987, April). *Home environment factors as predictors of child adjustment in mother-employed households: Results of a nationwide study.* Paper presented at the biennial meeting of the Society of Research in Child Development, Baltimore.

Gunter, N. C., & Gunter, B. G. (1990). Domestic division of labor among working couples. *Psychology of Women Quarterly, 14,* 355–370.

Hartmann, H. I. (1981). The family as the locus of gender, class, and political struggle: The example of housework. *Signs, 6*(2), 366–394.

Hayghe, H. (1986). Rise in mothers' labor force activity includes those with infants. *Monthly Labor Review, 109*(2), 43–45.

Hewlett, S. A. (1986). *A lesser life.* New York: William Morrow.

Hiller, D. V., & Dyehouse, J. (1987). A case for banishing "dual-career marriages" from the research literature. *Journal of Marriage and the Family, 49,* 787–795.

Hiller, D. V., & Philliber, W. W. (1986). The division of labor in contemporary marriage: Expectations, perceptions, and performance. *Social Problems, 33,* 191–201.

Hock, E. (1978). Working and nonworking mothers with infants: Their satisfaction with mothering. *Developmental Psychology, 14,* 37–43.

Hoffman, L. W. (1986). Work, family and the child. In M. S. Pallak & R. O. Perloff (Eds.), *Psychology and work: Productivity, change, and employment* (pp. 173–220). Washington, DC: American Psychological Association.

Hoffman, L. W. (1989). Effects of maternal employment in the two-parent family. *American Psychologist, 4*(2), 283–292.

Howe, C. (1990). Can the age of entry into child care and the quality of child care predict adjustment in kindergarten? *Developmental Psychology, 26*(2), 292–303.

Johnson, W. B. (1987). *Workforce 2000: Work and workers for the 21st century.* Indianapolis, IN: Hudson Institute.

Kahn, A. J., & Kamerman, S. B. (1987). *Childcare: Facing the hard choices.* Dover, MA: Auburn House.

Kamerman, S. B. (1986). Childcare services: A national picture. In C. H. Thomas (Ed.), *Current issues in child care* (pp. 4–8). Phoenix, AZ: Oryx Press.

Marks, S. R. (1977). Multiple roles and role-strain: Some notes on human energy, time and commitment. *American Sociological Review, 42,* 921–936.

Mason, K. O., & Kuhlthau, K. (1989). Determinants of child care ideals among mothers of preschool-aged children. *Journal of Marriage and the Family, 51,* 593–603.

Mason, K. O., & Yu, Y.-L. (1988). Attitudes toward women's familial roles: Changes in the United States, 1977–1985. *Gender and Society, 2,* 39–57.

Morgan, K. C., & Hock, E. (1984). A longitudinal study of psychosocial variables affecting the career patterns of women with young children. *Journal of Marriage and the Family, 46*(2), 383–392.

Nelson, M. (1988). Providing family day care: An analysis of home-based work. *Social Problems, 35,* 78–94.

Nock, L. (1987). The symbolic meaning of childbearing. *Journal of Family Issues, 8*(4), 373–393.

Ogden, A. s. (1986). *The great American housewife.* Westport, CT: Greenwood.

Owen, M. T., & Cox, M. J. (1988). Maternal employment and the transition to parenthood. In A. E. Gottfried & A. W. Gottfried (Eds.), *Maternal employment and children's development: Longitudinal research* (pp. 85–119). New York: Plenum.

Pistrang, N. (1984). Women's work involvement and experience of new mother-hood. *Journal of Marriage and the Family, 46*, 433–448.

Repetti, L., Matthews, A., & Waldron, I. (1989). Employment and women's health—effects of paid employment on women's mental and physical health. *American Psychologist, 44*(11), 1394–1401.

Rudkin, L. (1986, April). *Delayed childbearing among women aged 30–39 in the United States: 1971–80*. Paper presented at the annual meeting of the Population Association of America, San Francisco.

Sieber, D. (1974). Toward a theory of role accumulation. *American Sociological Review, 39*, 467–478.

Thoits, P. A. (1983). Multiple identities and psychological well-being: A reformulation and test of the social isolation hypothesis. *American Sociological Review, 48*, 147–187.

Tienda, M., & Glass, J. (1985). Household structure and labor force participation of black, Hispanic, and white mothers. *Demography, 22*, 381–394.

U.S. Bureau of the Census. (1990). *Statistical abstract of the United States*. Washington, DC: U.S. Government Printing Office.

Veevers, J. (1980). *Childless by choice*. Toronto: Butterworths.

Whitebook, M., Howes, G., Phillips, D., & Pemberton, C. (1989). Who cares? Child care teachers and the quality of care in America. *Young Children, 45*(1), 41–45.

Zaslow, M., Pederson, F., Suwalsky, J., & Rabinovich, B. (1983, April). *Maternal employment and parent-infant interaction*. Paper presented at meeting of the Society for Research in Child Development, Detroit.

■ Part 2
Impact on Family
Members

■ 4
The Employed Mother's Well-Being

Heather A. Sears and Nancy L. Galambos

The steady influx of women into the labor force in recent decades has been a dramatic trend, with important implications for the ways in which family members live. Although research on mothers' employment has been conducted since the 1930s, the literature has focused primarily on the effects of maternal employment on children; less attention has been given to the effects of employment on mothers. Recently, the association between women's employment and their well-being (i.e., physical and mental health) has received more empirical attention, as evidenced by a number of reviews (e.g., McBride, 1990; Repetti, Matthews, & Waldron, 1989; Rodin & Ickovics, 1990). This is an important area of inquiry, first, because society needs to know more about how the challenges, stresses, and rewards of employment affect women's well-being, and second, because it is partly through women's well-being that their employment may affect their partners and children.

To understand how participation in the workplace might affect women, it is important to characterize the jobs that women have. The majority of employed women are clustered in clerical and service positions,

*Completion of this chapter was supported by a Social Sciences and Humanities Research Council of Canada Grant to N. L. Galambos.
Address correspondence to Heather A. Sears, Department of Psychology, University of Victoria, P. O. Box 3050, Victoria, British Columbia, Canada V8W 3P5

many of which are part-time (LaCroix & Haynes, 1987; Voydanoff, 1987). There is no doubt that these occupations may be stressful. Clerical and service positions are frequently characterized by pay inequity, under-utilization of skills, and limited opportunities for promotion, all of which have been related to physical and psychological symptoms of stress (Greenglass, 1985). However, it is clear that few studies have examined the specific sources of and extent to which women experience stress related to their jobs; the benefits of being employed have also been neglected (Hoffman, 1989). Some women have moved up in the occupational hierarchy, assuming jobs with higher status and greater responsibility, and a number of women are entering jobs traditionally dominated by men (e.g., law, medicine, and engineering) (Harlan & Jansen, 1987; Matthews & Rodin, 1989). These jobs, too, bring with them unique sets of stressors and rewards that need to be studied.

The increase in the work force participation of women has called attention to the importance of investigating the processes by which women's employment conditions (e.g., work overload, opportunities for social interaction) are related to aspects of family functioning. Positive and negative events experienced at work, for example, may spill over to affect the quality of marital and family relations (Bolger, DeLongis, Kessler, & Wethington, 1989; Piotrkowski, 1979). Zedeck and Mosier (1990) have recently summarized the literature modeling the intersection of life at work with life at home. These models, however, fail to define what it is about work that influences family functioning and by what processes these influences occur. As illustrated in the following example, the employed woman is well aware of how intimately her work is tied to her physical and mental well-being and to family functioning.

> I've just spent the past four weeks working 12 to 15 hours a day on a book proposal. Last night, I swam my regular 24 laps between 9:15 and 10:00 p.m., then sat up till midnight chatting with my husband over a glass of wine (if we don't schedule these late-night talks, we can't get together at all). Between sips of Bordeaux, I fried a chicken breast for my daughter's school lunch and washed two loads of clothes. After falling into bed at 12:30 a.m., I was up again at 6:30 a.m. to drive my daughter to school (band starts at 7). Now, I sit here staring blearily at my typewriter. (Browder, 1991, p. 94)

Many employed women have similar stories to share. The purpose of this chapter is to review the literature that documents the links between work, well-being, and family functioning in samples of women. We begin by examining whether a woman's participation in the labor force is associated with health status.

LABOR FORCE PARTICIPATION AND HEALTH

As a result of women's increasing participation in the work force, researchers began asking whether there were negative effects of employment on women's health. The underlying assumption was that once women were exposed to the stressors of the workplace, they, like some employed men, would suffer poorer mental and physical health. The corollary to this assumption was that staying home and raising children was a positive experience, devoid of stress, fatigue, and boredom (Baruch, Biener, & Barnett, 1987). Thus, when studies found that, overall, employed women showed *fewer* signs of psychological distress than did nonemployed women (e.g., Kessler & McRae, 1982), the potential benefits of the work role and the potential strain of the homemaking role began to merit some empirical attention.

In recent years, an association between employment and better mental and physical health among women has been documented consistently in a variety of studies (LaCroix & Haynes, 1987; Verbrugge, 1989). Of course, it is difficult to argue that employment *causes* greater well-being (i.e., the social causation hypothesis) because it is also plausible that women who are of poorer health are less likely to seek, obtain, and remain in jobs (i.e., the social selection hypothesis) (Rodin & Ickovics, 1990). Recently, Adelmann, Antonucci, Crohan, and Coleman (1990) reported a reciprocal causal relationship between employment and health for midlife women: not only is part of the difference in health between employed and nonemployed women explained by the exclusion of unhealthy women from the labor force, but also women's health benefits from their involvement in employment. This finding suggests that the social causation and social selection hypotheses may operate simultaneously and are not necessarily mutually exclusive.

Research on women's employment and health is becoming increasingly sophisticated, focusing on women's multiple roles. In general, the more roles women occupy, the better their mental and physical health seems to be (Baruch et al., 1987). Although the role of mother may be a primary source of stress for women (Barnett & Baruch, 1985), on average, employed, married women who are parents are healthiest mentally and physically, whereas nonemployed, single women who are not parents are least healthy (Kandel, Davies, & Raveis, 1985; Verbrugge, 1983). Of course, some aspects of the parent role (e.g., having three or more children or having preschoolers at home) may offset some of the apparent advantages of employment (Voydanoff, 1987).

In this regard, Baruch et al. (1987) argues that it is not whether a woman occupies a given role that is important for her well-being. Rather, it is the *quality* of each of her roles (i.e., employee, spouse, parent) and the balance among them that will predict women's well-being. Verbrugge (1986) suggested that low-quality roles (e.g., a work role characterized by irregular schedules) may jeopardize women's health, whereas high-quality roles (e.g., a work role characterized by job complexity), even if these are numerous, may help maintain or enhance women's health. To better understand the quality of the work role, it is important to assess the nature of the work environment, a topic to which we now turn.

THE WORK ENVIRONMENT

Much of the research on women's employment has characterized the work role on the basis of employment status (i.e., employed full-time, part-time, or not at all) or occupational category (e.g., blue-collar). Studies investigating mothers' employment status initially compared employed mothers with nonemployed mothers and, later, mothers employed full-time with those employed part-time (Hoffman, 1989). This literature has been criticized because employment status alone fails to capture the complexity of mothers' work experiences.

With respect to studies of occupational category, the literature frequently compares blue-collar with white-collar workers (e.g., Waldron & Jacobs, 1988) or focuses on specific segments of the labor force, such as teachers or nurses (e.g., Dewe, 1987). Repetti et al. (1989), however, cautioned that differences in physical and mental health based on occupation may reflect differences in job characteristics or differences in personal characteristics and home situations of women who work in different occupations. They concluded that findings from this literature are difficult to compare because indices of occupations and health have been defined in different ways.

A focus on specific dimensions of occupational experiences (e.g., pay, routinization of tasks) is generally more informative than are studies of employment status and occupational category (LaCroix & Haynes, 1987; Miller, Schooler, Kohn, & Miller, 1979), but the specific aspects of paid work that are important for women's well-being have not been clearly identified (Adelmann, 1987). This is because, until recently, studies investigating the impact of work conditions on employees' adjustment have either excluded women as subjects (e.g., Hodapp, Neuser, & Weyer, 1988), have failed to analyze the data for sex differences (e.g., Sze & Ivker, 1986), or have not excluded measures that may be unique to women's experiences (e.g., sexual harassment, availability of child care) (Brief, Schuler, & Van Sell, 1981).

A popular approach to the study of work conditions has been to measure women's perceptions of the work environment and to relate these perceptions to measures of well-being (Caplan, 1985). A variety of work conditions have been considered in the research. Factors such as shift work, role ambiguity, technical changes, low job control, low or high job complexity, repetition and routinization, supervisory responsibilities, absence of social support, work overload, underutilization of skills, inadequate income, and low occupational status have been negatively associated with employed women's well-being (Adelmann, 1987; Bosch & deLange, 1987; Brief et al., 1981; Crohan, Antonucci, Adelmann, & Coleman, 1989; Hibbard & Pope, 1985; LaCroix & Haynes, 1987; Muller, 1986; O'Neill & Zeichner, 1985; Voydanoff & Donnelly, 1989). Although these conditions are relevant to men's and women's occupations, it is important to note that women may be exposed to some negative work conditions simply because they are women. Thus, sexual harassment and sexual discrimination are much more likely to be faced by female workers (Brief et al., 1981; Lips & Colwill, 1988).

Most studies of women's work conditions have evaluated the extent to which women's exposure to work conditions is associated with feelings of stress. Thus, we will present research linking employment to levels of stress. However, some work conditions (e.g., job complexity) may be beneficial for women's well-being. This leads us to consider, then, positive outcomes of employment, such as job satisfaction.

PHYSICAL AND PSYCHOLOGICAL STRESS

The strength of the evidence for employment as a source of stress varies, depending on the characteristics of the samples studied, the health outcomes examined, and the research designs used to draw conclusions (Caplan, 1985). Jobs most likely to result in feelings of stress combine high levels of demands with little control over work, for example, clerical or machine-paced assembly line work (Caplan, 1985; Haynes, 1991). Longitudinal data from the Framingham Heart Study indicate that high job demands, in combination with few clear expectations and little feedback from supervisors, may lead to an increased risk of coronary heart disease in women who are employed in clerical jobs (LaCroix & Haynes, 1987). Clerical or assembly line jobs typically have low status, low incomes, and few opportunities for advancement. Although these jobs fall to men as well as women, women are more likely to find themselves restricted to these positions by factors such as interrupted work histories, sex typing, and discrimination (Brief et al., 1981). Recent studies concur that the stressful aspects of women's employment may arise in part from their overrepresentation in low-level jobs (Barnett & Baruch, 1985; Harlan & Jansen, 1987).

Another potential source of stress for employed women, particularly white-collar and clerical workers, is the increasing computerization of the office environment. One in three of all such employees are currently using video display terminals (VDTs) (LaCroix & Haynes, 1987). Although computer technologies enhance efficiency and decrease time-consuming and repetitive tasks, studies have shown that prolonged and intense use of VDTs results in feelings of higher job strain and more frequent reports of eye strain, tension, and fatigue (see Haynes, 1991, for a summary). These effects may be exacerbated by conditions of high job demands and low job control. Environmental features of the office, like poor lighting, inadequate temperature and ventilation control, social isolation, and noise level, may also contribute to stress (Haynes, 1991; Stellman & Henifin, 1983).

Some women are exposed to physical, chemical, or biological hazards on the job. For instance, women have increased their participation in industrial jobs (e.g., textiles, electronics). Their subsequent exposure to a variety of organic solvents and carcinogenic materials has been associated with a number of health problems, ranging from nausea and dizziness to liver damage and cancer (Doyal, 1990). Stellman and Henifin (1983) reported that physical health hazards, such as radiation and respiratory or skin irritants, are frequently found in white-collar and service jobs. Other research (e.g., McDonald, 1988) suggests that exposure to certain chemicals, metals, and plastics is related to infertility, increased rates of spontaneous abortions, and a heightened risk of birth defects.

Workers who have direct responsibility for the well-being of others seem to suffer more stress than do those concerned only with inanimate objects (Doyal, 1990). This may be a particular issue for women because they are often employed in caregiving jobs or service positions that require employees to deal directly and constantly with the public. How many employees have been told that "the customer is always right"? Burnout is common among women in female-dominated "people" occupations like nursing or teaching (Greenglass, 1991).

Job complexity (i.e., high variety and low repetition in work tasks) is another condition that seems to be important for employed mothers' well-being. Lennon (1987) found that women whose occupations were characterized by low levels of job complexity reported high levels of demoralization. Miller et al. (1979) found that work conditions that constrain occupational self-direction (e.g., routinization, low complexity) or subject workers to job pressures and job insecurity were related to negative self-conceptions and rigid social orientations. Work conditions that encourage self-direction were related to positive self-evaluations and flexible orientations toward others. Similarly, Adelmann (1987) reported that job control (i.e., control over one's own and others' work) and job complexity contributed to women's self-confidence. According to Caplan (1985), it is the person-environment fit on job complexity (whether the absolute level of job complexity meets employees' need for complexity) that may be associated with well-being. A fit on complexity ensures that employees' skills are not underused and their abilities are not stretched too far.

Models have been proposed to help identify stressors at work and the pathways by which these stressors are related to employees' well-being (see Caplan, 1985; LaCroix & Haynes, 1987). For example, Karasek's (1979) two-dimensional model of job strain incorporates job demands and job control, asserting that job challenges can be either health-damaging or health-promoting, depending on the level of job control afforded by the work environment. Support for the job strain model in samples of women is developing. Alfredsson, Spetz, and Theorell (1985) found that hectic, monotonous work was associated with increased hospitilization rates for gastrointestinal illness, myocardial infarction, and alcohol-related illnesses. Karasek, Gardell, and Lindell (1987) reported that workload and conflict with supervisors were consistently associated with women's reports of depressed mood and physical symptoms (e.g., headaches, stomach problems), whereas job control and social support were associated with job satisfaction and few health problems.

Using Pearlin's life strains model of stress (Pearlin, Lieberman, Menaghan, & Mullan, 1981; Pearlin & Schooler, 1978), Kandel et al. (1985) found that, in addition to the four work strains conceptualized by Pearlin and colleagues (role overload, depersonalization, inadequate rewards, and noxious work environment), three other work strains were important to women: nonreciprocity (feeling exploited in the work situation), constriction of self (nonutilization of skills), and lack of control (undesirable job pressures). Furthermore, work strains (e.g., work overload, inadequate rewards) were associated with depression indirectly through their relations with work stress. That is, employed women's first response to work stressors is a role-specific stress (e.g., work stress or role strain), which may precede more global aspects of stress, such as depression.

Another aspect of stress that has received attention with respect to employed women's well-being is role strain, which refers to feelings of pressure or worry associated with adequately accomplishing work and family obligations (Bohen & Viveros-Long, 1981). Sometimes referred to as role conflict or role stress, the notion of role strain implies that the health of employed women may suffer in their attempts to combine the roles of spouse, parent, and employee (McBride, 1990). Because the presence of accessible child care and husbands' willingness to share household responsibilities have been directly related to decreased role strain in employed mothers (Ross & Mirowsky, 1988), one may expect role strain to be greatest in mothers with young children and in married women whose spouses contribute little to household work and child care (Repetti et al., 1989).

Although role strain has been associated with poor family relations and lower life satisfaction in women and men (Barling, 1986; Galambos & Silbereisen, 1989; Suchet & Barling, 1986), we need to recognize that multiple roles can also provide support, competence, and resources to women. In fact, multiple roles may enhance physical and mental health (Baruch et al., 1987). Clearly, it is essential to conduct further research targeting the specific combinations of work and family conditions that affect women's health (Doyal, 1990).

Establishing the links between women's work conditions and their levels of stress is a relatively new area of research. Initial studies suggest that specific work conditions (e.g., high workload, low job control) can be a source of stress for women. However, many other work conditions (e.g., co-worker relations, occupational status) still require exploration to better assess under what conditions the workplace affects women's well-being.

WORK RELATED SATISFACTIONS

Women's participation in paid work may be associated with some negative experiences, but employment may also contribute to good health by enhancing self-esteem, providing social contacts, and adding to financial resources. Participation in multiple roles (e.g., employee, spouse, parent) may offset some of the potentially negative effects of participation in a particular role (e.g., parent). Crucial to women's well-being is their role satisfaction, that is, the extent to which they occupy the roles that they want to occupy. Typically, role satisfaction has been operationalized as the congruence between whether women want to have paid jobs and whether they do have them. Waldron and Herold (1986) have suggested that whether women are employed or not, it is important for their health that their employment status be congruent with their attitude toward employment. Role satisfaction has been linked with higher life satisfaction, better physical health (Kopelman, Greenhaus, & Connolly, 1983;

Verbrugge, 1982), and more positive mothering (Lerner & Galambos, 1985).

Job satisfaction may also be important to well-being. Job satisfaction has been defined as employees' overall affective orientation toward the work role they occupy (Kalleberg, 1977). Employees' job satisfaction is positively correlated with their life satisfaction, happiness (Crohan et al., 1989), family cohesion, and decreased role strain (Anderson-Kulman & Paludi, 1986). Satisfaction with one's job, then, is linked to positive experiences in other domains.

Some research has identified conditions at work that may influence women's job satisfaction. For example, women's job satisfaction has been linked to work rewards (i.e., equality in pay, opportunity for promotion) (Kissman, 1990; Moore, 1985). Sears and Galambos (1990) found that greater work rewards (e.g., adequate income) were related to women's satisfaction with five aspects of their jobs: their general work, pay, promotions, supervision, and co-workers. In addition, higher work status (i.e., occupational prestige) predicted satisfaction with work and co-workers, and less work overload was associated with satisfaction with work, supervision, and co-workers. Experiences with sexual harassment, assembly line work, and part-time employment have been linked to lower job satisfaction (Clegg, Wall, & Kemp, 1987; Kissman, 1990; Miller and Terborg, 1979).

The quality of social relations at work is another feature of employment that has been associated with women's job satisfaction. Supervisory support as well as co-worker support has been associated with enhanced job satisfaction (Kissman, 1990). Repetti and Cosmas (1991) reported that supervisor support and a cohesive, respectful work environment best predicted job satisfaction; co-worker support and an emotionally supportive work environment were less important in their sample.

Job demands and job control have also been related to job satisfaction. McLaney and Hurrell (1988) found that, for nurses, job control was associated with increased job satisfaction independent of perceived job demands. Control over their work pace, the physical environment, and the availability of resources improved job satisfaction. Control over policies and hiring decisions, however, were not important for job satisfaction.

As researchers learn more about what types of work conditions contribute to job satisfaction, they are in a better position to make recommendations about how workplaces can enhance employees' well-being. This is important for women because so many are currently in or will join the labor force, and it is reasonable to assume that if women are satisfied with their work, they will be more likely to experience good health.

THE EMPLOYED MOTHER'S
MARITAL ADJUSTMENT

The increase in employment among married women has been substantially larger than the changes among never married women, divorced women, and widows (Statistics Canada, 1985). According to Scarr, Phillips, and McCartney (1989), women's employment status per se is not the major issue in marital relations. Rather, marital satisfaction in two-earner couples often depends on their attitudes about gender roles, their ability to set priorities for work and family, and the degree to which they can manage time and energy (Hochschild, 1989). Costs associated with women's paid employment include less leisure time, more time—on the husbands' part—spent on household tasks, and less sexual activity due to fatigue and lack of time (Voydanoff & Kelly, 1984). Gilbert (1985) suggested that the husband's marital satisfaction may depend primarily on the degree to which husbands feel inconvenienced by their wives' employment in exchange for a larger family income.

Little is known about which specific aspects of women's jobs are related to their marital relations. Dew, Bromet, Parkinson, Dunn, and Ryan (1989; cited in Bromet, Dew, & Parkinson, 1990) found that female assembly line workers who were experiencing high levels of occupational stress (e.g., working very fast; having a great deal to get done) reported marital stresses, such as husbands' unwillingness to listen to problems and husbands' failure to help with the housework. Repetti (1987) found that women who worked in an unpleasant social environment and overextended themselves with work and family commitments reported less satisfying family relations, more family conflict, and less cohesion at home. Coverman (1989) reported that lacking authority on the job was associated with low marital satisfaction in women. Finally, Wortman, Biernat, and Lang (1991) found that high work overload and lack of boundedness (i.e., "never finished," always something more to be done) was associated with high marital strain, low sexual satisfaction, and high psychological distress for women. The correlational nature of the data in these studies, however, prevents us from accurately assessing the direction of the relationship between work and marriage.

Stressors in women's work milieux may also be related to their spouses' adjustment (Billings & Moos, 1982). Although research has investigated how husbands' work experiences are related to their wives' well-being and marital satisfaction (e.g., Crouter, Perry-Jenkins, Huston, & Crawford, 1989; Repetti, 1989), the extent to which women's work experiences are related to their husbands' marital adjustment is an area of study sorely lacking in the literature, as few studies of employed women have also collected data from their spouses. Billings and Moos (1982) found that husbands of women who were highly stressed at work reported a greater number of physical symptoms (e.g., headaches, insomnia) and less cohesion in family functioning. Repetti (1987) reported that husbands' reports of marital and family relations were associated with their wives' descriptions of role overload and poor social climate in the work setting.

Generally, the research does not point to the way in which specific work conditions are associated with marital functioning for either spouse. Given that relations between work and marriage are likely to affect and be affected by women's well-being, it is important to consider *how* work and marriage come to be related. It is only recently that the processes by which work conditions and marital relations interact have been investigated.

PROCESSES CONNECTING WORK AND FAMILY

Studies have described at least two processes by which work experiences may be associated with family life: spillover and crossover (Bolger et al., 1989). The notion of *spillover* asserts that there is a similarity on a daily basis between what occurs in the work environment and what occurs at home for the same individual. Spillover from work to family life can be either positive or negative. Positive spillover occurs when job satisfaction or job challenges result in the creation of energy and enthusiasm that is carried over into family life. In negative spillover, problems and stress at work drain and preoccupy individuals, making it difficult to participate adequately in family interactions (Voydanoff, 1987). In a *crossover* process, stress experienced by one spouse at work or at home leads to stress for the other spouse in the other domain (Bolger et al., 1989). For instance, a wife's job demands may result in her having a bad day at work and subsequently arguing with her husband the same evening. When this interaction increases the husband's marital stress, crossover has occurred.

Piotrkowski (1979) examined positive and negative spillover from work to family in an in-depth study of 13 working-class and lower-middle-class families. She found that job stresses displaced the potential for positive family interaction and required family members to expend their personal resources to assist the employee in managing the strain. Jackson, Zedeck, and Summers (1985) reported that employees' emotional reactions to their jobs, as measured by indices of physical health and psychological mood, were related to decreased quality of family life and increased spouse dissatisfaction with employees' jobs.

Bolger et al. (1989) found significant spillover effects among men and women between work and home domains. These effects were bidirectional, with stresses at home (e.g., arguments) spilling over into the employment role, and stresses on the job (e.g., overload) spilling over into the family. They also reported that overload at work set in motion a process of dyadic adjustment at home, whereby wives increased their household involvement in response to their husbands' having a hectic day at work. On the other hand, evidence of this dyadic adjustment by husbands in response to wives' stress at work was weak, suggesting that even though women decreased their involvement in household tasks on stressful work days, their work at home was more often deferred to another day rather than being completed by their husbands (Bolger et al., 1989).

Sears (1991) found evidence for spillover and crossover from wives' work conditions to husbands' and wives' marital relations. She found that wives' feelings of stress mediated the relationship between wives' work conditions (e.g., work overload, low rewards, and work status) and their marital adjustment. Moreover, wives' work conditions were indirectly associated with husbands' marital adjustment through their relations with wives' stress and, in turn, wives' marital adjustment. No direct relation between wives' stress and husbands' marital adjustment was observed.

Women's feelings of well-being, positive or negative, then, may mediate a process in which their work experiences spill over into their marital relations or cross over into their spouses' perceptions of marital relations. With few exceptions, studies of husbands' or wives' work conditions and their spouses' marital adjustment have often failed to include measures of marital adjustment for both spouses and have typically studied the processes of spillover and crossover separately. Zedeck and Mosier (1990) have called for further examination of the processes by which work and family interact as well as for more specific measures of the sources of satisfying work and marital and family relations.

THE SINGLE EMPLOYED MOTHER

Studies of the effects of employment on mothers have focused primarily on married women. Although about 20% of all families with children are headed by single mothers (Mednick, 1987), the experiences of these women at work have not been adequately addressed in the literature. The majority of single mothers are either separated or divorced and began their childbearing at an early age; they typically have low education but are likely to be employed (Morrison, Page, Sehl, & Smith, 1986). Many single mothers, however, lack the resources often associated with well-being: they have little opportunity to develop their education and work experiences, and they lack partners to help maintain the home environment and to provide financial and emotional support. The simultaneous demands of parenting, employment, and home care often result in isolation and insufficient social support (Morrison et al., 1986).

Single-parent status has been associated with chronic, mild depressive symptoms (Hall, Williams, & Greenberg, 1985), and women who are financially strained and have responsibility for young children are at increased risk for depression (Pearlin & Johnson, 1977). About one half of single-mother families live below the poverty level (Mednick, 1987). Financial hardship, then, is one of the greatest difficulties for single mothers, and it is correlated with psychological distress (Belle, 1990; Hall et al., 1985; Pearlin & Johnson, 1977). Colletta (1979) found that income level alone was associated with the amount and source of stress reported by employed single mothers. Single mothers with more income, even though it was an amount that hardly lifted them above the poverty line, were more satisfied with their work and reported less stress than did the low-income group.

Beyond the importance of income for single mothers' well-being, little is known about the meaning of employment for single mothers and their families. Michelson (1983) found that single mothers who felt they had been forced into full-time employment were tense and unhappy; for others, tensions were due to the logistics of getting to work and arranging for child care. The cost of child care may nullify any financial benefits realized from working, and concerns about the quality or inadequacy of arrangements for shift workers are ongoing (Morrison et al., 1986). At the same time, employment has been associated with increased self-esteem in single mothers (Michelson, 1983), and may provide them with the opportunity to decrease their isolation and to establish social supports. It seems, then, that single mothers can benefit from employment even though their daily lives are complex and often strained.

JUGGLING WORK AND FAMILY LIFE

This review has shown that the challenges, stresses, and rewards of employment are associated with mothers' well-being. The relations, however, are complex. On the one hand, employment can provide mothers with needed material resources, greater financial independence, and important social contacts. On the other hand, employment may expose mothers to hazards (e.g., radiation) and conditions (e.g., low job control) that may hamper their mental and physical well-being. The picture is neither bright nor dismal; employment is a challenge for women that may sometimes be too demanding; but even in cases where employment is largely rewarding, the daily transition from work to family and back again can be made easier through the assistance of family members, particularly husbands, and social policies designed to provide support to employees with families.

One of the primary tasks of employed mothers is to allocate household and child care responsibilities. The expectation of an equitable division of labor between husbands and wives is not always practical, as husbands often resist sharing (Pleck, 1985) and some wives do not want more participation at home than they already receive (Hochschild, 1989; Wortman et al., 1991). Most employed mothers, however, are more than willing to have their husbands participate more actively in household tasks and child care. They are unlikely to get help, though, unless they hold strong beliefs about sharing household work and insist on it (Hardesty & Bokemeier, 1989; Hawkins & Crouter, 1991). Such an approach is not without its costs. Subsequent disagreements and increased frustration and resentment may make overload a more manageable alternative (Hochschild, 1989). When husbands do participate in child care, employed wives' mental health improves (Kessler & McRae, 1982; Pleck, 1985), and husbands may also benefit by developing closer relationships with their children (Almeida & Galambos, 1991). Clearly, responses from husbands are essential for making the day-to-day transition between work and family manageable.

Employers have also been slow to respond to the needs of employed mothers. Policies for mothers' well-being must address the concerns of employed mothers (e.g., child care, time management, inadequate pay) and foster the integration of work and family responsibilities. As these mothers also assume care of their aging parents, additional burdens are accumulated and also require consideration (Zedeck & Mosier, 1990). Policies, then, should attempt to ameliorate the costs to parents of combining work and family and enhance the benefits of this combination. Of course, these policies should not be limited to mothers. Fathers, too, need to be supported in their desires to nurture their families; mothers will undoubtedly benefit from programs that make fathering duties easier and more attractive.

Some employers have implemented policies designed to ease the tasks of working and caregiving among women and men. Such policies include job sharing, flexible work hours, telecommuting, compressed work weeks, parenting leave for childbirth or adoption, personal days, and employer-based child care (Zedeck & Mosier, 1990). Initial studies of these policies suggest positive ramifications for employers (e.g., lower absenteeism, higher morale), but little research on their effectiveness has been conducted. Even if these policies prove to be successful, they are found mostly within multinational corporations. The majority of employed mothers, however, are found in smaller businesses and factories and, as a result, may not benefit from their implementation.

In sum, employers need to monitor employee health and the presence or absence of specific work conditions so that risky conditions are reduced and health-enhancing aspects of jobs can be promoted (Doyal, 1990; Zedeck & Mosier, 1990). Nevertheless, organizations, government, and employed parents are jointly responsible for developing ways for employees to successfully combine work and family life.

REFERENCES

Adelmann, P. K. (1987). Occupational complexity, control, and personal income: Their relation to psychological well-being in men and women. *Journal of Applied Psychology, 72,* 529–537.

Adelmann, P. K., Antonucci, T. C., Crohan, S. E., & Coleman, L. M. (1990). A causal analysis of employment and health in midlife women. *Women and Health, 16,* 5–20.

Alfredsson, L., Spetz, C. L., & Theorell, T. (1985). Type of occupation and near-future hospitalization for myocardial infarction and some other diagnoses. *International Journal of Epidemiology, 14,* 378–388.

Almeida, D. M., & Galambos, N. L. (1991). Examining father involvement and the quality of father-adolescent relations. *Journal of Research on Adolescence, 1,* 155–172.

Anderson-Kulman, R. E., & Paludi, M. A. (1986). Working mothers and the family context: Predicting positive coping. *Journal of Vocational Behavior, 28,* 241–253.

Barling, J. (1986). Interrole conflict and marital functioning amongst employed fathers. *Journal of Occupational Behaviour, 7,* 1–8.

Barnett, R. C., & Baruch, G. K. (1985). Women's involvement in multiple roles and psychological distress. *Journal of Personality and Social Psychology, 49,* 135–145.

Baruch, G. K., Biener, L., & Barnett, R. C. (1987). Women and gender in research on work and family stress. *American Psychologist, 42,* 130–136.

Belle, D. (1990). Poverty and women's mental health. *American Psychologist,45,* 385–389.

Billings, A. G., & Moos, R. H. (1982). Work stress and the stress-buffering roles of work and family resources. *Journal of Occupational Behaviour, 3,* 215–232.

Bohen, H. H., & Viveros-Long, A. (1981). *Balancing jobs and family life: Do flexible work schedules help?* Philadelphia: Temple University.

Bolger, N., DeLongis, A., Kessler, R. C., & Wethington, E. (1989). The contagion of stress across multiple roles. *Journal of Marriage and the Family, 51,* 175–183.

Bosch, L. H. M., & deLange, W. A. M. (1987). Shift work in health care. *Ergonomics, 30,* 773–791.

Brief, A. P., Schuler, R. S., & Van Sell, M. (1981). *Managing job stress.* Boston: Little, Brown.

Bromet, E. J., Dew, M. A., & Parkinson, D. K. (1990). Spillover between work and family. In J. Eckenrode & S. Gore (Eds.), *Stress between work and family* (pp. 133–151). New York: Plenum Press.

Browder, S. (1991, October). Let it go. *New Woman*, pp. 94–98.

Caplan, R. D. (1985). Psychosocial stress in work. *Management and Labour Studies, 10*, 63–76.

Clegg, C., Wall, T., & Kemp, N. (1987). Women on the assembly line: A comparison of main and interactive explanations of job satisfaction, absence and mental health. *Journal of Occupational Psychology, 60*, 273–287.

Colletta, N. D. (1979). The impact of divorces: Father absence or poverty. *Journal of Divorce, 3*, 27–34.

Coverman, S. (1989). Role overload, role conflict, and stress: Addressing consequences of multiple role demands. *Social Forces, 67*, 965–982.

Crohan, S. E., Antonucci, T. C., Adelmann, P. K., & Coleman, L. M. (1989). Job characteristics and well-being at midlife: Ethnic and gender comparisons. *Psychology of Women Quarterly, 13*, 223–235.

Crouter, A. C., Perry-Jenkins, M., Huston, T. L., & Crawford, D. W. (1989). The influence of work-induced psychological states on behavior at home. *Basic and Applied Social Psychology, 10*, 273–292.

Dewe, P. J. (1987). Identifying the causes of nurses' stress: A survey of New Zealand nurses. *Work and Stress, 1*, 15–24.

Doyal, L. (1990). Waged work and women's well being. *Women's Studies International Forum, 13*, 587–604.

Galambos, N. L., & Silbereisen, R. K. (1989). Role strain in West German dual-earner households. *Journal of Marriage and the Family, 51*, 385–389.

Gilbert, L. A. (1985). *Men in dual-career families: Current realities and future prospects.* Hillsdale, NJ: Erlbaum.

Greenglass, E. R. (1985). Psychological implications of sex bias in the workplace. *Academic Psychology Bulletin, 1*, 227–240.

Greenglass, E. R. (1991). Burnout and gender: Theoretical and organizational implications. *Canadian Psychology, 32*, 562–572.

Hall, L. A., Williams, C. A., & Greenberg, R. S. (1985). Supports, stressors, and depressive symptoms in low-income mothers of young children. *American Journal of Public Health, 75*, 518–522.

Hardesty, C., & Bokemeier, J. (1989). Finding time and making do: Distribution of household labor in nonmetropolitan marriages. *Journal of Marriage and the Family, 51*, 253–267.

Harlan, C. L., & Jansen, M. A. (1987). The psychological and physical well-being of women in sex-stereotyped occupations. *Journal of Employment Counseling, 24*, 31–39.

Hawkins, A. J., & Crouter, A. C. (1991). Without map or compass: Finding the way in contemporary dual-earner marriages. In J. V. Lerner & N. L. Galambos (Eds.), *Employed mothers and their children* (pp. 211–235). New York: Garland.

Haynes, S. G. (1991). The effect of job demands, job control, and new technologies on the health of employed women: A review. In M. Frankenhaeuser, U. Lundberg, & M. Chesney (Eds.), *Women, work, and health* (pp. 157–169). New York: Plenum.

Hibbard, J. H., & Pope, C. R. (1985). Employment status, employment characteristics, and women's health. *Women and Health, 10*, 59–77.

Hochschild, A. (1989). *The second shift.* New York: Avon Books.

Hodapp, V., Neuser, K. W., & Weyer, G. (1988). Job stress, emotion, and work environment: Toward a causal model. *Personality and Individual Differences, 9*, 851–859.

Hoffman, L. W. (1989). Effects of maternal employment in the two-parent family. *American Psychologist, 44*, 283–292.

Jackson, S. E., Zedeck, S., & Summers, E. (1985). Family-life disruptions: Effects of job-induced structural and emotional interference. *Academy of Management Journal, 28*, 574–586.

Kalleberg, A. L. (1977). Work values and job rewards: A theory of job satisfaction. *American Sociological Review, 42*, 124–143.

Kandel, D. B., Davies, M., & Raveis, V. H. (1985). The stressfulness of daily social roles for women: Marital, occupational and household roles. *Journal of Health and Social Behavior, 26*, 64–78.

Karasek, R. A. (1979). Job demands, job decision latitude and mental strain: Implications for job redesign. *Administrative Science Quarterly, 24*, 285–308.

Karasek, R. A., Gardell, B., & Lindell, J. (1987). Work and non-work correlates of illness and behaviour in male and female Swedish white collar workers. *Journal of Occupational Behavior, 8*, 187–207.

Kessler, R. C., & McRae, J. A. (1982). The effects of wives' employment on the mental health of men and women. *American Sociological Review, 47*, 216–227.

Kissman, K. (1990). Women in blue-collar occupations: An exploration of constraints and facilitators. *Journal of Sociology and Social Welfare, 17*, 139–149.

Kopelman, R. E., Greenhaus, J. H., & Connolly, T. F. (1983). A model of work, family, and interrole conflict: A construct validation study. *Organizational Behavior and Human Performance, 32*, 198–215.

LaCroix, A. Z., & Haynes, S. G. (1987). Gender differences in the health effects of workplace roles. In R. C. Barnett, L. Biener, & G. K. Baruch (Eds.), *Gender and stress* (pp. 96–121). New York: Free Press.

Lennon, M. C. (1987). Sex differences in distress: The impact of gender and work roles. *Journal of Health and Social Behavior, 28*, 290–305.

Lerner, J. V., & Galambos, N. L. (1985). Maternal role satisfaction, mother-child interaction, and child temperament: A process model. *Developmental Psychology, 21*, 1157–1164.

Lips, H. M., & Colwill, N. L. (1988). Psychology addresses women and work: Canadian research in 1980s. *Canadian Psychology, 29*, 57–68.

Matthews, K. A., & Rodin, J. (1989). Women's changing work roles: Impact on health, family, and public policy. *American Psychologist, 44*, 1389–1393.

McBride, A. B. (1990). Mental health effects of women's multiple roles. *American Psychologist, 45*, 381–384.

McDonald, A. D. (1988). Work and pregnancy. *British Journal of Industrial Medicine, 45*, 577–580.

McLaney, M. A., & Hurrell, J. R. (1988). Control, stress, and job satisfaction in Canadian nurses. *Work and Stress, 3*, 217–224.

Mednick, M. T. (1987). Single mothers: A review and critique of current research. *Applied Social Psychology Annual, 7,* 184–201.

Michelson, W. (1983). *The logistics of maternal employment: Implications for women and their families* (Child in the City Report No. 18). Toronto: Ministry of National Health and Welfare.

Miller, J., Schooler, C., Kohn, M. L., & Miller, K. A. (1979). Women and work: The psychological effects of occupational conditions. *American Journal of Sociology, 85,* 66–94.

Miller, H. E., & Terborg, J. R. (1979). Job attitudes of part-time and full-time employees. *Journal of Applied Psychology, 64,* 380–386.

Moore, H. A. (1985). Job satisfaction and women's spheres of work. *Sex Roles, 13,* 663–678.

Morrison, W., Page, G., Sehl, M., & Smith, H. (1986). Single mothers in Canada: An analysis. *Canadian Journal of Community Mental Health, 5,* 37–47

Muller, C. (1986). Health and health care of employed adults: Occupation and gender. *Women and Health, 11,* 27–45.

O'Neill, C. P., & Zeichner, A. (1985). Working women: A study of relationships between stress, coping and health. *Journal of Psychosomatic Obstetrics and Gynaecology, 4,* 105–116.

Pearlin, L. I., & Johnson, J. (1977). Marital status, life strains, and depression. *American Sociological Review, 42,* 704–715.

Pearlin, L. I., Lieberman, M. A., Menaghan, E. G., & Mullan, J. T. (1981). The stress process. *Journal of Health and Social Behavior, 22,* 337–356.

Pearlin, L. I., & Schooler, C. (1978). The structure of coping. *Journal of Health and Social Behavior, 19,* 2–21.

Piotrkowski, C. S. (1979). *Work and the family system.* New York: Macmillan.

Pleck, J. H. (1985). *Working wives/working husbands.* Beverly Hills, CA: Sage.

Repetti, R. L. (1987). Linkages between work and family roles. *Applied Social Psychology Annual, 7,* 98–127.

Repetti, R. L. (1989). Effects of daily workload on subsequent behavior during marital interaction: The roles of social withdrawal and spouse support. *Journal of Personality and Social Psychology, 57,* 651–659.

Repetti, R. L., & Cosmas, K. A. (1991). The quality of the social environment at work and job satisfaction. *Journal of Applied Social Psychology, 21,* 840–854.

Repetti, R. L., Matthews, K. A., & Waldron, I. (1989). Employment and women's health: Effects of paid employment on women's mental and physical health. *American Psychologist, 44,* 1394–1401.

Rodin, J., & Ickovics, J. R. (1990). Women's health: Review and research agenda as we approach the 21st century. *American Psychologist, 45,* 1018–1034.

Ross, C. E., & Mirowsky, J. (1988). Child care and emotional adjustment to wives' employment. *Journal of Health and Social Behavior, 29,* 127–138.

Scarr, S., Phillips, D., & McCartney, K. (1989). Working mothers and their families. *American Psychologist, 44,* 1402–1409.

Sears, H. A. (1991). *A process model for understanding links between women's work conditions and marital adjustment in two-earner couples.* Unpublished master's thesis, University of Victoria, Victoria, British Columbia.

Sears, H. A., & Galambos, N. L. (1990, May). *Mothers' work conditions as sources of psychological well-being*. Paper presented at the annual meeting of the Canadian Psychological Association, Ottawa, Ontario.

Statistics Canada. (1985). *Women in Canada: A statistical report*. Ottawa: Ministry of Supply and Services Canada.

Stellman, J. M., & Henifin, M. S. (1983). *Office work can be dangerous to your health*. New York: Pantheon.

Suchet, M., & Barling, J. (1986). Employed mothers: Interrole conflict, spouse support and marital functioning. *Journal of Occupational Behavior, 4*, 167–168.

Sze, W. C., & Ivker, B. (1986). Stress in social workers: The impact of setting and role. *Social Casework, 67*, 141–148.

Verbrugge, L. M. (1982). Work satisfaction and physical health. *Journal of Community Psychology, 7*, 62–83.

Verbrugge, L. M. (1983). Multiple roles and physical health of women and men. *Journal of Health and Social Behavior, 24*, 16–30.

Verbrugge, L. M. (1986). Role burdens and physical health of women and men. *Women and Health, 11*, 47–77.

Verbrugge, L. M. (1989). The twain meet: Empirical explanations of sex differences in health and mortality. *Journal of Health and Social Behavior, 30*, 282–304.

Voydanoff, P. (1987). *Work and family life*. Beverly Hills, CA: Sage.

Voydanoff, P., & Donnelly, B. W. (1989). Work and family roles and psychological distress. *Journal of Marriage and the Family, 51*, 923–932.

Voydanoff, P., & Kelly, R. F. (1984). Determinants of work-related family problems among employed parents. *Journal of Marriage and the Family, 46*, 881–892.

Waldron, I., & Herold, J. (1986). Employment, attitudes toward employment, and women's health. *Women and Health, 11*, 79–98.

Waldron, I., & Jacobs, J. A. (1988). Effects of labor force participation on women's health: New evidence from a longitudinal study. *Journal of Occupational Medicine, 30*, 977–983.

Wortman, C., Biernat, M., & Lang, E. (1991). Coping with role overload. In M. Frankenhaeuser, U. Lundberg, & M. Chesney (Eds.), *Women, work, and health* (pp. 85–110). New York: Plenum.

Zedeck, S., & Mosier, K. L. (1990). Work in the family and employing organization. *American Psychologist, 45*, 240–251.

■ 5
Maternal Employment:
Effects on Children

Claire Etaugh*

The labor force participation of mothers has increased steadily for over 40 years. By 1988, 72.5% of married mothers of 6–17-year-old children were employed, as were 57.1% of married mothers of children under 6, including 51.9% of those with infants under 1 year of age (U.S. Bureau of the Census, 1990).

In this chapter, I review the effects on children of a mother's employment, concentrating on the research since the mid-1970s.

INFANTS

Parent and Child Interaction

Studies generally have found few or no differences in parent–infant interactions related to mothers' employment status (Cohen, 1978; Davis & Stith, 1983; Owen & Cox, 1988; Pedersen, Cain, Zaslow, & Anderson, 1982; Pedersen, Zaslow, Suwalsky, & Cain, 1982; Rabinovich, Suwalsky, & Pedersen, 1986; Schubert, Bradley-Johnson, & Nuttal, 1980; Zaslow, Pedersen, Suwalsky, & Rabinovich, 1983).

*The author thanks Andrea Etaugh, Harold Rosenberg, and William Wilsen for commenting on earlier drafts of this chapter.

Attachment

Other studies have focused on attachment behaviors. Most of these have not found any relationship between maternal employment status and the security of mother–infant attachment (Ansul, DiBiase, & Weinraub, 1987 [for girls]; Chase-Lansdale & Owen, 1987; Goldberg & Easterbrooks, 1988; Hock, 1980; Owen, Easterbrooks, Chase-Lansdale, & Goldberg, 1984; Owen & Cox, 1988; Tulkin, 1973; Weinraub, Jaeger, & Hoffman, 1988; Wille, 1989).

Two studies report evidence of less secure mother–infant attachment when the mother is employed (Barglow, Vaughn, & Molitor, 1987 [for firstborns only]; Belsky & Rovine, 1988). Some research finds that full-time maternal employment is related to more insecure father–infant attachment in sons but not daughters (Belsky & Rovine, 1988; Chase-Lansdale & Owen, 1987 [for 12-month-old but not 18-month-old sons]). Other studies, however, report few or no differences in father–infant attachment associated with maternal employment (Easterbrooks & Goldberg, 1985; Lamb, Frodi, Hwang, & Frodi, 1982; Volling & Belsky, 1989).

Maternal job satisfaction was unrelated to mother–infant attachment in one study (Funk, 1984). Another found that maternal role satisfaction was positively related to secure mother–infant attachment (Jaeger, Weinraub, Becker, & Jaeger, 1989).

The infant's age when the mother returns to work is associated in complex ways with mother–infant attachment. Less secure attachment has been associated with the mother's return to work before an infant is 6 months (Goldberg & Easterbrooks 1988) or 8 months (Weinraub & Jaeger, 1988) old. Benn (1986), however, found less secure mother–son attachment when the mother returned to work later in the first year as opposed to earlier. Finally, the mother's return to work when the child is 12.5 to 19.5 months old has been associated with either more *or* less secure attachment (Thompson, Lamb, & Estes, 1982).

PRESCHOOLERS

Adjustment and Interaction

Several studies have found that preschoolers with working mothers show better social adjustment than do those with nonworking mothers (Gold & Adres, 1978c; Gold, Andres, & Glorieux, 1979; Schacter, 1981). Other research has found no relationship between maternal employment status and psychosocial functioning (Gottfried, Gottfried, & Bathurst, 1988;

Henggeler & Borduin, 1981; LeVine, 1981; Taylor, 1980) or mother–child social interaction (Henggeler & Borduin, 1981; Weiskopf-Bock, 1983). In longitudinal research reported by Goldberg and Easterbrooks (1988), when significant effects of maternal employment emerged, the outcomes sometimes were favorable (e.g., more adaptive ego resiliency among sons, more secure attachment among daughters) and sometimes were less favorable (e.g., less ego resiliency among daughters, less secure attachment among sons).

Cognitive Development

Findings regarding cognitive development are mixed. Some data indicate higher IQ scores for children of nonemployed mothers (Blau & Grossberg, 1990 [when mother worked during the child's second and subsequent years]; Cohen, 1978; Gold & Andres, 1978c [for English-speaking boys]; Schacter, 1981). Other research, however, finds no relationship between maternal employment status and preschoolers' cognitive development (Desai, Chase-Lansdale, & Michael, 1989 [for girls, lower-income children, and children whose mothers resumed work after the child was 1 year old]; Gold and Andres, 1978c [for English-speaking girls]; Gold et al., 1979; Goldberg & Easterbrooks, 1988 [for language development]; Gottfried et al., 1988; Poresky & Whitsitt, 1985; Schacter, 1981 [for language development]). Two studies found a negative effect of maternal employment when the mother worked during the child's first year (Blau & Grossberg, 1990; Desai et al., 1989 [for high-income boys only]).

Sex-Role Concepts

Two studies reported no relationship between maternal employment and preschoolers' sex-role stereotypes (MacKinnon, Stoneman, & Brody, 1984; Seegmiller, 1980). Others, however, have found that children of employed mothers show less sex typing (Gold & Andres, 1978c; Gold et al., 1979) and greater sex-role flexibility (Levy, 1989 [for daughters but not sons]). One study found that traditionality of the mother's occupation was related to traditionality of children's vocational interests (Barak, Feldman, & Noy, 1991).

Parental Behavior and Attitudes

Several studies of the home environment of preschoolers revealed no differences in the quantity and quality of cognitive and social stimulation in households with and without employed mothers (Gottfried et al., 1988; MacKinnon, Brody, & Stoneman, 1982; Owen & Cox, 1988; Stuckey, McGhee, & Bell, 1982). One study reported that employed mothers used less negative control and that mothers who worked more hours were more responsive to their children and used more guidance (Crockenberg & Litman, 1989).

Three studies indicated that parental behavior and attitudes may be less favorable toward boys than girls in families with employed mothers, whereas the opposite pattern may be seen in families with nonemployed mothers. Stuckey et al. (1982) found that, in families with nonworking mothers, preschool sons received more parental attention than did daughters, whereas daughters received more attention in families with working mothers. Zaslow et al. (1983) obtained similar results for 12 month-olds. Along the same lines, Bronfenbrenner, Alvarez, and Henderson (1984) found that 3-year-old daughters were described most favorably and 3-year-old sons were described least favorably by mothers working full-time and their husbands. Greenberger (1989) failed to replicate these results, however.

Gottfried et al. (1988) found that mothers of preschoolers who were satisfied with their work had more favorable perceptions of the influence of maternal employment on children's development than did mothers who were not satisfied. Harrell and Ridley (1975) reported that mothers' work satisfaction was positively related to the quality of mother–child interaction. Similarly, Galambos and Lerner (1984) found that mothers of 3-year-olds who were dissatisfied with their roles (i.e., with being employed or nonemployed) showed more rejection of their children and in turn had more difficult children. Along the same lines, Barling and Van Bart (1984) reported that maternal job satisfaction was associated with daughters' greater self-control and fewer conduct problems, whereas maternal role conflict was related to greater conduct problems for boys and immaturity for girls. Stuckey and associates (1982) reported that parental negative affect directed toward the child was seen more frequently in both mothers and fathers whose attitudes toward dual roles for women were not congruent with the mother's employment status. Gold and her colleagues (Gold & Andres, 1978c; Gold et al., 1979) found that employed mothers and their husbands were happier with mothers' roles than were nonemployed mothers and their husbands. The children of these more satisfied working mothers and husbands showed better social adjustment. The results of these studies are consistent with previous research, which showed a positive association between mothers' satisfaction with their roles and the adjustment of elementary school children (see Etaugh, 1974).

ELEMENTARY SCHOOL CHILDREN

Adjustment

Recent studies of elementary school children generally have found no differences in adjustment related to maternal work status, in line with earlier research (see Etaugh, 1974). Studies of kindergartners have yielded no difference in self-concept (Al-Timini, 1977) or self-esteem (Miller, 1975). Studies of older elementary school children (ranging in age from 7 to 12 years) similarly have found no relationship between maternal employment and children's self-concept (Barling, Fullagar, & Marchl-Dingle, 1988; Colangelo, Rosenthal, & Dettmann, 1984; Rosenthal & Hansen, 1981), self-perceptions of competence (Baruch, 1976), family adjustment (Warshaw, 1976), personal problems (Dellas, Gaier, & Emihovich, 1979), and social-emotional adjustment (Gold & Andres, 1978b, 1980; Guidubaldi, Nastase, Cleminshaw, & Perry, 1986). Mothers' work-related stress also is unrelated to adjustment (Galambos & Maggs, 1990).

In his longitudinal study of British children, Moore (1975) found few personality differences for girls at age 11 as a function of maternal employment. Some differences in personality (but not overall adjustment) emerged for boys: sons of working women were more fearless and aggressive but less sensitive, fastidious, and conforming than sons of nonworking women.

On the other hand, maternal employment has been shown to be related to higher self-esteem in daughters (Amato, 1987), lower fear of success in daughters (Gilroy, Talierco, & Steinbacher, 1981); more positive subjective states (Duckett & Richards, 1989 [for children in one-parent but not two-parent families]), and lower levels of both maternal depression and reported child behavior problems (Walker, Ortiz-Valdes, & Newbrough, 1989).

SCHOOL ACHIEVEMENT AND INTELLIGENCE

Recent data support earlier research findings that maternal employment is unrelated to academic achievement for elementary school girls and either unrelated or negatively related for boys (see Etaugh, 1974). Most of these data, however, have been collected from predominantly white, two-parent families. Studies using black samples, some of them including low-income, single-parent families, have consistently demonstrated that maternal employment is positively associated with academic achievement (e.g., Avery, 1975; Cherry & Eaton, 1977; Milne, Myers, Rosenthal, & Ginsburg, 1986; also see Etaugh, 1974).

Several studies primarily using white children found no relationship between maternal work status and school grades, IQ, or academic achievement (Colangelo et al., 1984; Farel, 1980; Gold & Andres, 1980; Moorehouse 1991 [if mother-child activities were frequent]; Rosenthal & Hansen, 1981; Stevenson, 1983; Warshaw, 1976). One study found negative effects of maternal employment for both boys and girls but only if they were from white two-parent families (Milne et al., 1986). Two studies have shown no effects of maternal employment for girls but negative effects for boys. Moore (1975) reported better reading achievement at age 7 years for sons of nonworking women than for sons of working women. Gold and Andres (1978b) found that middle-class boys with employed mothers had lower scores on language and mathematics achievement tests than did middle-class boys with nonemployed mothers. For lower-class boys, maternal employment was associated with a greater dislike of school and lower self-report grades but not with lower objective test data. Earlier studies (see Etaugh, 1974) had shown lower academic achievement and IQ scores for both elementary-school-age and adolescent middle-class boys with working mothers.

Finally, two studies reported positive associations between maternal employment and achievement motivation (Gorman, 1980), academic achievement, and IQ (Guidubaldi et al., 1986).

Educational and Career Aspirations

Studies of elementary school children generally reveal no differences in educational and occupational attitudes and aspirations for either girls or boys as a function of maternal employment (Colangelo et al., 1984; Dellas et al., 1979; Gold & Andres, 1978b, 1980; Lavine, 1982; Rosenthal & Hansen, 1981; Taylor, 1984). Selkow (1984), however, found that kindergarten and first-grade girls whose mothers were in nontraditional fields aspired to nontraditional careers themselves.

Sex-Role Concepts

Maternal employment generally is associated with less stereotyped sex role concepts for both girls and boys (Bacon & Lerner, 1975; Cheles-Miller, 1974; Cordua, McGraw, & Drabman, 1979; Dellas et al., 1979; Gold and Andres, 1978b, 1980; Jones & McBride, 1980; Marantz & Mansfield, 1977; Miller, 1975; Nelson & Keith, 1990 [for girls but not boys]; Perloff, 1977; Robb & Raven, 1981; Rollins & White, 1982). A few studies have found no effect of maternal employment on children's perceptions of adult male and female roles (Baruch & Barnett, 1986; Meyer, 1980; Rodgon, Gralewski, & Hetzel, 1977; Warshaw, 1976).

Household Tasks

In line with earlier research (Etaugh, 1974), more recent studies report that children of employed mothers perform more household chores and spend more time on them than do children of nonemployed mothers (Crouter & McHale, 1989; Medrich, Roizen, Rubin, & Buckley, 1982).

Perceptions of Parental Behavior

Early studies found that maternal employment was largely unrelated to elementary school children's perceptions of various maternal behaviors (see Etaugh, 1974). More recent research generally is consistent with these conclusions and also extends the pattern of results to perceptions of paternal behavior (Bankart & Bankart, 1985; Colangelo et al., 1984; Dellas et al., 1979; Klecka & Hiller, 1977; Rosenthal & Hansen, 1981).

Another group of studies suggests that the elementary school child's identification with the mother is enhanced by maternal employment. Gold and Andres (1978b) found that 10-year-old sons and daughters perceived themselves as equally similar to an employed mother; if the mother was not employed, however, daughters perceived themselves as more similar to her than did sons. Studies of girls in kindergarten (Miller, 1975) and eighth grade (Klecka & Hiller, 1977) reported a positive relationship between maternal employment and daughters' desire to be like their mothers. Earlier studies had produced the same results for adolescent daughters of working mothers (see Etaugh, 1974).

Parental Attitudes

Recent data on maternal attitudes are consistent with both the earlier data for elementary school children (see Etaugh, 1974) and the recent data for preschoolers (Gold & Andres, 1978c; Gold et al., 1979; Harrell & Ridley, 1975; Stuckey et al., 1982) in finding that favorable child outcomes are positively related to mothers' satisfaction with their roles. Farel (1980) found that kindergarten children of nonworking women who did not want to work performed better in school than did children of nonworking mothers who wanted to work. Avery (1975) reported better adjustment and achievement for white fifth-graders whose mothers were working by choice than for those mothers who were working as a necessity. Williamson (1970) found that the children of mothers with positive attitudes toward their work or nonwork status had a higher grade point average for the first six grades. Trimberger and MacLean (1982) reported that 9–12-year-olds who perceived that their mothers had positive feelings about their jobs were more likely to feel positively affected by their mothers' employment.

ADOLESCENTS

Adjustment

Early research indicated that the mother's working had no harmful effects on adolescent adjustment, except occasionally for lower-class boys (Etaugh, 1974). Recent studies tend to corroborate the conclusion that there are no adverse effects (Armistead, Wierson, & Forehand, 1990; Dellas et al., 1979; Hillman, Sawilowsky, Becker, & Ogilivie, 1990; Joy & Wise, 1983; Lerner & Galambos, 1988; Mitchell, 1981; Moore, 1975; Oakes & Oliver, 1984; Rosenthal & Hansen, 1981; Wise & Joy, 1982). In some instances, maternal employment or commitment to a career is found to be related positively to adolescent adjustment (Baruch, 1973; Crandall & Crandall, 1983; Duckett & Richards, 1989; Gibbons & Kopelman, 1977; Gold & Andres, 1978a; Walker et al., 1989).

The only negative finding was reported by Collins (1975). Lower-class ninth-graders with full-time working mothers did not differ in personality adjustment from those with nonworking mothers. Children of part-time working mothers, particularly the boys, showed poorer adjustment, however.

School Achievement and Intelligence

Recent data indicate that maternal employment is either unrelated or positively related to academic achievement for adolescent girls and is unrelated for adolescent boys (Alwin & Thornton, 1984; Baldwin, 1984; Gold & Andres, 1978a; Marcek, 1976; Mitchell, 1981; Nichols & Shauffer, 1975; Rosenthal & Hansen, 1981). Although some earlier studies had reported poorer school performance for middle-class adolescent sons of working mothers (see Etaugh, 1974), this finding has not emerged from the newer research.

Educational and Career Aspirations

Most of the earlier studies of the effect of maternal employment on children's educational and career aspirations dealt with daughters, and the results consistently showed that maternal employment was positively related to daughters' educational and career aspirations (Etaugh, 1974). The more recent studies yield the same pattern of mostly female samples and generally positive outcomes for daughters (Amstey & Whitbourne, 1988; Baldwin, 1984; Bielby, 1978; Corder & Stephan, 1984; Foon, 1988; Smith, 1980; Stevens & Boyd, 1980). One study found higher career aspirations among both sons and daughters of employed mothers (Mitchell, 1981). Several studies that used samples of both sexes, however, found no differences in educational and career aspirations, academic orientation, study habits or future life plans of adolescents as a function of mothers' work status (Dellas et al., 1979; Falbo & Aida, 1987; Ramarao, Parvathy, & Swaminathan, 1983; Rosenthal & Hansen, 1981). Similarly, maternal employment was not related to the work orientation of either black or white high school senior girls (Macke & Morgan, 1978), college women's career orientation (Komarovsky, 1982) or job and home attitudes (Stake & Rogers, 1989), or adult women's work activity (Mott, Statham, & Maxwell, 1982).

Three studies have found that the number of years of maternal employment is positively correlated with career aspirations and orientations in college-age and adult women (D'Amico, Haurin, & Mott, 1983; Ridgeway, 1978; Stein, 1973), as well as with choosing a nontraditional career (Sandberg, Ehrhardt, Mellins, Ince, & Meyer-Bahlburg, 1987).

Still other studies have suggested the importance of perceived maternal satisfaction on career aspirations. Pearlman (1981) found that adolescent daughters of working mothers were more career-oriented than were daughters of nonworking mothers. A more important predictor of career orientation in daughters of working mothers, however, was their perception of their mothers' satisfaction with a working life-style. Similarly, Leslie (1986) reported that the more satisfied mothers were with their employment, the more positively daughters valued employment. Other studies, however, indicate that maternal job satisfaction may be inversely related to daughters' career aspirations. Oakes and Oliver (1984) found that postsecondary students of both sexes were more likely to select a higher-status career if their mother's job satisfaction was perceived as low. Similarly, Altman and Grossman (1977) found not only greater career orientation for college women with working mothers but also higher aspirations in daughters who perceived their mothers as relatively dissatisfied with their lower-status jobs. This same pattern of results had been obtained for college women in an earlier study by Frieze, Parsons, and Ruble (1972), who suggested that mothers who were dissatisfied with the types of jobs available to them might encourage their daughters to achieve more than they themselves had achieved.

Others studies have focused on the relationship between maternal employment and the type of occupation chosen. Earlier studies had shown that adult women in professional occupations were more likely to have had working mothers (see Etaugh, 1974). Both Almquist (1974) and Tangri (1972) reported that college women who preferred traditionally masculine occupations more often had working mothers than did those who preferred traditionally feminine occupations. Lemkau (1983, 1984) found that both women and men in sex-atypical professions were more likely to have had employed mothers than were individuals employed in sex-typical professions. Other research shows that daughters of employed women aspire to and choose occupations similar to those of their mothers (Burlin, 1976; Stevens & Boyd, 1980; Zuckerman, 1981).

Sex-Role Concepts

As was the case for elementary school children, maternal employment generally is associated with less stereotyped sex-role concepts among adolescents (Acock, Barker, & Bengston, 1982; Altman & Grossman, 1977; Baldwin, 1984; Bielby & Bielby, 1984; Chandler, Sawicki, & Stryffeler, 1981; Galambos, Petersen, & Lennerz, 1988; Gardner & LaBreque, 1986; Gold & Andres, 1978a; Herzog, Bachman, & Johnston, 1983; Morgan & Grube, 1987; Powell & Steelman, 1982 [sons only]; Stephan & Corder, 1985; Stoloff, 1973). College students also hold less traditional sex-role attitudes if their mothers worked by choice rather than necessity (Etaugh & Gerson, 1974).

Other research yields no relationship between maternal employment status and sex-role ideology among either high school students (Dellas et al., 1979) or college and other postsecondary students (Dempewolff, 1974; Oakes & Oliver, 1984; Tallichet & Willits, 1986).

Perceptions of Parental Behavior

Some studies have found no perceived differences in parent-child relationships as a function of maternal employment (Dellas et al., 1979; Mitchell, 1981; Richards & Duckett, 1989). These results are in line with earlier findings for adolescents (Etaugh, 1974) and with the more recent results for elementary school children discussed above. Gold and Andres (1978a) reported that adolescent children of employed women perceived their parents' behavior as similar in household activities. This result is consistent with the finding that children of employed mothers have fewer stereotyped sex-role concepts.

Some research indicates that maternal employment may be associated with less favorable perceptions of parental behavior. Female college students whose mothers were employed full-time reported more tension and anger at home and less close relationships with their fathers than did daughters of nonemployed women (Jensen & Borges, 1986). Tenth-grade sons (but not daughters) reported more arguments with their mothers and siblings when their mothers were employed (Montemayor, 1984). Perceptions vary by developmental level. In one study, 7th through 10th graders perceived full-time employed mothers as less accepting and as granting less autonomy than did nonemployed mothers; however, this pattern was reversed for 11th and 12th graders (Dusek & Litovsky, 1988).

Research also indicates that maternal identification and sex-role socialization of adolescent women are positively affected by maternal employment variables, in line with earlier findings (see Etaugh, 1974). Baruch (1974) found that college women with working mothers hoped to emulate the life pattern of their mothers rather than their fathers more often than did daughters of nonworking mothers. In addition, mothers who preferred to work (even if not employed) were perceived by their daughters to be more similar to themselves than were mothers who preferred not to work. Pasquali and Callegari (1978) reported that high school girls identified more strongly with satisfied mothers, whether or not they were employed. Finally, two studies have found that androgynous college women were more likely to have working mothers (Gilroy, et al., 1981; Hansson, Chernovetz, & Jones, 1977).

Parental Behavior and Attitudes

The findings of Gold and Andres (1978a) concerning the behaviors of parents of Canadian adolescents closely parallel their results for parents of elementary school children (Gold & Andres, 1978b, 1980). Employed mothers and their husbands were more likely than nonemployed mothers and their husbands to see their behaviors in the home as similar and to report joint supervision of the children. Working women and their husbands also had lower child rejection scores.

Once again, the recent data on attitudes of parents of adolescents are consistent with both the recent and the older findings for younger children. Maternal satisfaction generally is related to favorable consequences for the children (Gold & Andres, 1978a; Pasquali & Callegari, 1978; Pearlman, 1981; Stoloff, 1973).

SUMMARY AND CONCLUSIONS

Research with infants and preschoolers has found few or no differences in parent or child behaviors as a function of the mother's work status. For elementary school children, maternal employment is unrelated to academic achievement for daughters and either unrelated or negatively related for sons. Academic performance of black children, however, is enhanced when the mother works. Adjustment and perceptions of parental behavior generally are unaffected by maternal employment. Children of working mothers have less stereotyped sex-role concepts. In adolescence, maternal employment is either unrelated or positively related to personality and social adjustment. In contrast to earlier research, recent studies do not indicate adjustment problems for lower-class adolescent boys with working mothers. Maternal employment is either unrelated or positively related to school achievement for adolescent girls and, in recent research, is unrelated for boys. Adolescent girls with working mothers have higher educational and career aspirations. As in middle childhood, sex-role concepts of both sexes are less stereotyped when the mother is employed.

A key factor at all ages is the mother's attitude toward her various roles. Mothers who are satisfied with their roles—whether employed or not—have the best-adjusted children. An employed mother's satisfaction, in turn, appears to depend in part on a number of factors, including characteristics of her job, her attitude toward her work, her husband's attitude toward her being employed, and the extent to which her husband shares in domestic activities (Moen, 1982). Clearly, the impact of maternal employment on the child can be understood by examining it within the larger context of work and family circumstances.

REFERENCES

Acock, A. C., Barker, D., & Bengtson, V. L. (1982). Mother's employment and parent-youth similarity. *Journal of Marriage and the Family, 45,* 441–455.

Almquist, E. M. (1974). Sex stereotypes in occupational choice: The case for college women. *Journal of Vocational Behavior, 5,* 13–21.

Al-Timini, S. (1977). Self-concepts of young children with working and nonworking mothers. *Dissertation Abstracts International, 38,* 4972A–4973A.

Altman, S. L., & Grossman. F. K. (1977). Women's career plans and maternal employment. *Psychology of Women Quarterly, 1,* 365–376.

Alwin, D. F. & Thornton, A. (1984). Family origins and the schooling process: Early versus late influence of parental characteristics. *American Sociological Review, 49,* 784–802.

Amato, P. R. (1987). Maternal employment: Effects on children's family relationships and development. *Australian Journal of Sex, Marriage & Family, 8,* 5–16.

Amstey, F. H. & Whitbourne, S. K. (1988). Work and motherhood: Transition to parenthood and women's employment. *The Journal of Genetic Psychology, 149,* 111–118.

Ansul, S. E., DiBiase, R., & Weinraub, M. (1987, April). *Separation distress: The effects of maternal employment and child sex.* Paper presented at the meeting of the Society for Research in Child Development, Baltimore.

Armistead, L., Wierson, M., & Forehand, R. (1990). Adolescents and maternal employment: Is it harmful for a young adolescent to have an employed mother? *Journal of Early Adolescence, 10,* 260–278.

Avery, C. D. (1975). Academic achievement and personal-social adjustment of elementary school students with working mothers (Doctoral dissertation, Fordham University, 1975). *Dissertation Abstracts International, 36,* 1380A.

Bacon, C., & Lerner, R. M. (1975). Effects of maternal employment status on the development of vocational-role perception in females. *Journal of Genetic Psychology, 126,* 187–193.

Baldwin, B. (1984, April). *A causal model of the effects of maternal employment on adolescent achievement.* Paper presented at the meeting of the American Educational Research Association, New Orleans.

Bankart, C. P. & Bankart, B. M. (1985). Japanese children's perceptions of their parents. *Sex Roles, 13,* 679–690.

Barak, A., Feldman, S., & Noy, A. (1991). Traditionality of children's interests as related to their parents' gender stereotypes and traditionality of occupations. *Sex Roles, 24,* 511–524.

Barglow, P., Vaughn, B. E., & Molitor, N. (1987). Effects of maternal absence due to employment on the quality of infant-mother attachment in a low-risk sample. *Child Development, 58,* 945–954.

Barling, J., Fullagar, C., & Marchl-Dingle, J. (1988). Employment commitment as a moderator of the maternal employment status/child behavior relationship. *Journal of Organizational Behavior, 9,* 113–122.

Barling, J., & Van Bart, D. (1984). Mothers' subjective employment experiences and the behaviour of their nursery school children. *Journal of Occupational Psychology, 57,* 49–56.

Baruch, G. K. (1973). Feminine self-esteem, self-ratings of competence and maternal career-commitment. *Journal of Counseling Psychology, 20,* 487–488.

Baruch, G. K. (1974). Maternal career-orientation as related to parental identification in college women. *Journal of Vocational Behavior, 4,* 173–180.

Baruch, G. K. (1976). Girls who perceive themselves as competent: Some antecedents and correlates. *Psychology of Women Quarterly, 1,* 38–49.

Baruch, G. K. & Barnett, R. C. (1986). Fathers' participation in family work and children's sex-role attitudes. *Child Development, 57,* 1210–1223.

Belsky, J., & Rovine, M. J. (1988). Nonmaternal care in the first year of life and the security of infant-parent attachment. *Child Development, 59,* 157–167.

Benn, R. K. (1986). Factors promoting secure attachment relationships between employed mothers and their sons. *Child Development 57,* 1224–1231.

Bielby, D. D. (1978). Maternal employment and socioeconomic status as factors in daughters' career salience: Some substantive refinements. *Sex Roles, 4,* 249–265.

Bielby, D. D. & Bielby, W. T. (1984). Work commitment, sex-role attitudes, and women's employment. *American Sociological Review, 49,* 234–247.

Blau, F. D., & Grossberg, A. J. (1990). *Maternal labor supply and children's cognitive development* (Working Paper No. 3536) Cambridge, MA: National Bureau of Economic Research.

Bronfenbrenner, U., Alvarez, W. F., & Henderson, C. R., Jr., (1984). Working and watching: Maternal employment status and parents' perceptions of their three-year-old children. *Child Development, 55,* 1362–1378.

Burlin, F. (1976). The relationship of parental education and maternal work and occupational status to occupational aspiration in adolescent females. *Journal of Vocational Behavior, 9,* 99–104.

Chandler, T. A., Sawicki, R. F., & Stryffeler, J. M. (1981). Relationship between adolescent sexual stereotypes and working mothers. *Journal of Early Adolescence, 1*, 72–83.

Chase-Lansdale, P. L., & Owen, M. T. (1987). Maternal employment in a family context: Effects on infant-mother and infant-father attachments. *Child Development, 58*, 1505–1512.

Cheles-Miller, P. (1974, April 17–20). *An investigation of whether the stereotypes of husband and wife presented in television commercials can influence a child's perception of the role of husband and wife.* Paper presented at the meeting of the International Communication Association, New Orleans.

Cherry, F. F., & Eaton, E. L. (1977). Physical and cognitive development in children of low-income mothers working in the child's early years. *Child Development, 48*, 158–166.

Cohen, S. (1978). Maternal employment and mother-child interaction. *Merrill-Palmer Quarterly, 24*, 189–197.

Colangelo, N., Rosenthal, D. M., & Dettmann, D. F. (1984). Maternal employment and job satisfaction and their relationship to children's perceptions and behaviors. *Sex Roles, 10*, 691–700.

Collins, S. W. (1975). The effects of maternal employment upon adolescent personality adjustment. *Graduate Research in Education and Related Disciplines, 8*, 5–44.

Corder, J., & Stephan, C. W. (1984). Females' combination of work and family roles: Adolescents' aspirations. *Journal of Marriage and the Family, 50*, 391–400.

Cordua, G. D., McGraw, K. O., & Drabman, R. S. (1979). Doctor or nurse: Children's perception of sex typed occupations. *Child Development, 50*, 590–593.

Crandall, V. C., & Crandall, B. W. (1983). Maternal and childhood behaviors as antecedents of internal-external control perceptions in young adulthood. In H. M. Lefcourt (Ed.), *Research with the locus of control construct* (pp. 53–69). New York: Academic Press.

Crockenberg, S., & Litman, C. (1989, April). *Effects of maternal and two-year old child behavior.* Paper presented at the meeting of the Society for Research in Child Development, Kansas City, MO.

Crouter, A. C., & McHale, S. M. (1989, April). *Childrearing in dual- and single-earner families: Implications for the development of school-age children.* Paper presented at the meeting of the Society for Research in Child Development, Kansas City, MO.

D'Amico, R. J., Haurin, R. J., & Mott, F. L. (1983). The effects of mothers' employment on adolescent and early adult outcomes of young men and women. In C. Hayes & S. Kamerman (Eds.), *Children of working parents: Experiences and outcomes* (pp. 130–219). Washington, DC.: National Academy Press.

Davis, A. J., & Stith, S. M. (1983, April). *Infant caregiving behaviors of employed mothers, non-employed mothers and substitute caregivers in unregulated family day care homes.* Paper presented at the meeting of the Society for Research in Child Development, Detroit.

Dellas, M., Gaier, E. L., & Emihovich, C. A. (1979). Maternal employment and selected behaviors and attitudes of preadolescents and adolescents. *Adolescence, 14*, 579–589.

Dempewolff, J. A. (1974). Some correlates of feminism. *Psychological Reports, 34,* 671–676.

Desai, S., Chase-Lansdale, P. L., & Michael, R. T. (1989). Mother or market? Effects of maternal employment on the intellectual ability of 4-year-old children. *Demography, 26,* 545–561.

Duckett, E., & Richards, M. H. (1989, April). *Maternal employment and young adolescents' daily experience in single-mother families.* Paper presented at the meeting of the Society for Research on Child Development, Kansas City, MO.

Dusek, J. B., & Litovsky, V. G. (1988, March). *Maternal employment and adolescent adjustment and perceptions of child bearing.* Paper presented at the meeting of the Society for Research on Adolescence, Alexandria, VA.

Easterbrooks, M. A., & Goldberg, W. A. (1985). Effects of early maternal employment on toddlers, mothers, and fathers. *Developmental Psychology, 21,* 774–783.

Etaugh, C. (1974). Effects of maternal employment on children: A review of recent research. *Merrill-Palmer Quarterly, 20,* 71–98.

Etaugh, C., & Gerson, A. (1974). Attitudes toward women: Some biographical correlates. *Psychological Reports, 35,* 701–702.

Falbo, T., & Aida, Y. (1987, August). *Quality vs. quantity time: Mother's employment and children's outcomes.* Paper presented at the meeting of the American Psychological Association, New York.

Farel, A. M. (1980). Effects of preferred maternal roles, maternal employment, and sociodemographic status on school adjustment and competence. *Child Development, 51,* 1179–1186.

Foon, A. E. (1988). Effect of mother's employment status on adolescents' self perceptions and academic performance. *Educational Studies, 14,* 265–274.

Frieze, I., Parsons, J., & Ruble, D. (1972). *Some determinants of career aspirations in college women.* Paper presented at the UCLA Symposium on Sex Roles and Sex Differences, Los Angeles.

Funk, E. (1984). The relationship between work satisfaction and maternal attitudes of infants' attachment to their mothers. *Dissertation Abstracts International, 44,* 2915B.

Galambos, N. L., & Lerner, J. V. (1984, August). *Maternal role satisfaction, mother-child interaction, and child temperament.* Paper presented at the meeting of the American Psychological Association, Toronto.

Galambos, N. L. & Maggs, J. L. (1990). Putting mothers' work-related stress in perspective: Mothers and adolescents in dual-earner families. *Journal of Early Adolescence, 10,* 313–328.

Galambos, N. L., Petersen, A. C., & Lenerz, K. (1988). Maternal employment and sex typing in early adolescence: Contemporaneous and longitudinal relations. In A. E. Gottfried & A. W. Gottfried (Eds.), *Maternal employment and children's development: Longitudinal research* (pp. 155–189). New York: Plenum.

Gardner, K. E., & LaBrecque, S. V. (1986). Effects of maternal employment on sex role orientation of adolescents. *Adolescence, 21,* 875–885.

Gibbons, P. A., & Kopelman, R. E. (1977). Maternal employment as a determinant of fear of success in females. *Psychological Reports, 40,* 1200–1202.

Gilroy, F. D., Talierco, T. M., & Steinbacher, R. (1981). Impact of maternal employment on daughters' sex-role orientation and fear of success. *Psychological Reports, 49*, 963–968.

Gold, D., & Andres, D. (1978a). Developmental comparisons between adolescent children with employed and non-employed mothers. *Merrill-Palmer Quarterly, 24*, 243–254.

Gold, D., & Andres, D. (1978b). Developmental comparisons between 10-year-old children with employed and nonemployed mothers. *Child Development, 49*, 75–84.

Gold, D., & Andres, D. (1978c). Relations between maternal employment and development of nursery school children. *Canadian Journal of Behavioral Science, 10*, 116–129.

Gold, D., & Andres, D. (1980). Maternal employment and development of ten-year-old Francophone children. *Canadian Journal of Behavioral Science, 12*, 233–240.

Gold, D., Andres, D., & Glorieux, J. (1979). The development of Francophone nursery school children with employed and nonemployed mothers. *Canadian Journal of Behavioral Science, 11*, 169–173.

Goldberg, W. A., & Easterbrooks, M. A. (1988). Maternal employment when children are toddlers and kindergartners. In A. E. Gottfried, & A. W. Gottfried (Eds.), *Maternal employment and children's development: Longitudinal research* (pp. 121–154). New York: Plenum.

Gorman, L. K. (1980). The relationship between independence training and achievement motivation in children of career women. *Dissertaion Abstracts International, 42*, 768–B.

Gottfried, A. E., Gottfried, A. W., & Bathurst, K. (1988). Maternal employment, family environment, and children's development: Infancy through the school years. In A. E. Gottfried & A. W. Gottfried (Eds.), *Maternal employment and children's development: Longitudinal research* (pp. 11–58). New York: Plenum.

Greenberger, E. (1989, August). *Bronfenbrenner et al. revisited: Maternal employment and perceptions of young children.* Paper presented at the meeting of the American Psychological Association, New Orleans.

Guidubaldi, J., Nastasi, B. K., Cleminshaw, H. K., & Perry, J. D. (1986, August). *Maternal employment and child adjustment: Results of a nationwide study.* Paper presented at the meeting of the American Psychological Association, Washington, DC.

Hansson, R. O., Chernovetz, M. E., & Jones, W. H. (1977). Maternal employment and androgyny. *Psychology of Women Quarterly, 2*, 76–78.

Harrell, J. E., & Ridley, C. A. (1975). Substitute child care, maternal employment, and the quality of mother-child interaction. *Journal of Marriage and the Family, 37*, 556–564.

Henggeler, S. W., & Borduin, C. M. (1981). Satisfied working mothers and their preschool sons: Interaction and psychosocial adjustment. *Journal of Family Issues, 2*, 322–335.

Herzog, A. R., Bachman, J. G., & Johnston, L. D. (1983). Paid work, child care, and housework: A national survey of high school seniors' preferences for sharing responsibilities between husband and wife. *Sex Roles, 9,* 109–133.

Hillman, S. B., Sawilowsky, S., Becker, M. J., & Ogilvie, L. A. (1990, August). *Effects of maternal employment on adolescent substance use.* Paper presented at the meeting of the American Psychological Association, Boston.

Hock, E. (1980). Working and nonworking mothers and their infants: A comparative study of maternal caregiving characteristics and infant social behavior. *Merrill-Palmer Quarterly, 26,* 79–101.

Jaeger, E., Weinraub, M., Becker, N., & Jaeger, M. (1989, April). *Attachment, dependency, and separation distress in infants of employed mothers.* Paper presented at the meeting of the Society for Research in Child Development, Kansas City, MO.

Jensen, L., & Borges, M. (1986). The effect of maternal employment on adolescent daughters. *Adolescence, 21,* 659–666.

Jones, L. M., & McBride, J. L. (1980). Sex-role stereotyping in children as a function of maternal employment. *Journal of Social Psychology, 111,* 219–223.

Joy, S. S., & Wise, P. S. (1983). Maternal employment, anxiety, and sex differences in college students' self-descriptions. *Sex Roles, 9,* 519–525.

Klecka, C. O., & Hiller, D. V. (1977). Impact of mothers' life style on adolescent gender-role socialization. *Sex Roles, 3,* 241–255.

Komarovsky, M. (1982). Female freshmen view their future: Career salience and its correlates. *Sex Roles, 8,* 299–314.

Lamb, M. E., Frodi, A., Hwang, P., & Frodi, M. (1982). Mother- and father-infant interaction involving play and holding in traditional and non-traditional Swedish families. *Developmental Psychology, 18,* 215–221.

Lavine, L. O. (1982). Parental power as a potential influence on girls' career choice. *Child Development, 53,* 658–663.

Lemkau, J. P. (1983). Personality and background characteristics of women in male-dominated professions. *Psychology of Women Quarterly, 8,* 144–165.

Lemkau, J. P. (1984). Men in female-dominated professions: Distinguishing personality and background features. *Journal of Vocational Behavior, 24,* 110–122.

Lerner, J. V., & Galambos, N. J. (1988). The influences of maternal employment across life: The New York longitudinal study. In A. E. Gottfried & A. W. Gottfried (Eds.), *Maternal employment and children's development: Longitudinal research* (pp. 59–83). New York: Plenum.

Leslie, L. A. (1986). The impact of adolescent females' assessments of parenthood and employment on plans for the future. *Journal of Youth and Adolescence, 15,* 29–49.

LeVine, B. K. (1981). Familial parameters of the adjustment of preschool children to maternal employment. *Dissertation Abstracts International, 42,* 776B.

Levy, G. D. (1989). Relations among aspects of children's social environments, gender schematization, gender role knowledge, and flexibility. *Sex Roles, 21,* 803–823.

Macke, A. S., & Morgan, W. R. (1978). Maternal employment, race, and work orientation of high school girls. *Social Forces, 57,* 187–204.

MacKinnon, C. E., Brody, G. H., & Stoneman, Z. (1982). The effects of divorce and maternal employment on the home environments of preschool children. *Child Development, 53,* 1392–1399.

MacKinnon, C. E., Stoneman, Z., & Brody, G. H. (1984). The impact of maternal employment and family form on children's sex-role stereotypes and mothers' traditional attitudes. *Journal of Divorce, 8,* 51–60.

Marantz, S. A., & Mansfield, A. F. (1977). Maternal employment and the development of sex-role stereotyping in five- to eleven-year-old girls. *Child Development, 48,* 668–673.

Maracek, J. (1976, April). *Predictors of women's career attainment: A longitudinal study.* Paper presented at the meeting of the Eastern Psychological Association, New York.

Medrich, E. A., Roizen, J., Rubin, V., & Buckley, S. (1982). *The serious business of growing up: A study of children's lives outside school.* Berkeley: University of California Press.

Meyer, B. (1980). The development of girls' sex-role attitudes. *Child Development, 51,* 508–514.

Miller, S. M. (1975). The effects of maternal employment on sex role perceptions, interests and self-esteem in kindergarten children. *Developmental Psychology, 11,* 405–406.

Milne, A. M., Myers, D. E., Rosenthal, A. S., & Ginsburg, A. (1986). Single parents, working mothers, and the educational achievement of school children. *Sociology of Education, 59,* 125–139.

Mitchell, T. E. (1981). Relationship of maternal employment to adolescent adjustment. *Dissertation Abstracts International, 41,* 2572B.

Moen, P. (1982). The two-provider family: Problems and potentials. In M. E. Lamb (Ed.), *Nontraditional families: Parenting and child development* (pp. 13–43). Hillsdale, NJ: Erlbaum.

Montemayor, R. (1984). Maternal employment and adolescents' relations with parents, siblings, and peers. *Journal of Youth and Adolescence, 13,* 543–557.

Moore, T. W. (1975). Exclusive mothering and its alternatives: The outcome to adolescence. *Scandanavian Journal of Psychology, 16,* 255–272.

Moorehouse, M. J. (1991). Linking maternal employment patterns to mother-child activities and children's school competence. *Developmental Psychology, 27,* 295–303.

Morgan, M., & Grube, J. W. (1987). Consequences of maternal employment for adolescent behaviour and attitudes. *The Irish Journal of Psychology 8,* 85–98.

Mott, F. L., Statham, A., & Maxwell, N. L. (1982). From mother to daughter: The transmission of work behavior patterns across generation. In F. L. Mott (Ed.), *The employment revolution: Young American women in the 1970's* (pp. 66–79). Cambridge, MA: MIT Press.

Nelson, C., & Keith, J. (1990). Comparisons of female and male early adolescent sex role attitude and behavior development. *Adolescence, 25,* 183–204.

Nichols, I. A., & Shauffer, C. B. (1975, August). *Self-concept as a predictor of performance in college women.* Paper presented at the meeting of the American Psychological Association, Chicago.

Oakes, R., & Oliver, J. (1984, August). *Maternal employment, personality and career variables in a post high school population*. Paper presented at the meeting of the American Psychological Association, Toronto.

Owen, M. T., & Cox, M. J. (1988). Maternal employment and the transition to parenthood. In A. E. Gottfried & A. W. Gottfried (Eds.), *Maternal employment and children's development: Longitudinal research* (pp. 85–119). New York: Plenum.

Owen, M. T., Easterbrooks, M. A., Chase-Lansdale, L., & Goldberg, W. A. (1984). The relation between maternal employment status and the stability of attachments to mother and to father. *Child Development, 55*, 1894–1901.

Pasquali, L., & Callegari, A. I. (1978). Working mothers and daughters' sex-role identification in Brazil. *Child Development, 49*, 902–905.

Pearlman, V. A. (1981). Influences of mothers' employment on career orientation and career choice of adolescent daughters. *Dissertation Abstracts International, 41*, 4657A.

Pedersen, F. A., Cain, R. L., Zaslow, M. J., & Anderson, B. J. (1982). Variation in infant experience associated with alternative family roles. In L. Laosa & I. Sigel (Eds.), *Families as learning environments for children* (pp. 203–219). New York: Plenum.

Pedersen, F. A., Zaslow, M. J., Suwalsky, J. T. D., & Cain, R. L. (1982). *Infant experiences in traditional and dual wage earner families*. Paper presented at the International Conference on Infant Studies, Austin, TX.

Perloff, R. M. (1977). Some antecedents of children's sex-role stereotypes. *Psychological Reports, 40*, 463–466.

Poresky, R. H., & Whitsitt, T. M. (1985). Young girls' intelligence and motivation: Links with maternal employment and education but not systems theory. *Journal of Psychology, 119*, 475–480.

Powell, B., & Steelman, L. C. (1982). Testing an undertested comparison: Maternal effects on sons' and daughters' attitudes toward women in the labor force. *Journal of Marriage and the Family, 48*, 349–355.

Rabinovich, B. A., Suwalsky, J. T. D., & Pedersen, F. A. (1986). The effects of maternal employment on infants: A pretest-posttest design. *Journal of Genetic Psychology, 147*, 283–285.

Ramarao, P., Parvathy, S., & Swaminathan, V. D. (1983). Study habits of adolescent boys and girls of employed and non-employed mothers. *Psychological Studies, 28*, 44–47.

Richards, M. H., & Duckett, E. (1989, April). *Maternal employment and young adolescents' daily experience with family*. Paper presented at the meeting of the Society for Research on Child Development, Kansas City, MO.

Ridgeway, C. (1978). Parental identification and patterns of career orientation in college women. *Journal of Vocational Behavior, 12*, 1–11.

Robb, B., & Raven, M. (1981). Maternal employment and children's sex-role perceptions. *Educational Research, 23*, 223–225.

Rodgon, M. M., Gralewski, C., & Hetzel, J. (1977, April). *Maternal attitudes toward sex roles related to children's attitudes toward maternal roles in second and sixth grade children*. Paper presented at the meeting of the Society for Research in Child Development, New Orleans.

Rollins, J., & White P. N. (1982). The relationship between mothers' and daughters' sex-role attitudes and self-concepts in three types of family environment. *Sex Roles, 8,* 1141–1155.

Rosenthal, D., & Hansen, J. (1981). The impact of maternal employment on children's perceptions of parents and personal development. *Sex Roles, 7,* 593–598.

Sandberg, D. E., Ehrhardt, A. A., Mellins, C. A., Ince, S. E., & Meyer-Bahlburg, H. F. L. (1987). The influence of individual and family characteristics upon career aspirations of girls during childhood and adolescence. *Sex Roles, 16,* 649–668.

Schacter, F. F. (1981). Toddlers with employed mothers. *Child Development, 52,* 958–964.

Schubert, L., Bradley-Johnson, S., & Nuttal, J. (1980). Mother-infant communication and maternal employment. *Child Development, 51,* 246–249.

Seegmiller, B. R. (1980). Sex-role differentiation in preschoolers: Effects of maternal employment. *Journal of Psychology, 104,* 185–189.

Selkow, P. (1984). Effects of maternal employment on kindergarten and first-grade children's vocational aspirations. *Sex Roles, 11,* 677–690.

Smith, E. R. (1980). Desiring and expecting to work among high school girls: Some determinants and consequences. *Journal of Vocational Behavior, 17,* 218–230.

Stake, J. E., & Rogers, L. L. (1989). Job and home attitudes of undergraduate women and their mothers. *Sex Roles, 20,* 445–463.

Stein, A. W. (1973). The effects of maternal employment and educational attainment on the sex typed attributes of college females. *Social Behavoir and Personality, 1,* 111–114.

Stephan, C. W., & Corder, J. (1985). The effects of dual-career families on adolescents' sex-role attitudes, work and family plans, and choices of important others. *Journal of Marriage and the Family, 51,* 921–929.

Stevens, G., & Boyd, M. (1980). The importance of mother: Labor force participation and intergenerational mobility of women. *Social Forces, 59,* 186–199.

Stevenson, N. G. (1983). The role of maternal employment and satisfaction level in children's cognitive performance. *Dissertation Abstracts International, 43,* 3377B.

Stoloff, C. (1973). Who joins women's liberation? *Psychiatry, 36,* 325–340.

Stuckey, M. F., McGhee, P. E., & Bell, N. J. (1982). Parent-child interaction: The influence of maternal employment. *Developmental Psychology, 18,* 635–644.

Tallichet, S. E., & Willits, F. K. (1986). Gender-role attitude change of young women: Influential factors from a panel study. *Social Psychology Quarterly, 49,* 219–227.

Tangri, S. S. (1972). Determinants of occupational role innovation among college women. *Journal of Social Issues, 28,* 177–200.

Taylor, E. S. (1984). Components of achievement in latency age daughters of career women. *Dissertation Abstracts International, 44,* 3947B.

Taylor, J. S. (1980). The relationship of empathy and self-concept in four-year-old nursery school boys and girls correlated with maternal employment. *Dissertation Abstracts International, 41,* 2435A–2436A.

Thompson, R. A., Lamb, M. E., & Estes, D. (1982). Stability of infant-mother attachment and its relationship to changing life circumstances in an unselected middle-class sample. *Child Development, 53,* 144–148.

Trimberger, R., & MacLean, M. J. (1982). Maternal employment: The child's perspective. *Journal of Marriage and the Family, 44,* 469–475.

Tulkin, S. R. (1973). Social class differences in attachment behaviors of ten-month-old infants. *Child Development, 44,* 171–174.

U. S. Bureau of the Census. (1990). *Statistical abstract of the United States: 1990* (110th ed.). Washington, DC: U. S. Government Printing Office.

Volling, B. L., & Belsky, J. (1989, April). *Infant, father, and marital antecedents of infant-father attachment security in dual-earner and single-earner families.* Paper presented at the meeting of the Society for Research in Child Development, Kansas City, MO.

Walker, L. S., Ortiz-Valdes, J. A., & Newbrough, J. R. (1989). The role of maternal employment and depression in the psychological adjustment of chronically ill, mentally retarded, and well children. *Journal of Pediatric Psychology, 14,* 357–370.

Warshaw, R. (1976). The effects of working mothers on children. *Dissertation Abstracts International, 37,* 1933B.

Weinraub, M., & Jaeger, E. (1988, September). *The timing of mothers' return to the workplace: Effects on the developing mother-infant relationship.* Paper presented at the meeting of the Wingspread Conference, "Parental Leave and Childcare: Setting a Research and Policy Agency," Racine, WI.

Weinraub, M., Jaeger, E., & Hoffman, L. (1988). Predicting infant outcome in families of employed and nonemployed mothers. *Early Childhood Research Quarterly, 3,* 361–378.

Weiskopf-Bock, S. (1983, April). *The effects of maternal employment on mother-child interaction and parental childrearing attitudes.* Paper presented at the meeting of the Society for Research in Child Development, Detroit.

Wille, D. E. (1989, April). *The effect of maternal employment on maternal separation and reunion behavior.* Paper presented at the meeting of the Society for Research in Child Development, Kansas City, MO.

Williamson, S. Z. (1970). The effects of maternal employment on the scholastic performance of children. *Journal of Home Economics, 60,* 609–613.

Wise, P.S., &Joy, S. S. (1982). Working mothers, sex differences, and self-esteem in college students' self descriptions. *Sex Roles, 8,* 785–790.

Zaslow, M., Pedersen, F., Suwalsky, J., & Rabinovich, B. (1983, April). *Maternal employment and parent-infant interaction.* Paper presented at meeting of the Society for Research in Child Development, Detroit.

Zuckerman, D. M. (1981). Family background, sex-role attitudes, and life goals of technical college and university students. *Sex Roles, 1,* 1109–1126.

■ 6
Family Work of Husbands and Fathers in Dual-Earner Marriages

Joe F. Pittman and Jennifer L. Kerpelman

Studying the participation of men in family work, defined as the unpaid work involved in the maintenance of the home and in the care and monitoring of children, is a challenge. There are at least two reasons for this assertion. First, the fact that gender is overwhelmingly the center predictor of who does what family work and how much may well be the best-documented fact in the family literature. By itself, this fact hardly makes research on family work a challenge. Indeed, it leads one to wonder why people continue to invest such energy in its study. In combination with this fact, however, is a second detail that makes the research finding seem somehow unauthentic. Everyone reading this chapter will be able to think readily of both men and women who do not fit the mold. It is this direct experience, seemingly at odds with the research, that sets the serious researcher to puzzling. Why are these apparent exceptions so difficult for researchers to isolate? Does their existence hold implications for the otherwise incredible consistency in the linkage between gender and family work? Why does virtually every study designed to test hypotheses that theoretically should account for greater male participation reveal disappointingly small results? Are the right questions being asked? These are some of the factors that, when combined with the dominant thrust of the research literature, make the study of men and family work challenging and exciting.

This chapter is organized around a brief review of recent research providing continuing support for the dominance of gender in predicting family work. Some tentative suggestions for moving our understanding of gender and family work forward are also advanced. Although this book is oriented to dual-earner families with children, our focus is necessarily somewhat wider because, by necessity, family work takes place regardless of the presence of children and because the research does not often distinguish between the family work associated with spousal versus parental roles.

The research literature reads as an indictment of husbands and fathers, as numerous careful analyses consistently establish that wives and mothers do far more family work than men do (Antill & Cottin, 1988; Berk, 1985; Hardesty & Bokemeier, 1989; Hiller & Philliber, 1986; Leslie & Anderson, 1988; Rexroat & Shehan, 1987; Spitze, 1986). Berk (1985), in a summary of the empirical findings of the time-use studies conducted in the 1970s, reports that men spend approximately 10–15 hours a week in household work. This contribution amounts, on average, to about 15% of the total time invested by all household members. A study using a more recent sample (but a less precise method of estimating time) revealed that in the late 1980s husbands continued to invest approximately 14 hours a week and that the allocation of tasks was highly segregated by sex (Blair & Lichter, 1991). Little seems to have changed in the decade of the 1980s.

Although the gender difference in the distribution of family work is well established, the literature does not paint a completely clear picture of what factors influence men's participation rates. When studying gender differences in the distribution of family work responsibilities, a number of contextual dimensions are often considered. First, structural factors related to men's families and jobs are typically considered (Berk, 1985, Pleck, 1985). Equally important in explaining men's family work, however, are psychosocial factors, such as self-role congruence and gender-role ideology (Chassin, Zeiss, & Reaven, 1985; McDermid, Huston, & McHale, 1990). Our first task will be to review this literature and to consider its implications for the understanding of fathers' participation in family work in dual-earning families.

THE INFLUENCE OF STRUCTURAL FACTORS ON FAMILY WORK

Structural factors are typically conceptualized as "given" aspects of a situation. In other words, they are background variables that, if considered, add definition to a situation. For instance, time invested in work, income, and education levels of husbands and wives can be considered structural elements of a working family member's situation. Knowing a person's work schedule, income, and educational background may facilitate the development of predictions about the decisions that person is likely to make. Similarly, the presence, as well as the ages, of children in a family are easily understood as elements of family structure. A structural examination of the allocation of family work in dual-earning families requires consideration of family patterns, the organizational culture of the workplace, and the linkages between these domains. Families must accommodate these arrangements.

Time Invested in Paid Work

If one were to guess what single factor would make the difference in whether husbands and fathers participate more in family work, the first suggestion ventured would probably be that the wife/mother's participation in the work force should lead directly to greater participation by her mate in the family work. The weight of the evidence supports this assertion (Barnett & Baruch, 1987; Coverman, 1985; Huber & Spitze, 1981; Leslie & Anderson, 1988; Leslie, Anderson, & Branson, 1991; Ross, 1987; Smith & Reid, 1986) but in a surprisingly limited way. When women join the work force, their time investment in family work declines. This results in a scenario in which men increase their share in the work done while potentially not increasing their actual time investment. Several time-use studies (Meissner, Humphreys, Meis, & Scheu, 1975; Shelton, 1990) reveal that husbands of employed wives do not spend more time on housework than do husbands of housewives. Limited support is found for the conclusion that working fathers do increase their time investments in child care (Bird, Bird, & Scruggs, 1984; Coverman, 1985; Douthitt, 1989) but only by small margins.

Whereas the wife/mother's participation in the provider role only minimally affects the husband/father's involvement in family work, his own investment in paid work substantially affects his commitment to family work. The more hours a husband spends in his paid job, the less he participates in household labor (Antill & Cottin, 1988; Atkinson & Huston, 1984; Coverman, 1985; Coverman & Sheley, 1986). Hardesty and Bokemeier (1989) showed that when a husband/father commits less time to paid labor, his proportionate contribution to family work increases as well. Atkinson and Huston (1984) suggest that it is spouses' relative investments in paid labor that affect the husband/father's family work contribution. They found that the more hours the husband was employed, in comparison to the wife, the less he was involved in family work.

In families with children, fathers tend to have considerably longer work days than mothers have (Kingston & Nock, 1985; Voydanoff, 1988).

This fact serves to keep men away from home longer than women each day, decreasing their availability (and willingness) to take care of regular household and child care tasks (Antill & Cottin, 1988). It is interesting to note that when dual-earner couples commit greater time to work, both parents recognize that this commitment translates into a loss of time with children, but husbands tend to expect their wives, rather than themselves, to moderate schedules to be more available to the children (Kingston & Nock, 1985).

Income

About half of the relevant literature suggests that, as a working woman's income approaches that of her husband's, the probability of greater husband participation in family work increases (Antill & Cottin, 1988; Bird et al., 1984; Model, 1981; Ross, 1987). However, this hypothesis is not supported or receives mixed support in about as many studies as support it (Hardesty & Bokemeier, 1989; Huber & Spitze, 1981; Spitze, 1986). Much more consistent support is obtained for the assertion that men with higher incomes participate less in family work than do those who earn lower incomes (Antill & Cottin, 1988; Ericksen, Yancey, & Ericksen, 1979; Model, 1981; Smith & Reid, 1986). Model's (1981) findings suggest that these two factors may operate together. She found that high-earning husbands (making over $25,000 per year in 1978) whose wives' earnings were similar were the highest male family-work participants in her sample. Men in this same income category, however, showed the lowest involvement when their wives did not work for pay or earned considerably less. Overall, Model (1981) found that lower-income husbands exhibited much higher levels of responsibility taking for specific household tasks, such as laundry, dinner preparation, and vacuuming, in comparison to their high-earning counterparts.

Education

Another notable structural influence on husbands' participation in family work is education, that of both the husband and the wife. A number of studies have found a positive relationship between the husband's/father's education level and his performance of family work (Antill & Cottin, 1988; Hardesty & Bokemeier, 1989; Huber & Spitze, 1983; Indelicato, Cooney, Pederson, & Palkovitz, 1991; Ross, 1987). The husband/father's education level is especially important in explaining his participation in the traditionally female household tasks. More highly educated men are considerably more likely to share tasks with their wives than are less well educated men (Antill & Cottin, 1988). Interestingly, when predicting participation in child care, the husband's education level appears to interact with other variables. Indelicato et al. (1991) found that becoming a father at an older age, when combined with higher levels of education, produced an alliance of factors leading to greater father involvement with the children.

Wives' education may also play a role in affecting the husband's level of participation in family work, although, as usual, findings are inconclusive. Huber and Spitze (1981) found that when both spouses are highly educated, wives receive more help from their husbands. Nyquist, Slivken, Spence, and Helmreich (1985) reported that an increase in wives' education has a positive effect on husbands' sharing of family work. In contrast, Ross (1987) reported that the wife's education level is unrelated to the division of household labor, and Coverman's (1985) results indicated that the higher the wife's education, the less the husband performs family work tasks.

Societal factors

So far we have considered only the most immediate factors that characterize any working person: they have work schedules, they earn incomes, and they bring educational backgrounds with them. It is also possible to consider structural factors that transcend the worker and seem to exist at the most general level; we refer to social forces and to organizational reactions to them. A recent economic analysis, conducted by Bergen (1991), revealed that the condition of one's local economy affects the allocation of time to paid work and family work for both spouses but in different ways. Although men respond to strong economies by working more hours when opportunities arise, women do not. Women's, but not men's, involvement in domestic labor varies on the basis of local context, with the lowest rates seen in urban settings compared to suburban and rural settings.

In recent decades societal conditions have demanded the participation of mothers in the work force. Bergen (1991) reported that, whereas men's market and domestic labor is constant in the face of varying family financial need, women respond to this need with increased market work. Children decrease their mother's investment in the labor market but increase the demand for domestic services by a margin considerably greater than the time freed by the work cutback (Bergen, 1991). Incredibly, workplace policies in the United States to date have failed miserably in the provision of support to either employed parent (Silverstein, 1991; Stipek & McCroskey, 1989; Zedeck & Mosier, 1990). The vast majority of employers do not offer any form of job-protected parental leave. Indeed, workplace policies are designed to reinforce the traditional segregation of work and family domains, despite the near total abandonment of this traditional role allocation.

Pleck (1977) identifies two sets of cultural buffers that operate between the domains of work and family and that limit the effects that role changes in one area have on the other. One set of buffers consists of gender-based "market mechanisms," which translate into inequitable job qualities and opportunities for men and women (e.g., men have higher-paying, higher-status jobs than do women). These buffers encourage husbands/fathers to emphasize their work role, often at the expense of their family role. The same market mechanisms press women who have become successful in male-dominated jobs to take on the more typically male pattern of values: work first, family second.

The second set of buffers Pleck (1977) calls "asymmetrically permeable boundaries" between work and family roles. These boundaries legitimate the emphasis on the family role, as against the work role, for women. For men the opposite pattern is legitimized; men are allowed (expected) to place priority on their work role at the expense of their family role. Consequently, policies that support the father's taking on paternal role demands are extremely rare in the United States. Bowen and Orthner (1991) argue that until very recently there was little reason for researchers to study the relationship between organizational policy and fathers' role performance, as neither domain allowed much variation from the traditional mold. They imply that much of the more recent corporate "responsiveness" to families may more likely represent a paternalistic reaction to perceived needs of working women than an effort to develop family- or father-supportive policies. Because of the financial needs of families and the barriers that employing organizations impose, fathers often find it difficult to allocate time and energy to parenting activities (Lamb, 1987). Silverstein (1991) seems to summarize well this apparent cultural impasse as well as its impact on families: "Until our culture includes nurturing and attachment as highly valued qualities of male gender identity formation and defines child care as central to fathering, the achievement of equality within the confines of heterosexual marriage will remain elusive" (p. 1030).

Children and Father's Family Work

When considering the influence of children on the participation of fathers in family work, it is important to distinguish domestic labor from child care. In families with children, mothers invest considerably more time and are considered to be more responsible for both types of family work. For fathers, however, the research reveals quite a different pattern. When focusing on domestic labor, the presence of young children seems to have no effect, or may even have a negative effect, on fathers' contributions to domestic labor (Hardesty & Bokemeier, 1989; Huber & Spitze, 1981; Leslie & Anderson, 1988; Ross, 1987). Only Coverman's (1985) results support the notion that fathers increase their participation in domestic labor when there are small children at home. The apparent lack of responsiveness of fathers to domestic labor may be partly the result of two opposing processes common to families with young children. Although children increase the amount of domestic labor that must be done, parents often respond to the transition to parenthood with a move toward greater role specialization, with fathers increasing their work hours and mothers decreasing theirs (Cowan & Cowan, 1988). This pattern would edge both parents, on average, toward a more traditional pattern.

The ages of children are important to fathers' domestic labor rates. The weight of the evidence suggests that having small children produces no net effect on fathers' participation, whereas having older children in the home is related to a rather sharp drop in fathers' involvement in domestic tasks (Hardesty & Bokemeier, 1989; Model, 1981; Rexroat & Shehan, 1987).

Child care needs to be considered separately from domestic labor in families with young children because there are some interesting but subtle patterns in the rates and types of father involvement that could be obscured in a study that simply collapsed the behavioral categories together. First, the care of children can be separated into two clearly differentiated sets of behaviors. One set can be defined as the routine care of the child (bathing, feeding, dressing); the other is oriented more to play and being responsively available to the child. A recent study by Biernat and Wortman (1991) is especially interesting because it focuses on dual-earning relationships in which both partners are highly committed to their jobs, the least traditional arrangement for families with very young children. This family structure should maximize the pressures toward egalitarianism in the family. Nevertheless, the fathers and mothers in this study revealed a rather traditional pattern in the sharing of child care. Only play was equally shared. Two other child care tasks that are easily classified as relationship-oriented, responding to and teaching the child, were nearly equally shared. Tasks that are more routine or that required an interface with the work role (such as arranging care for the child or staying home from work with a sick child) tended to be more the responsibility of mothers than of fathers. Given this imbalanced pattern, it is somewhat surprising that two thirds of the mothers were satisfied with the amount of the fathers' involvement, and nearly 14% said their husbands were doing too much. Only 24% of the mothers in the sample felt that their husbands were involved too little in child care.

Another recent study, by Volling and Belsky (1991), sheds more light on the question of which fathers are more involved in the care of young children. Considering more relationship-oriented participation first, Volling and Belsky found that more mature, occupationally stable fathers, who had higher self-esteem and were more sensitive to the feelings of others, also were the most responsive and affectionate with their infants. Affection appeared to depend on more than the characteristics of the father, however. Less affectionate fathers had more temperamentally difficult infants. Further, the marriages of less affectionate fathers were more conflictual and ambivalent. Fathers were more invested in routine-maintenance child care tasks, according to Volling and Belsky, when they had participated more in traditionally female household chores prior to the baby's birth. However, these fathers had more difficulty balancing their work and family roles and experienced greater marital conflict after the birth of the baby.

Lamb (1987) identifies four factors that facilitate understanding the father's investment in child care. First is the father's motivation to spend time with his children. Lamb cites research suggesting that at least 40% of fathers would like to be more involved with their children; the rest are either satisfied with their involvement or would prefer less. Skills and self-confidence comprise the second factor. Fathers are less likely to engage in active child care if they are unsure of themselves when performing the tasks. Although child care tasks can be learned readily, another factor critical to skill and confidence is the father's ability to read his child's cues and to respond appropriately. The father competent in these ways is much more likely to have rewarding father–child interactions and increased motivation to participate. The third factor determining father involvement is support, especially from his wife. Even though survey studies suggest that many women want more actively involved husbands, men who do increase their involvement sometimes upset the balance of power in the domestic sphere (Polatnick, 1974). Because motherhood and the role of home manager have traditionally been the unquestioned province of women, increased involvement by men in these domains could represent a threat as much as a source of sustaining support. Lamb's final factor is institutional practices. Because the father's performance in the provider role satisfies the major portion of the family's financial needs and because there is little support in the workplace for increased participation in fathering, men view their employment situation as an obstacle to increased involvement with their children's care.

Life Cycle Changes

Families with children of different ages represent families at different stages of the family life cycle (Aldous, 1978). Family members of different ages are at different life-course phases (Elder, 1974), meaning that they may experience similar events in different ways because of their unique histories. There is a tendency in the literature to talk about dual-earner couples as if their spousal roles were static. Moen (1982) suggests that a life-course perspective helps place the two-provider family within a context of change.

Parents of young children are the most likely to experience conflicts between work and family obligations. These external pressures may facilitate the traditionalization of couples around the transition to parenthood. Cowan and Cowan (1988) find that after the birth of a first child parents' roles become more traditional regardless of where the couple was on the traditional-egalitarian continuum prior to the birth of the child. In relation to household tasks, this shift translates into changes in task assignments following the transition. As the children grow older, the career trajectories of working parents also mature, producing changes in time demands— the experience of role overload—and the earning potential of the family. Families with adolescents have more people capable of contributing to family work but also higher income requirements, which add to the financial pressure on working parents. Having two earners in a family increases the complexity of the family's life course.

In using a life-course perspective, one must consider both present and historical (earlier in one's life) factors related to the couple's division of family work. Surprisingly few studies of family work recognize the value of considering personal or marital history. One interesting study, by Barnett and Baruch (1987) found that fathers were *more* active in child care when they recalled their own fathers being relatively *less* involved in these activities. Weingarten (1978) examined two family employment patterns, one in which both spouses worked full-time and continuously and one in which the husband worked full-time and continuously while the wife worked only part-time or temporarily. When both spouses consistently work full-time, Weingarten found that husbands did a greater portion of family work, in terms of both child care and domestic tasks. Clearly, aspects of one's personal history can be important to decisions affecting the allocation of family work.

To this point, the focus has been on the role of structural factors in explaining fathers/husbands' involvement in family work. Many factors clearly enhance our understanding of who participates in family work. Nevertheless, all of these factors combined do not approach the predictive power of the single structural variable, gender (Berk, 1985; Pleck, 1985). This should not come as a great surprise, however, because no attention has yet been given to factors that lead individuals to interpret their sets of given conditions and decide what their behavior should be within the highly personal realm of family relationships. Next we will consider some of the psychosocial factors that researchers have considered when attempting to understand and explain fathers/husband's commitment to family work.

THE INFLUENCE OF PSYCHOSOCIAL FACTORS ON FAMILY WORK

Several psychosocial factors seem to dominate research on the family work participation of husbands and fathers. The factor that has received the most attention is gender-role ideology. Gender-role research builds on the assumption that role behavior is learned and that a person's sex is a major determinant of the role behavior he or she is taught and, consequently, adopts. Although the process is organized less by biology than by the cultural tendency to associate gender with notions of who *should* do what, it is an easy step to move from beliefs about what a gender *should* do to a program of training and sanctions. Mixed in with the concept of gender-role ideology is another psychosocial issue—power. If one gender is defined as more powerful in a culture, it is in a better position to control the programs of training and sanctions used to teach gender-role behavior. Spousal support constitutes another psychosocial factor. Families in which all adult members are expected to shoulder multiple, heavy, social roles can be expected to maximize their performance and enhance their relationships when they support one another rather than fight about who does what. Yet another important psychosocial concept focuses on conceptualizations of fairness or equity. Some definitions of fairness are organized around symmetric conceptions of equal task sharing, such that the only equitable arrangements are those in which all tasks are evenly shared. Other definitions of equity focus more on spouses' attitudes about the overall fairness of the allocation of tasks. A final psychosocial element has received less research attention, but is growing in importance; satisfaction with the allocation of roles appears to be related to who does what and how much of it. This research suggests spouses may be motivated less by culturally prescribed work loads than by their own satisfaction with the allocation of roles and their performance in them.

Gender-Role Ideology

Gender-role ideology is the product of a socialization process by which families transmit to their members the cultural and family values that are organized around biosocial issues. Gender-role identity, another product of this process, specifies one's self-definition in terms of these biosocial issues. Gender-role ideology extends the construct of gender beyond the self and into the larger world of relationships. Researchers studying the allocation of family work tend to use these constructs in highly similar ways. Often, in fact, one's gender-role "identity" is inferred from an ideological statement about the role of women in the family or the society. Both gender-role ideology and identity are assumed to connect in important ways to individuals' definitions of appropriate role behavior.

According to Pleck (1985), gender-role identity delimits the range of roles that a person is willing to assume. His research suggests that gender roles are the strongest psychosocial predictors of the allocation of family work. He maintains that although structural variables are critically important, the role placed by one's definition of self is even more fundamental in determining who does what family work. Pleck's argument asserts that a grand social experiment that revolutionized workplace policies overnight, producing strong policy support for egalitarian family roles, would *not* effect change in the allocation of family work. Not until ideological support for the more basic maintaining factor is undermined will the allocation actually change, that is, the traditional division of family work by sex. This extremely interesting position claims that the *primary* constraint on change is ideological rather than structural. The structural demands of the work role are real and significant, but, in Pleck's argument, they simply reinforce the more basic and more intransigent gender-based ideology that defines family work as outside men's purview.

The primacy of ideology has received rather impressive empirical support. Lamb and Levine (1983) evaluated the Swedish parental insurance policy that was engineered to encourage fathers to become more involved with their newborn children. The thrust of their report states that "despite the availability of paid paternal leave, the bulk of child-rearing responsibilities are still assumed by mothers" (p. 47). In Sweden, as in other Western cultures, infant care is predominantly defined as the function of women. This ideological stance prevents large numbers of men from taking advantage of policies deliberately targeted to minimize the structural barriers to greater family-work participation.

Traditional gender-role ideologies continue to be heavily entrenched in American culture. Stein (1984) reported that husbands who increase their involvement in family work are sometimes confronted with mixed messages from relatives and colleagues. Although kin and co-workers often find something "cute" in being more involved, they often consider the commitment "unprofessional" or even "unmanly." Oddly, and unfortunately, rather than being encouraged for this role behavior, the personal adjustment of the more active father, and by extension the adjustment of the dual-earner family, is determined in part by how well he can withstand the view of others about his family role.

Criticism based on gender roles, of course, may not be entirely external. Indeed, in all likelihood, the most important attitudes are those of immediate family members. Gender-role orientations can cause conflict when either spouse is perceived by the other to be moving in on one's preferred role domain. Husbands and wives with traditional attitudes seem to find it difficult to accept less traditional behavior from their spouses. When such unacceptable behavior changes occur, the former balance in role behavior in the couple is upset, further increasing interpersonal tension (Baruch & Barnett, 1986; Chassin et al., 1985; Lamb, 1987). What happens when, for instance, the traditional husband of a mother who has recently taken a job is pressured to participate in family work that was formerly exclusively within the traditional mother's domain? What about when the traditional wife, who has just joined the work force, gives up or deemphasizes her more comfortable, familiar roles. In this situation both spouses are stressed. The mother faces the partial loss of a known role, one for which she may still feel responsible, while confronting a new life role. Concomitantly, events at home likely conspire to reduce her husband's supportiveness. His frustration emerges from the choice of engaging in behavior inconsistent with self-definitions or finding tasks going undone.

Under any of these conditions, pressures mount and marital tension can result. McDermid et al. (1990), in their study of the transition to parenthood, found that fathers with more traditional sex-role attitudes who were more involved in child care and household tasks felt less love for their wives and were more negative about their marriages. A similar pattern approached statistical significance for the mothers in the study but fell just short. Chassin et al. (1985) suggest that traditionally oriented dual-earner parents of preschoolers are dissatisfied with their marriages when their spouses either fail to perform adequately the traditional roles they hold or seem to fulfill nontraditional roles "too well." On the other hand, when nontraditional couples are compared with more conventionally oriented couples, the former are *more* satisfied with their marriages if they judge their partners to be "competent in opposite-sex-typed roles" (Terry & Scott, 1987, p. 215). Moen (1982), however, suggests that traditional values are tacitly understood to underlay most marriages: "The hidden contract in most marriages contains certain implicit expectations regarding the roles played by husbands and wives . . . . When working couples develop relationships that radically depart from those in conventional single-provider families, both spouses may be dissatisfied with the marriage" (p. 28). Taken together, these studies suggest that combining traditional attitudes with nontraditional behavior is detrimental to marital health.

Spousal Support

Spouses are surprisingly unsympathetic observers of one another. It is common for employed spouses, regardless of gender, to perceive family responsibilities as interfering with their own paid work responsibilities. However, few recognize that family responsibilities may interfere with their spouses' paid work responsibilities (Baruch & Barnett, 1986). Apparently, each spouse is better able to monitor his or her own experience of role conflict than to sense the clash of roles experienced by the partner. It is relatively easy to understand how this imbalance in perception occurs. Work/family role conflict increases for both genders with increases in the hours worked and when children are present in the home (Voydanoff, 1988), but not all predictors of work/family conflict are so easily observed. Voydanoff (1988), for instance, found that the pressure of work overload, the feeling that there is more to do than one can do in the time allocated, contributes to the work/family conflict of both genders. These perceptions are difficult for spouses to monitor. In addition, having some control of one's schedule influences one's experience of work/family conflict; greater control considerably decreases some aspects of work/family conflict. Spouses, however, may not always accurately assess their partners' schedule control.

Spousal support is a crucial factor in dual-earner parents' satisfaction with work and family roles. For wives and mothers, satisfaction with their dual-earner role is greatest when their husbands are supportive of their working (Chassin et al., 1985; Houseknecht & Macke, 1981; Repetti, 1987). For husbands and fathers in dual-earner couples who are highly involved in child care, the effect of spousal support is less clear. Many fathers receive mixed messages from their wives about how involved they should be in fathering (Baruch & Barnett, 1986; Lamb, 1987). Greater participation is encouraged, until it happens. At this point, some mothers become ambivalent about the fathers' involvement.

Emmons, Biernat, Tiedje, Lang, and Wortman (1990) examined spousal support in dual-earner, upper-middle-class white couples with preschool children. The wives in their sample felt well supported by their husbands, who were good at listening, encouraging, conveying understanding, and engaging in helping behaviors in the area of household and child care tasks. Given this support, employed mothers found that their career roles enhanced their relationships with their husbands, but unfortunately they felt that those roles conflicted with their relationships with their children.

Support from husbands, in both attitude and behavior, is important to women who are both raising a family and working at a full-time job

(Chassin et al., 1985; Houseknecht & Macke, 1981). Similarly, having the support of wives is important to husbands who take on child care tasks. Chassin et al. (1985) concluded, however, that women tend not to be highly supportive of the father role. The authors suggested that this lack of support may contribute to fathers' feeling that their parenting efforts are undervalued. This feeling may perpetuate stress for dual-earner couples.

Just as men are socialized to legitimate high involvement in employment, even at the expense of family work, women's socialization legitimates greater investment in their children. This pattern places women in a bind (Tribble, 1987). Many send their husbands mixed messages about how involved to be in the care of their children (Lamb, 1987). Men are more willing to increase their involvement in child care than in any other type of family work. Still, the majority of mothers are not enthusiastic about this involvement. Some may feel the father is incompetent in the role and that his greater involvement will simply increase her work. Others recognize that women's bases of power in the family are built on relationships and nurturing (Kranichfeld, 1987), and they may see increased paternal involvement as a threat to their domain.

Lamb (1987) implies that this loss of power is especially difficult for working women in low-status jobs because of the lack of alternate opportunities for social power. These mothers may need a place in their social lives where they feel empowered even if they experience greater exhaustion. Having the lead role in family work fulfills this need for some. Additionally, employed mothers may want to compensate for the limited time they have with their children (Piotrkowski & Repetti, 1984). Satisfying this need may, at times, result in crowding the father out, which can further complicate the situation.

Satisfaction with the Division of Family Work

Satisfaction with the allocation of family work is another psychosocial variable that has received growing attention in recent research. This emerging area of interest assumes that satisfaction with role allocations is reinforcing. Two consequences are liable to occur from being satisfied with the division of family work. First, role performance may conform to a higher standard, and second, a couple's stress may be lower, due to the absence of underlying resentment of the need to perform undesired tasks.

Research by Cowan and Cowan (1988) appears to support the idea that stress is inversely related to satisfaction with the division of family work, at least in the transition to parenthood. Mothers of infants in their sample were most satisfied in their marriages when the fathers were highly involved in the paternal role *and* when they (the mothers) had relatively lower interest in parenting. The ability to adjust the allocation of family work to become more consistent with one's preferences, even when the adjustment differs from the traditional allocation, appears to represent a satisfying relief for mothers. This relief, in turn, translates into greater marital satisfaction. Obviously, this exchange works best when the preferences of both partners can be accommodated. This is not always the case, unfortunately.

Fathers in dual-earner marriages who are highly involved in family roles often feel that their wives' work interferes with family responsibilities (Baruch & Barnett, 1986). When these high-participating fathers spend a lot of time in solo child care tasks, they are substantially less satisfied with their wives' work schedule and their time spent in family roles. The mothers in Baruch and Barnett's (1986) sample, whose husbands were highly involved in child care, praised their husbands' parenting abilities (implying recognition of their support) but were lower in life satisfaction and more self-critical about their balance of work and family responsibilities. Presumably, these mothers did not have the lower interest level that some of Cowan & Cowan's (1988) new mothers had. Rather, the active fathers in Baruch and Barnett's sample evaluated their wives' parenting less favorably than did the less active fathers. Two possible reasons for these trends are offered. Perhaps high-participant fathers are more confident of their own parenting skills, leading them to poorer impressions of their wives' parenting skills. Alternatively, highly involved fathers may resent what they perceive to be inequitable over-involvement.

Defining and Valuing Equity and Exchange

The research on satisfaction with the allocation of family work suggests that the ways in which couples define an equitable allocation depend on existing preferences, which then determine their satisfaction with the division. Much research on the allocation of family work seems to assume that people are motivated by the desire to establish an appropriate exchange based on personal and professional competencies and their relative value. This position is represented most formally by Becker (1981). An alternative approach that still builds upon an exchange notion assumes the wish to establish and maintain an equitable balance (Thompson, 1991).

Rachlin (1987) defines equity as "a feeling of fairness derived from the individual's perception of the overall balance of rewards and constraints in the relationship" (p. 188). Equity so defined does not necessarily assume equality. Rachlin's study indicated that for husbands and wives the perception of marital equity is related to greater marital adjustment. By far the most research, however, places a greater emphasis on equality, defined as a 50–50 division of labor, when defining equity. Hiller and Philliber (1986) examined men's and women's attitudes and behaviors about sharing family work. Sharing was defined in terms of the equality of the partners' responsibilities for given tasks. They found remarkable consistency in attitude among the spouses but surprisingly large discrepancies in the relation between attitude and behavior. Although 84% of the couples said that child care should be shared, only one third to one half of fathers were equally responsible with mothers for any of the tasks of child care. Fifty-eight percent of husbands indicated a belief that housework should be shared, but only a third were responsible for any regular household tasks. Although these findings appear to represent an extremely unfair situation, the couples in the study appeared not to feel this way on the whole. Perhaps this feeling resulted from the fact that a majority of the men in the study felt that it was their obligation to be better at earning income than their wives were, whereas 40% of the wives considered it important to excel at housework and 43% thought it important to exceed their husbands in child care. In another recent study (Biernat & Wortman, 1991), both spouses reported valuing equality in playful child care tasks more than in other child care tasks.

Using a definition of equity that emphasizes perceived fairness, spouses who satisfy their obligation and feel that their partners are also satisfying theirs would be happy regardless of the equality of the division of family work. Tension would be expected to grow when spouses felt that they were being overbenefited (guilt) or underbenefited (anger). By a definition of equity emphasizing equality, spouses would be happy only when both spouses perceived a relatively equal level of performance in the tasks of family work.

Benin and Agostinelli (1988) conducted an intriguing analysis to examine whether satisfaction with the allocation of tasks is affected by the relative balance in the allocation of tasks. They defined equity in terms of equal time investments and hypothesized that equity-motivated spouses would show greatest satisfaction when performance was equal between the partners. Another motive, labeled exchange, predicted that respondents would be happiest when doing the least relative to their partners. Their findings suggested that husbands and wives, in their highly educated sample, differed. Husbands were best described by an equity orientation, expressing greatest happiness when the division of tasks was equal. For wives, the exchange motive was significant: the greater their share of family work, the less satisfied they were with the division. Although intriguing, these results have not been replicated in a recent analysis performed on a nationally representative sample of couples (Carpenter, 1992). Indeed, this study found some spouses of each gender were most satisfied with a near-equal arrangement. A small tendency was noted among the remaining women, however, to be more satisfied when they did *more* family work than their husbands did. Among men not characterized by the equity motive, the greatest satisfaction tended to be associated with being overbenefited (i.e., doing less than their wives did). Together these studies suggest not only that men and women may differ in their motives but that, within gender, differing motives may also affect the allocation of family work.

Family Work Standards

When it is highly important to the wife or to both spouses that the house remain orderly, such wives spend more time cleaning the house than do wives who have low standards (Hernandez, 1990). Additionally, having higher standards for a particular household task increases the likelihood of performing it (Smith & Reid, 1986). Given these findings, it is surprising that more research has not taken into consideration the role of standards in explaining the allocation of tasks. Do men have lower family work standards than women do? Shaw (1988) found men to be more likely to define family work as leisure and less likely to define it as work than were women. In addition, men perceived more freedom of choice in their family-work participation and were less likely than women to evaluate their own family-work performances.

Smith and Reid (1986) suggest that standards may be important in the development of a more egalitarian balance in family work. To achieve this balance, must spouses negotiate a set of compromise standards? The potential for frustration is evident in families in which one spouse refuses to lower his or her expectations. Their partners are less likely to participate in family work because of either an unwillingness or an inability to perform up to the higher standard. Ferree (1988) found that when employed women are viewed as family breadwinners, their family work standards tend to be lower than other women. Perhaps this helps account for the increase in men's participation as wives' work hours increase (Leslie et al., 1991).

WHITHER RESEARCH ON FAMILY WORK?

It is clear that our understanding of the man's role in family work has come a long way. Our empirical understanding of the allocation is better, and the sophistication in our thinking about family work is significantly improved. There is an increasing recognition that the allocation of tasks, which shows remarkable consistency in its patterning across the population, is also highly idiosyncratic when specific family patterns are compared in detail (Ferree, 1991). Nevertheless, there are a number of biases that seem to be persistent and that limit our thinking about family work and men's roles in it. These biases force our views of gender and family work into narrowed channels.

An excellent example of such a limiting assumption is the nearly pervasive postulate that family work is noxious, to both men and women. This assumption is grounded in the fact that most family work is routine and often invisible. There can be no doubt that the presumption of the unpleasant nature of family work is warranted for many people. Still, would not a better approach consider people's preferences for family-work tasks when attempting to understand their allocation rather than defining them, in an a priori fashion, as distasteful? Incorporating preferences into assessments of the allocation of tasks and the quality of their performance could transform the way we think about who does what.

Another related bias can be seen in the tendency to define spouses as victimizers and victims with regard to family work. Thompson and Walker (1989), in their excellent discussion of gender in families, assert that the allocation of family work is best conceptualized "as a source and an occasion for power" (p. 864). When one considers family work an onerous burden thrust by oppressors upon the oppressed, then, clearly, the power approach is only reasonable. Similarly, but from a quite disparate position, if one considers family work the single domain of power for an otherwise less powerful family member, the concepts of power and conflict again attain ascendancy. The legitimacy of power-oriented perspective to the understanding of family work is entirely supportable, given the definition of power as one's ability to shape the behavior of another. Furthermore, in families in which both spouses work and are raising children, the problem of power in the allocation of tasks, either as male dominance or as female dominion, may be particularly important. But the centrality of the power approach is less tenable when matters of preference are considered. Daniels (1987), in commenting about the invisibility of family work, says that, in addition to being done largely by women, family work is both private and commonplace; it is the product of both love and leisure. These do not seem to be the images of victimization.

Also common is leaping from the recognition of substantial differences between the genders in family work to the assumption that different patterns will not be found within genders. More attention needs to be given to those who do not seem to fit the mold. Can one assume that all members of a gender will behave according to a single pattern? One of Margaret Mead's (1949) conclusions from her classic 1948 study of gender is that the variability within genders is greater than the differences between genders when considering culturally or socially derived characteristics and practices. Benin and Agostinelli (1988) contribute to our thinking on the allocation of tasks by considering that the two genders may respond differently to the motives of exchange and equity. Yet they are willing to assume that all members of each gender will respond to only one of these motives. Recent research (Bergmann, 1986; Feree, 1991) shows considerable variation in the patterns of allocation within couples. Furthermore, Carpenter (1992) suggests that there may be different groups within each gender that operate according to different motives as the tasks of family work are allocated.

A final problematic bias that may characterize researchers' thinking less than it does their methodology is the treatment of family-work allocations and standards as static. Could men and women overestimate their own involvement and underestimate their partner's partly because of selective attention to behavior discrepant from typical patterns? A father thinks of the "extra" help he gave his wive last week when she was under higher than average work pressure, and he adds this help to his performance estimate. The working mother, recognizing last week's involvement as extraordinary, discounts the aid in her estimate. As Ferree (1991) notes, there are considerable qualitative data that support the notion that greater variability exists in the allocation of family work and the standards brought to this work than the quantitative research suggests. We submit that the allocation is negotiated through a dynamic process. However, to identify the elements of this emergent family process, intensive longitudinal research, oriented to the interaction of stress levels and performance standards played out against a background of a couple's history, will be necessary (Solheim & Pittman, 1991).

CONCLUSIONS

This review has considered both structural and social psychological aspects of the extent to which husbands and fathers are involved in unpaid family work. The consistency with which the allocation is based primarily on gender, and the resistance of this general trend to modification through the inclusion of other explanatory variables, had led in recent years to the conceptualization of family work exclusively as a "gendered" phenomenon, meaning that it is a socially constructed arrangement (see Feree, 1990).

Research designed to appreciate the constructed quality o the allocation and performance of unpaid family work will have to go far beyond the type of research reviewed in this chapter. To date, the allocation of resources in the family has been a major organizer of research and theorizing. Resources, however, although showing modest results consistent with predictions, have been woefully inadequate to the task of explaining family work. Social-psychological variables, as Pleck (1985) argues, appear to be the more basic constraints on who does what. Yet the relevant source of these values remains an issue. Are families of origin the important source of the social construction of gender? We would argue, with Ferree (1990), that the important constructive process is ongoing in the relationship between the spouses. Although these processes occur against the backdrop of a cultural ideology and a history of socialization, as Berger and Kellner (1964) assert, marriage is a reality constructed in ongoing interaction between people who bring these separate histories to a unique sphere of their own making.

This process of dynamically creating and maintaining an allocation of family work remains a seriously understudied area. Virtually all research in the area examines the products of the construction (responsibility for and/or time spent in tasks) rather than the constructive process. Little is known about the process drivers. Whereas power is posited as the primary driver by many (see Thompson & Walker, 1989), others find power connected to too many of the problematic biases noted earlier to serve as the organizing orientation to research on family work. If marriages are constructed, they are, by definition, assembled by both relevant parties. These parties may have differing standards, preferences, and definitions of fairness. The nearly exclusive emphasis in the research on resources and traditional attitudes fails to account for the uniqueness of couples. The stress on mean differences similarly misses those who fail to fit the patterns.

Having made these points, however, it remains that the balance of family work falls to women, even more so in families with children. If our culture is developing toward increasing gender equality and egalitarianism in marriage relationships, this imbalance in the allocation of unpaid family work represents a dilemma and stands in the way of opportunity. When we understand the dynamic negotiation of the tasks of family work, then we will also better understand the limits and avenues to change.

REFERENCES

Aldous, J. (1978). *Family careers*. New York: Wiley.

Antill, J. K., & Cottin, S. (1988). Factors affecting the division of labor in households. *Sex Roles, 18*, 531–553.

Atkinson, J., & Huston, T. L. (1984). Sex role orientation and division of labor early in marriage. *Journal of Personality and Social Psychology, 46*, 330–345.

Barnett, R. C., & Baruch, G. K. (1987). Determinants of fathers' participation in family work. *Journal of Marriage and the Family, 49*, 29–40.

Baruch, G. K., & Barnett, R. C. (1986). Consequences of fathers' participation in family work: Parents' role strain and well-being. *Journal of Personality and Social Psychology, 51,* 983–992.

Becker, G. S. (1981). *A treatise on the family.* Cambridge, MA: Harvard University.

Benin, M. H., & Agostinelli, J. (1988). Husbands' and wives' satisfaction with the division of labor. *Journal of Marriage and the Family, 50,* 349–361.

Bergen, E. (1991). The economic context of labor allocation: Implications for gender stratification. *Journal of Family Issues, 12,* 140–157.

Berger, P., & Kellner, H. (1964). Marriage and the construction of reality: An exercise in the microsociology of knowledge. *Diogenes, 46,* 1–23.

Bergmann, B. (1986). *The economic emergence of women.* New York: Basic Books.

Berk, S. (1985). *The gender factory.* New York: Plenum Press.

Biernat, M., & Wortman, C. B. (1991). Sharing of home responsibilities between professionally employed women and their husbands. *Journal of Personality and Social Psychology, 60,* 844–860.

Bird, G. W., Bird, G. A., & Scruggs, M. (1984). Determinants of family task sharing: A study of husbands and wives. *Journal of Marriage and the Family, 46,* 245–255.

Blair, S. L., & Lichter, D. T. (1991). Measuring the division of household labor: Gender segregation of housework among American couples. *Journal of Family Issues, 12,* 91–113.

Bowen, G. L., & Orthner, D. K. (1991). Effects of organizational culture on fatherhood. In F. W. Bozett & S. M. H. Hanson (Eds.), *Fatherhood and families in cultural context* (pp. 187–217). New York: Springer Publishing Co.

Carpenter, H. E. (1992). *The effects of relative time expenditures in family and employment tasks upon spouses' satisfaction with domestic chore arrangement: An analysis of relevant theoretical models.* Unpublished manuscript.

Chassin, L., Zeiss, A. & Reaven, J. (1985). Role perceptions, self-role congruence and marital satisfaction in dual-worker couples with preschool children. *Social Psychology Quarterly, 48,* 301–311.

Coverman, S. (1985). Explaining husbands' participation in domestic labor. *Sociological Quarterly, 26,* 81–97.

Coverman, S., & Sheley, J. F. (1986). Change in men's housework and child-care time, 1965–1975. *Journal of Marriage and the Family, 48,* 413–422.

Cowan, C. P., & Cowan, P. A. (1988). Who does what when partners become parents: Implications for men, women, and marriage. *Marriage and Family Review, 12,* 105–131.

Daniels, A. K. (1987). Invisible work. *Social Problems, 34,* 403–415.

Douthitt, R. A. (1989). The division of labor within the home: Have gender roles changed? *Sex Roles, 20,* 693–704.

Elder, G. H. (1974). *Children of the Great Depression.* Chicago: University of Chicago.

Emmons, C., Biernat, M., Tiedje, L. B., Lang, E. L., & Wortman, C. B. (1990). Stress, support, and coping among women professionals with preschool children. In J. Echenrode & S. Gore (Eds.), *Stress between work and family* (pp. 61–93). New York: Plenum Press.

Ericksen, J. A., Yancey, W. L., & Ericksen, E. P. (1979). The division of family roles. *Journal of Marriage and the Family, 41,* 301–313.

Ferree, M. M. (1988, November). *Negotiating household roles and responsibilities: Re-*

sistance, conflict and change. Paper presented at the annual meeting of the National Council on Family Relations, Philadelphia.

Ferree, M. M. (1990). Beyond separate spheres: Feminism and family research. *Journal of Marriage and the Family, 52,* 866–884.

Ferree, M. M. (1991). The gender division of labor in two-earner marriages: Dimensions of variability and change. *Journal of Family Issues, 12,* 158–180.

Hardesty, C., & Bokemeier, J. (1989). Finding time and making do: Distribution of household labor in nonmetropolitan marriages. *Journal of Marriage and the Family, 51,* 253–267.

Hernandez, S. A. (1990). The division of housework: Choice and exchange. *Journal of Consumer Policy, 13,* 133–154.

Hiller, D. V., & Philliber, W. W. (1986). The division of labor in contemporary marriage: Expectations, perceptions, and peformance. *Social Problems, 33,* 191–201.

Houseknecht, S. K., & Macke, A. S. (1981). Combining marriage and career: The marital adjustment of professional women. *Journal of Marriage and the Family, 43,* 651–674.

Huber, J., & Spitze, G. (1981). Wives' employment, household behaviors, and sex-role attitudes. *Social Forces, 60,* 150–169.

Huber, J., & Spitze, G. (1983). *Sex stratification: Children, housework, and jobs.* New York: Academic Press.

Indelicato, S., Cooney, T. M., Pederson, F. A., & Palkovitz, R. (1991, November). Timing of fatherhood: Is "onetime" optimal? Paper presented at the annual conference of the National Council on Family Relations, Denver.

Kingston, P. W., & Nock, S. L. (1985). Consequences of the family work day. *Journal of Marriage and the Family, 47,* 619–629.

Kranichfeld, M. L. (1987). Rethinking family power. *Journal of Family Issues, 8,* 42–56.

Lamb, M. E. (1987). Introduction: The emergent American father. In M. E. Lamb (Ed.), *The father's role: Cross cultural perspectives* (pp. 3–25). Hillsdale, NJ: Lawrence Erlbaum.

Lamb, M. E., & Levine, J. A. (1983). The Swedish parental insurance policy: An experiment in social engineering. In M. E. Lamb & A. Sagi (Eds.), *Fatherhood and family policy* (pp. 39–52). Hillsdale, NJ: Lawrence Erlbaum.

Leslie, L. A., & Anderson, E. A. (1988). Men's and women's participation in domestic roles: Impact on quality of life and marital adjustment. *Journal of Family Psychology, 2,* 212–226.

Leslie, L. A., Anderson, E. A., & Branson, M. P. (1991). Responsibility for children: The role of gender and employment. *Journal of Family Issues, 12,* 197–210.

McDermid, S. M., Huston, T. L., & McHale, S. M. (1990). Changes in marriage associated with the transition to parenthood: Individual differences as a function of sex-role attitudes and changes in the division of labor. *Journal of Marriage and the Family, 52,* 475–486.

Mead, M. (1949). *Male and female: A study of the sexes in a changing world.* New York: William Morrow.

Meissner, M., Humphreys, E. W., Meis, S. M., & Scheu, W. J. (1975). No exit for wives: Sexual division of labor and the cumulation of household demands. *Canadian Review of Sociology and Anthropology, 12*, 424–459.

Model, S. (1981). Housework by husbands: Determinants and implications. *Journal of Family Issues, 2*, 225–237.

Moen, P. (1982). The two-provider family: Problems and potentials. In M. E. Lamb (Ed.), *Nontraditional families: Parenting and child development* (pp. 13–43). Hillsdale, NJ: Lawrence Erlbaum.

Nyquist, L., Slivken, K., Spence, J. T., & Helmreich, R. L. (1985). Household responsibilities in middle-class couples: The contribution of demographic and personality variables. *Sex Roles, 12*, 15–34.

Piotrkowski, C. S., & Repetti, R. L. (1984). Dual-earner families. In B. B. Hess & M. Sussman (Eds.), *Marriage and Family Review* (pp. 99–124). New York: Haworth Press.

Pleck, J. H. (1977). The work-family role system. *Social Problems, 24*, 417–427.

Pleck, J. H. (1985). *Working wives/working husbands.* Beverly Hills, CA: Sage.

Polatnick, M. (1974). Why men don't rear children: A power analysis. *Berkeley Journal of Sociology, 18*, 44–86.

Rachlin, V. C. (1987). Fair versus equal role relations in dual-career and dual-earner families: Implications for family interventions. *Family Relations, 36*, 187–192.

Repetti, R. L. (1987). Linkages between work and family roles. *Applied Social Psychology Annual, 7*, 98–127.

Rexroat, C., & Shehan, C. (1987). The family life cycle and spouses' time in housework. *Journal of Marriage and the Family, 49*, 737–750.

Ross, C. E. (1987). The division of labor at home. *Social Forces, 65*, 816–833.

Shaw, S. M. (1988). Gender differences in the definition and perception of household labor. *Family Relations, 37*, 333–337.

Shelton, B. A. (1990). The distribution of household tasks: Does wife's employment status make a difference? *Journal of Family Issues, 11*, 115–135.

Silverstein, L. B. (1991). Transforming the debate about child care and maternal employment. *American Psychologist, 46*, 1025–1032.

Smith, A. D., & Reid, W. J. (1986). Role expectations and attitudes in dual-earner families. *Social Casework, 67*, 394–402.

Solheim, C. A., & Pittman, J. F. (1991). *Standards and stress as drivers of family work performance.* Unpublished manuscript.

Spitze, G. (1986). The division of task responsibility in U. S. households: Longitudinal adjustments to change. *Social Forces, 64*, 689–701.

Stein, P. J. (1984). Men in families. *Marriage and Family Review, 7*, 143–162.

Stipek, D., & McCroskey, J. (1989). Investing in children: Government and workplace policies for parents. *American Psychologist, 44*, 416–423.

Terry, D. J. & Scott, W. A. (1987). Gender differences in correlates of marital satisfaction. *Australian Journal of Psychology, 39*, 207–221.

Thompson, L. (1991). Family work: Women's sense of fairness. *Journal of Family Issues, 12*(2), 181–196.

Thompson, L., & Walker, A. J. (1989). Gender in families: Women and men in marriage, work, and parenthood. *Journal of Marriage and the Family, 51*, 845–871.

Tribble, R. G. (1987). Dual-career marriages: Problems, satisfactions, and therapeutic considerations. *Pastoral Psychology, 35,* 211–220.

Volling, B. L., & Belsky, J. (1991). Fathers' involvement with infants in single- and dual-earner families. *Journal of Marriage and the Family, 53,* 461–474.

Voydanoff, P. (1988). Work role characteristics, family structure demands, and work/family conflict. *Journal of Marriage and the Family, 50,* 749–761.

Weingarten, K. (1978). The employment pattern of professional couples and their distribution of involvement in the family. *Psychology of Women Quarterly, 3,* 43–52.

Zedeck, S., & Mosier, K. L. (1990). Work in the family and employing organization. *American Psychologist, 45,* 240–251.

■ Part 3
Diversity of Employed Mothers' Experiences

■ 7
Families of
Lower-Income
Employed Mothers

Dolores A. Stegelin and Judith Frankel

This chapter addresses the coping mechanisms and life-styles of lower-income employed mothers and their families. For purposes of this chapter, low-income, working-class mothers are defined as women with natural or adopted children living in families in which the adults are employed in blue-collar service and/or nonsupervisory clerical jobs. This broad framework includes dual-parent families in which both father and mother have these kinds of jobs, dual-parent and female single-parent families that depend on a combination of wages and unemployment insurance payments, and families of employed, divorced mothers who have experienced downward economic mobility caused by the loss of ex-husbands' incomes (H. Benenson, private communication, February 15, 1991).

A great deal has been written about female employment in relationship to numerous variables, but there is a need to explore further the coping skills and dynamics of mothers who are employed in lower-income occupations and the issues around their ability to provide for their families, cope with stressors, and, in a sense, develop survival skills. Women have worked outside the home since the industrial revolution; however, it was not until the mid-1970s and the return of middle-class mothers to the work force that the issue of maternal employment surfaced as a major research and policy issue (Ferree, 1990). Most of the literature that addresses dual-career families focuses on middle-class families; thus, the lower-income employed maternal population has been overlooked as a separate group or research issue.

Myths about working-class families are beginning to be dispelled, according to Piotrkowski and Katz (1983), but there is still a lack of research-based information about working-class families in general and working-class mothers in particular. Two specific myths about low-status workers discussed by Piotrkowski and Katz include the notion of "separate worlds," which asserts the clear and natural separation of work and family realms. Although this myth is no longer tenable for professionals and managers, it seems to prevail in the thought processes regarding workers' family relations. In essence, this myth suggests that working-class families somehow segment their working worlds from their personal worlds. However, in research conducted by Piotrkowski (1979), work *"did* intrude on family relations" (p. 190) in working class families, even though workers believed that work and family life should be kept separate. Rather than being "natural," what separation existed appeared to result from active coping mechanisms. The second myth, derived from the 19th-century notion that the home is a "haven in the heartless world" (Piotrkowski & Katz, 1983, p. 189), implies that for the low-status worker, the family is still viewed as compensating him or her for deprivations experienced in the occupational world.

Other myths about working-class families also abound, including the myth that working-class women are not feminists, when actually, according to Ferree (1980), they simply express their feminism differently. The fact is that all women who hold jobs tend to be feminists. For working-class women, feminism surfaces as a function of their employment. One of the most intriguing myths is that working-class women work only because they must for financial and economic reasons and, if given a preference, would opt to assume full-time homemaking and domestic responsibilities. A study by Hiller and Dyehouse (1987) refutes this myth and documents the fact that working-class women are committed to their jobs and would not leave even if they did not need the money.

The number of working mothers in lower-income occupations represents a significant proportion of the female employment force in the United States, and, from an economic perspective, the poorest people in America are single mothers. Young children 4 years or younger, represent the largest segment of poverty in our country. The Children's Defense Fund (1990) states that approximately 25% of preschool children live in poverty conditions. Many of these young children are in single-parent households headed by their mothers, an increasingly number of whom are teenage, never-married mothers. Because the term "lower-income employed mothers" is variously defined, the authors find it difficult to identify in an inclusive manner all individuals who fit this economic and sociological population. The terminology is shifting, and the definitions of poverty, low income, and working-class families are in flux. The government may define this group within a financial framework, that is, within set income parameters, but families are hard-pressed to exist on this defined level of income. Therefore, the authors focus on (a) working-class mothers in low-status occupations, including women who have always been single; (b) the 50% of mothers who do not receive child support to which they are entitled; and (c) women in intact families where the family income level is still subsistent.

The theme of this chapter is that, because of economic restraints, women who have less income have fewer choices and more stressors. Therefore, coping skills and strategies must of necessity be pragmatic. The authors support the tenet that these women demonstrate unusual resilience, problem-solving skills, and personal strength in the face of limited energy, resources, and structural support systems. Second, as a result of this ability to cope, the working class family *does* survive.

STRESSORS OF WORKING-CLASS, LOWER-INCOME MOTHERS

Common stressors of working-class lower-income employed mothers are now identified and discussed. Many of these stressors relate to the lack of resources: money, time, and adequate child care. In addition, the women face constant demands that place them in role-overload situations. Some mothers are employed in shift work that places additional strains on them and their families. Finally, unemployment as a stressor will be discussed. All of these stressors are exacerbated for mothers who head single-parent households.

Lack of Resources

Financial Constraints

Perhaps the most common issues for lower-income, working-class mothers are related to the severe financial limitations in which they must live and support their families. R. R. Cherry and E. L. Eaton (1977; cited in Hoffman, 1987) examined the variables related to maternal employment and per capita income, as well as subsequent child development measures. Maternal employment, as opposed to nonemployment, was found to be related to higher measures of per capita income; and higher per capita income was related to children's higher cognitive and physical development scores, at least for the low-income families included in their study. Thus, the overall level of income is a predictor of individual and family financial well-being and is related indirectly to developmental outcomes for children. Thus, for lower-income mothers, there is a subsequent concern for the developmental outcomes of their young children.

For lower-income families, money management means "allocating shortages and forestalling creditors" (J. Pahl, 1983; cited in Ferree, 1990, p. 878). The implications for dealing with money in this manner are obviously stressful because of the negative and defensive posture that the mothers are required to maintain regarding their finances. In a capitalist society, money is power. Thus, there are families who have lost their power through lack of money. How the money is managed in the family is also a demonstration of power. When there is limited or no money, women tend to be primary managers, whereas when surpluses of money develop, men tend to manage (Ferree, 1990).

In all families, women's incomes are generally used for child care, replacing domestic services, and extra spending money, although in the lowest-income families, the women's income is used for more basic financial needs. In all families, one bargains with money, but in the lower-income family, women do not have this capability, and that also diminishes their sense of power. Women in both working-class and middle-income families do not have a sense of their true economic contribution and power. There is a need to study this phenomenon further, and "a central element of the feminist research agenda is to recover a more accurate accounting of the variation in women's economic contributions across time, place, class, race, and culture" (Ferree, 1990, p. 872).

For single mothers, financial stressors are even more extreme. The poorest segment of the U.S. population is represented by single mothers and their children (Children's Defense Fund, 1990; Norton & Glick, 1986). Single mothers include teenage mothers, never married mothers, and mothers who are separated, divorced, or widowed. Some of the latter were of middle-income status prior to the loss of their spouses but have suffered major financial declines of up to 60% of their previous income. "Regardless of the type of income measure that is used, the same conclusion is reached, namely, that men who maintain one-parent families are much better situated economically than their female counterparts" (Norton & Glick, 1986, p. 14). The median income of father-child families in 1983 ($19,950) was more than twice as high as that for mother-child families ($9,153) (Norton & Glick, 1986). Although child support is one source of family income for single-parent families, many fathers do not provide this income on a consistent, predictable basis, and some do not provide it at all.

Time as a Resource

There is a clear relationship between money and time resources. The more money the family has, the more extracurricular activities the children are engaged in, requiring more parent time for transporting and supervising. Mothers in lower-income families have fewer options for how they spend their time; many must work longer hours, and even when time is available, financial resources limit their choices in the use of time.

Single parents experience even more chronic shortages of time. Having to shoulder all child care and domestic responsibilities alone frequently requires the single mother to sacrifice attention to her own needs. Single mothers' work schedule demands are often in conflict with the needs of preschool and older children. The resolution is often a painful one—the mother can choose to work at a less desirable job that has more flexible hours but lower pay, or she may be forced to neglect or compromise her children's care, leading to strong feelings of guilt (Quinn & Allen, 1989).

Managing work and family responsibilities is a challenge for all employed mothers. According to Fassinger (1989), a certainty is that most single mothers feel strained from managing work and family responsibilities. However, Fassinger (1989; citing D. Burden [1986]), reports that single mothers find excessive time spent at work and feelings of fatigue less of a problem than do employed mothers with husbands. Managing family responsibilities is a challenge for employed mothers; in working-class families, fathers' increased participation in child care responsibilities was related to decreased satisfaction with the marital relationship, further straining the employed mother (Crouter, Perry-Jenkins, Huston, & McHale, 1987).

Child Care Issues

The mother's time on the job may affect the quality of mother-child interaction as well as its quantity. According to Hoffman (1987), the time spent at work might improve the mother's morale or contribute to a feeling of work overload. Obtaining adequate child care becomes a necessity for the employed mother, and because of the limited financial resources available to this population, a common individual concern, shared by the public, is that many of these children may go without adequate care or supervision. Public policy continues to attempt to address the plight of the lower-income employed mother who is in need of dependable, quality child care, primarily through child care vouchers and supplemental funds. However, much still needs to be done in the area of policy development to assure better options for lower-income employed parents.

The research clearly documents that high-quality child care is a desirable option and can provide the young child with positive developmental outcomes. Unfortunately for many low-income employed mothers, high-quality child care is unaffordable, and they must turn to more informal and less reliable forms of child care. These informal sources may include the use of extended family, neighbors, qualified and unqualified sitters, and other makeshift means of providing care for the child (Stegelin, 1990). Depending on the availability of these informal sources, child care arrangements may become an additional and significant stressor for the lower-income employed mother.

Different women view their child care responsibilities and arrangements in different ways. For example, a study by Fassinger (1989) of single, divorced, and employed mothers showed that mothers who had been in traditional marriages where there were clear-cut roles (the father being the breadwinner and the mother being the domestic caretaker) were most unhappy in not being able to provide full-time care for their children. For lower-income employed mothers, the options for quality child care are limited. Galinsky (1989), in a study of middle-class parents who earned between $40,000 and $50,000 per year, found that the process of finding day care was a difficult one; thus, it is even more difficult for lower-income parents.

Role Strain and Overload

Regardless of income level, today's working family is a busy one. However, the strain placed on lower-income employed mothers, particularly if they are single, is greatly intensified, thus leading to role strain and overload. Because financial resources limit their options to purchase support services, such as domestic help and child care, these mothers must of necessity fulfill responsibilities associated with many different roles. D'Ercole (1988) found that role overload, along with a low income and inadequate standard of living, predicted stress in the lives of their single-mother employed subjects. How they handled this strain depended on the social support system available to them.

Ferree (1990), in examining the theoretical basis for feminism and family research, found that being responsible for housework has "measurable occupational costs for men and women of all classes" (p. 873). These costs include exclusion from jobs because of long hours, inflexible scheduling, inability to travel, and inability to assume a position on the fast track. Role strain affects both men and women. For women, being a sole or co-provider is often experienced as a "loss of freedom of choice" and perceived as a failure of men to live up to their "proper" role (p. 874).

Shift Work

An issue perhaps unrecognized or underestimated in the lives of working-class mothers is the phenomenon of shift work. In a 1980 sample of U.S. nonfarm households with children and with both spouses employed full-time, one third of the couples included at least one spouse who worked other than a regular dayshift. In about one tenth of the couples, the spouses worked entirely different shifts with no overlap in hours (Presser & Cain, 1983). This apparently unnoticed phenomenon of shift workers—individuals who work on other than a regular day shift—is more common than usually realized. On the basis of their study, Presser and Cain, (1983) recommend a more refined approach to studying shift work by examining the number of hours of spouse overlap in their full-time principal jobs. Because shift work tends to be most common among couples with young children, issues around child care arrangements are often solved or remediated through the shift work arrangement. However, these couples also tend to be younger, thus in lower-wage-earning positions. As children become older, the issues around child care become less intense as children are more able to manage time on their own. Presser and Cain conclude that research is still needed to understand better such issues as commuting time, overlap time, and quality of time together as a couple and as a family. Because shift work seems to be increasing in labor demands, there is a growing need to be aware of its effects on the quality and dynamics of spousal and parent-child relationships. Other questions related to shift work, still to be addressed, include the following: "What is the quality of child care in shift-work households? To what extent do the parent caretakers sleep during the children's awake hours? What are the quality and stability of marriages among shift-work couples as compared to marriages without shift work pressures?" (Presser & Cain, 1983, p. 878). Another question raised in this study relates to possible gender differences in the effects of shift work.

Stress of Unemployment

Working-class employees hold jobs that are more susceptible to the ravages of unemployment than are those of middle-class or upper-income employees, one example of which has been the recession of the early 1990s. Unemployment affects men and women differently. The effect of employment on working-class men (Larson, 1984) appears to lead to more negative marital and family relations but is less damaging to the worker's self-esteem. The nature of the marital relationship determines the extent of the intensity of the negative effect. Men who were unemployed and had more traditional marital expectations fared worse than did men who had egalitarian expectations of the marital relationship. "Unemployment seems to splinter an already susceptible marital system in blue-collar families. Future research should be directed at determining the more specific kinds of marital strains induced by unemployment" (Larson, 1984, p. 510).

The outcomes for unemployment for women have not been studied extensively enough to make general statements. Marshall (1984) believes there are good sociological reasons that women react so differently from men to unemployment, and there is a need for systematic research to determine these sociological origins and differences and their impact on the family systems involved.

Summary

This litany has reviewed the myriad of stressors that impact on the lower-income employed mother and her family. They are powerful, and their impact is pervasive, yet these families manage to cope and make decisions in the face of great adversity. As cited by numerous authors, there is still a need to study further the dynamics of these stressors, particularly those issues around shift work, differential impacts of unemployment on men and women, and the complexity of role strain and overload. As reflected in this writing, all of these stressors are exacerbated for the single mother, who must somehow negotiate these stresses and strains by herself.

As we reviewed the research on these families, we were impressed by their managing and coping styles and strengths. In the face of continuous hardship and adversity, the women exhibit extraordinary problem-solving skills and tenacity in providing for their families and themselves.

COPING SKILLS AND STRATEGIES

Support Systems

One of the primary coping mechanisms for lower-income working mothers is the use of various support systems. D'Ercole (1988) cites the following as major sources of informal social support, particularly for single mothers: co-workers and friends, spouses, families, and extended family members.

Friends, Co-workers, and Church

In a study of the social support systems of 83 single mothers (average age, 34), 75% of whom were employed, with a median annual income between $10,000 and $14,999, D'Ercole (1988) identified nine factors that contributed forms of social support. The most significant source of social support was from neighbors and friends; other sources identified were children, co-workers, mother, father, lover, former husband, and others. Consistent with other research findings, she found that a low income, an inadequate standard of living, and role overload were the three significant predictors of strain in the lives of these single mothers. According to D'Ercole,

> Financial stressors accounted for nearly a quarter of the variance in each measure of strain, while role overload accounted for only about 10% of the variance. Social support for single mothers in this sample, when available, came from few people rather than from a larger, generally supportive network. (p. 50)

In accordance with other research, this study also revealed that supportive relationships with friends and co-workers contributed more to the well-being of single mothers than did task-related support provided by family and neighbors. Finally, D'Ercole reports that the importance of co-worker support may lie in the role that the workplace plays in being able to provide a fresh respite from the demands of home and family, as well as being a source of personal and occupational recognition and competence.

Quinn and Allen (1989) describe the resources of the single women in their study as including families, friends, and the church.

> An unexpected finding from the women in the study was their use of the church as a safe place for socialization and friendship. They turned to the church for contacts with people who had similar values and interests; some hoped these contacts would lead to dating relationships or even marriage. (p. 394)

In addition, participation in some form of individual or group counseling served as a resource for 24 of the women. Attending school or seeking assistance for their children's problems were other avenues of social support. When asked to describe their lives, single-parent employed women in Quinn and Allen's study characterized themselves as being involved in a "paradoxical bind" resulting from their need to survive in a male-dominated work environment while searching for the ideal of the "ever-happy two-parent family they feel they have been promised" (p. 390).

Rapp (1978) describes the sometimes invisible yet frequently effective support provided by the network of friends that the lower-income mother defines simply be extending and expanding the circle of individuals into what she considers the family. By stretching the definition of the family to be more inclusive, the lower-income mother enables herself to barter, trade, and assist with a larger number of individuals. Even when talking about very poor individuals, such noted analysts as Hannerz, Valentine, and Stack (Rapp, 1978) note that there are multiple household types based on domestic cycles and the relative ability to draw on resources. Thus, the family may be a conscious construction of its participants, described as "fictive kinship"(Rapp, 1978). Although this coping strategy may, on the surface, appear to have enormous benefits, it also has enormous costs. "One of the most obvious (costs) is leveling: resources must be available for all and none may get ahead" (Rapp, 1978, p. 178). Thus, the process of sharing of resources results in trade-offs for all participants.

Spousal Support

Marriage has the potential to provide an emotional support system for women. A deciding factor is the quality of the marital relationship, which has a very direct effect on the mother's parenting attitudes (Schachere, 1990) and therefore on the quality of their children's development. Women who felt intimate support from their spouses were much more satisfied with their lives and were more responsive to their infants (K. Crinic, M. Greenberg, A. Ragozin, N. Robinson, & R. Basham [1983], cited in Schachere, 1990). However, for working-class families, contradictions do exist. One form of spousal support can be thought of as fathers taking care of their children. Unfortunately, the greater involvement in the parenting role on the part of working-class fathers does not always correlate with greater marital satisfaction (Schachere, 1990). In a study by Crouter, Perry-Jenkins, Huston, and McHale (1987), mentioned earlier in the chapter, it was found that working-class husbands who were involved in high levels of child care exhibited less marital satisfaction. The attitude of these fathers seemed to be that, although they favored their wives' employment and income, they did not wish to assume additional responsibilities and an expanded domestic role.

Mothers, on the other hand, carry over positive feelings from the job to the home and the marriage (Piotrkowski & Katz, 1983). Indicators of job satisfaction and job-related mood were particularly predictive of home satisfaction for employed women (Piotrkowski & Crits-Christoph, 1981). Given this discrepancy between men's and women's perceptions of the spousal support role, more research is indicated to understand better the origins of these attitudes. Some single mothers, lacking this form of spousal support, still manage, usually, to adapt to their situations and to cope well (Fassinger, 1989).

Grandparent Support

In spite of the mobility and apparent fragmentation of the American family, the role of grandparents in intergenerational support continues to be significant. Wilson (1987) surveyed the role of grandparents in providing a continuing level of material support in 61 households with dependent children in an inner city area. Wilson concludes that "assistance is structured by gender, income level, household financial organization, residential proximity, need, and ideology"(p. 702). It appears that grandmothers provide more tangible support than do grandfathers and that they have the capacity to direct the support where it is most needed. The network of female relatives, especially mothers and mother-in-laws, is critical, particularly for working-class families and mothers. In contrast, in professional families characterized by higher income levels, the unit of support is the grand*parents* rather than the grandmother or other female relatives.

Accommodations and Compromise

Because of the complexity of their lives, the lower-income employed mother makes considerable adaptation and compromise to maintain an adequate quality of life. Gould and Werbel (1983) and Quinn and Allen (1989) describe the kinds of compromises characteristic of these women. Some of these adaptations include taking lower-level jobs, moving to lower-level positions that provide flextime, and, in general, placing a priority on job flexibility rather than on professional advancement. Second, in their social lives, they place limits on their own socialization needs in order to meet the time and energy demands of their work and families. Most of the women in Quinn and Allen's study reported that their social life was the area in which they were forced to make the most compromises and sacrifices.

Because the workplace makes few accommodations for the female worker, the lower-income employed mother must make these difficult adjustments herself. For example, if a child becomes ill, the mother must decide between providing personal care for the child by staying at home—meanwhile running the risk of jeopardizing job advancement and job security—and hoping that makeshift arrangements for the ill child will not have harmful consequences.

EFFECTS ON FAMILY MEMBERS

In this chapter we have discussed common stressors of lower-income, working-class mothers. We have identified these stressors as multiple and complex. In response, we have also identified some of the coping strategies of these mothers. Working-class families take many forms, ranging from the nuclear family to a much larger, extended family. The complexity of working-class families is apparent. The effects on and outcomes for the members of these families are now discussed.

Effects on Mothers

In spite of the constancy of stressors, many working-class mothers demonstrate resilience and an outstanding ability to solve problems in an effort to adapt, cope, and maintain family stability. Quinn and Allen's (1989) study portrayed single working-class women as being strong, resourceful, and "managing at least in a marginally successful manner" (p. 394).

Working-class mothers also reflect certain health problems, as documented by research conducted in England by Parry (1986, 1987). Although Parry did not find significant general differences in health status between employed and unemployed mothers, she did find that working-class mothers were more prone to mental health problems, particularly if they had suffered at least one major life event and lacked adequate social support.

Effects on Fathers

In our review of the literature on working-class families in general and lower-income employed mothers in particular, we found a dearth of information on the role of fathers. The research we found focused primarily on the father's marital satisfaction, household responsibilities, attitude toward his wife's employment, and some father-child relationship data. Our conclusion is that fathers need to be studied in much greater detail. We believe that work life is clearly related to family relationships, with both spouses and children, and that mediating factors are involved in overall father adjustment and happiness. Some of these factors include the degree of autonomy with work, the level of satisfaction or challenge with work, and the attitude toward spousal employment. "Important differences may exist between them [families] in the types of strains suffered as well as in the solutions found" (Piotrkowski & Katz, 1983, p. 196). Two important qualitative studies by Hochschild (1989) and Rubin (1976) found that working-class husbands expressed intense hostility toward their employed wives when their own breadwinner role was felt to be weakened. Thus, their own insecurity thrust them into the position of feeling challenged or threatened by their wives.

Effects on Children

Numerous studies have been conducted in an effort to understand better the relationship between lower-income employed mothers and their children. Schachere (1990) reviewed the literature on attachment between working mothers and their infants in order to understand family processes more fully. A central issue for working-class mothers is the effect of day care, or any other alternative caregiving during the first year of life, on the infant's socioemotional development. Some research suggests that early and long-term child care (35 hours a week or more) may result in more anxious and insecurely attached infants. However, more refined research suggests that mediating variables, such as the quality of child care, parent-child relationships, and others, affect the attachment process. There is clearly a need to study this issue further.

In a study conducted by Baker and Entwisle (1987), the focus was on the influence of middle- versus lower-income mothers on their children's academic expectations. In this study, Baker and Entwisle did not find significant overall differences in middle-class mothers' influence on their children's academic self-concept versus that of lower-income mothers, but they did find that middle-class mothers imposed less of a gender difference expectation than did lower-income mothers. For example, they found that working-class mothers strongly expected their daughters to exhibit better school conduct than their sons.

In a study of developmental comparisons between 10-year-old children with employed and nonemployed mothers, Gold and Andres (1978) hypothesized that maternal employment had an impact on children's development that was dependent on the gender of the child and the socioeconomic level of the family. Gold and Andres predicted that children of employed mothers would have broader, less differentiated conceptions of sex roles than would children with nonemployed mothers. They also predicted more mother–daughter distance, and that usually leads to a better cognitive outcome for the daughter. The results of this study provide some support for the study's hypotheses that maternal employment "is differentially associated with the development of children depending on the social class of the family and the gender of the child" (p. 82). In general, Gold and Andres found employed mothers to be more content with their roles than were nonemployed mothers, and it appears that "the employed mothers who are most content with their roles have children with the most egalitarian sex-role concepts" (p. 82).

Hoffman's (1987) classic review of the effects on children of maternal and paternal employment indicated that there are selective factors related to the effects on children of maternal employment. One effect of maternal employment appears to be a diminishing of sex-role stereotypes in relationship to the division of labor in the household. Both sons and daughters of employed mothers appear to be less stereotyped in their views of men and women (Gold & Andres, 1978; Hoffman, 1987). Gold and Andre's (1978) study also suggested that working-class boys with employed mothers have more adjustment difficulties. According to Gold and Andres, these boys are described more negatively by fathers, exhibit more shyness and nervousness, and are less successful in school. Thus, this study did confirm the sex-role differentiation for boys and girls related to maternal employment, with more research clearly needed to understand why some of the more negative outcomes appear for boys but not for girls.

Research has been done with middle-class working mothers and the impact on their children's development. A study of maternal employment and parent-child relations in middle-income families of seventh-graders was conducted by Paulson, Koman, and Hill (1990). Subjects were 100 seventh-grade boys and 100 seventh-grade girls and their parents who were recruited through the cooperation of several school districts in a large midwestern metropolitan area. Subjects were measured on maternal employment status, closeness, involvement in family activities, and number of rules and disagreements over rules. The seventh-grade sons in this study reported no differences in closeness with employed and non-employed mothers but did report greater closeness with fathers when mothers were employed than when mothers were not employed. When mothers had higher levels of satisfaction with their job status, more closeness with their children was reported by parents. Although this study focused on middle-income families, there are variables that are common also for the working-class family.

CONCLUSIONS

Working-class families and employed mothers face great difficulties, and they respond pragmatically and with great strengths. However, to enable better coping, the following policy recommendations are made:

1. *Policy changes related to working conditions.* These changes include continuing efforts to address the needs of the family as an entire unit. Examples include the establishment of leave policies that include fathers as well as mothers. This type of leave policy can apply to both maternity and paternity leave as well as to sick leave to care for children. Another work-related policy recommendation is to expand flexible work schedules to allow families more options. Giving workers, particularly

single, working-class mothers, more choices in their work hours, setting work goals within the employment environment, and providing support for them as an important part of the workplace decision-making process is critical.

2. *Improved child care options and support.* Research clearly shows the relationship between the quality of child care provided and the mother's level of satisfaction with her employment status and her child's well-being. However, low-income families do not have the financial options or access to quality child care options that higher-income families often do. Therefore, there is a continued need for business and government to initiate policies that either provide quality day care directly or provide options for the employed mother, such as vouchers or employee benefits and benefit-menu options.

3. *More refined research on working-class families and employed mothers.* Although there is considerable research on dual-career families of the middle-class, there is still a dearth of information about working-class families, particularly the working-class employed mother. In addition, information on the father's role and those of other family members and on the well-being of the working-class mother is lacking. Researchers are gaining some insight into the development outcomes for children of employed mothers, but there is a need to refine the research to look more closely at the interactions of multiple variables that affect the working-class family. Along with quantitative approaches, the authors would encourage the use of case studies and other qualitative research strategies to understand better the many consequences of working-class family lifestyles.

REFERENCES

Baker, D. P., & Entwisle, D. R. (1987). The influence of mothers on the academic expectations of young children: A longitudinal study of how gender differences arise. *Social Forces, 65*(3), 672–694.

Children's Defense Fund. (1990). *The nation's investment in children.* Washington, DC: Author.

Crouter, A. C., Perry-Jenkins, M., Huston, T. L., & McHale, S. M. (1987). Processes underlying father involvement in dual-earner and single-earner families. *Developmental Psychology, 23*(3), 431–440.

D'Ercole, A. (1988). Single mothers: Stress, coping, and social support. *Journal of Community Psychology, 16*, 41–54.

Fassinger, P. A. (1989). Becoming the breadwinner: Single mothers' reactions to changes in their paid work lives. *Family Relations, 38*, 404–411.

Ferree, M. M. (1980). Working class feminism: A consideration of employment. *Sociological Quarterly, 21,* 173–184.

Ferree, M. M. (1990). Beyond separate spheres: Feminism and family research. *Journal of Marriage and Family, 52,* 866–884.

Galinksy, E. (1989). Parent/Teacher study: Interesting results. *Young Children, 45,* 2–3.

Gold, D., & Andres, D. (1978). Developmental comparisons between ten-year-old children with employed and nonemployed mothers. *Child Development, 49,* 75–84.

Gould, S., & Werbel, J. D. (1983). Work involvement: A comparison of dual wage earner and single wage earner families. *Journal of Applied Psychology, 68,* 313–319.

Hiller, D. V., & Dyehouse, J. (1987). A case for banishing "dual-career marriages" from the research literature. *Journal of Marriage and the Family, 49,* 787–795.

Hochschild, A. (1989). *The second shift.* New York: Viking.

Hoffman, L. (1987). The effects on children of maternal and paternal employment. In N. Gerstel & H. Gross (Eds.), *Families and work* (pp. 362–395). Philadelphia: Temple University Press.

Larson, J. H. (1984). The effect of husband's unemployment on marital and family relations in blue-collar families. *Family Relations, 33,* 503–511.

Marshall, G. (1984). On the sociology of women's unemployment, its neglect and significance. *Sociological Review, 32,* 235–259.

Norton, A. J., & Glick, P. C. (1986). One parent families: A social and economic profile. *Family Relations, 35,* 9–17.

Parry, G. (1986). Paid employment, life events, social support and mental health in working-class mothers. *Journal of Health and Social Behavior, 27,* 193–208.

Parry, G. (1987). Sex-role beliefs, work attitudes and mental health in employed and non-employed mothers. *British Journal of Social Psychology, 26,* 47–58.

Paulson, S. E., Koman, J. J., & Hill, J. P. (1990). Maternal employment and parent-child relations in families of seventh graders. *Journal of Early Adolescence, 10*(3), 279–295.

Piotrkowski, C. S. (1979). *Work and the family system.* New York: Macmillan.

Piotrkowski, C. S., & Crits-Cristoph, P. (1981). Women's jobs and family adjustment. *Journal of Family Issues, 2*(2), 126–147.

Piotrkowski, C. S., & Katz, M. H. (1983). Work experience and family relations among working-class and lower-middle-class families. *Research in the Interweave of Social Roles: Jobs and Families, 3,* 187–200.

Presser, H. B., & Cain, V. S. (1983). Shift work among dual-earner couples with children. *Science, 219,* 876–879.

Quinn, P., & Allen, K. R. (1989). Facing challenges and making compromises: How single mothers endure. *Family Relations, 38,* 390–395.

Rapp, R. (1978). Family class in contemporary America: Notes toward an understanding of ideology. In B. Thorne & M. Yalom (Eds.), *Rethinking the family* (pp. 168–187). New York and London: Longman.

Rubin, L. B. (1976). *Worlds of pain: Life in the working class family.* New York: Basic Books.

Schachere, K. (1990). Attachment between working mothers and their infants: The influence of family processes. *American Journal of Orthopsychiatry, 60*(1), 19–34.

Stegelin, D. A. (1990). Kentucky's statewide parent survey on child care needs and resources: Implications for policy and research. *Dimensions, 18*(2), 9–12.

Wilson, G. (1987). Women's Work: The role of grandparents in inter-generational transfers. *Sociological Review, 35,* 703–720.

■ 8
Educational and Economic Outcomes for Adolescent Mothers

Nancy E. Barbour, Rhonda A. Richardson, and Donald L. Bubenzer

Much of the writing about adolescent mothers begins with a similar form of rhetoric depicting the extent of this "overwhelming social problem." For example, many articles begin by quoting the half-million-per-year figure for adolescent births, an astounding number on its own. Yet when one examines the teen birthrates from 1955 to 1989, there was a decrease in the rates in the 1960s and 1970s, with an increase since 1986 that still does not exceed even the 1970 figures (Moore, 1992). We read so often of an increase in adolescent childbearing and the disastrous effects that this event has on the individual's life course in terms of educational and economic outcomes that we begin to believe, unquestioningly, the "truths" repeated in a wide range of media. Are we being misled by the repetition of inaccuracies? Or do we need to apply more attention to the problem in an attempt to discern an informed picture of the phenomenon of adolescent childbearing and its relationship to the educational and economic outcomes for these women?

In this chapter the authors will explore the likely educational and economic outcomes to be experienced by adolescent mothers through the examination of demographic trends and confounds, antecedent family systems variables, and intervention programs. The review of the literature raises questions about gaps in knowledge about adolescent childbearing and parenting, the family variables that seem to have an impact on these outcomes, the foci of intervention programs, and implications for future research and intervention. The existing interventions have focused on the phenomenon of adolescent childbearing in a piecemeal rather than a holistic manner. For instance, interventions of choice have included foci on preventing adolescent pregnancy, increasing the likelihood of high school completion, enhancing parenting skills through education, and increasing potential for economic self-sufficiency. The authors will examine the success or lack of success of these programs.

PORTRAITS OF ADOLESCENT MOTHERS

Prior to the late 1960's, adolescent pregnancy and childbearing was not a topic readily found in the social science literature (Furstenberg, 1991). With the publication of the Alan Guttmacher Institute report *Eleven Million Teenagers* (1976), academic as well as public circles began to view this phenomenon as a national dilemma. According to Furstenberg (1991), the statistics were decreasing rather than increasing during the 1970s. What, then, precipitated the shift in perceptions about adolescent childbearing? Vinovskis (1988) suggests that the "epidemic" character of adolescent childbearing was a false perception created by researchers' and social service providers' misreading of the statistical trends. It is suggested that disregard of the social and historical context of the post-1960s period may explain why the problem has been viewed out of reasonable proportions. Furstenberg (1991), for instance, believes that the alarmists neglected to consider the increase in the adolescent population in general during this time as a result of the developing baby boom generation. Likewise, those adolescents who did become pregnant did not automatically choose the traditional solution of marriage upon the discovery of their pregnancy. This shift in choice to not marry but still have the baby created a new group in need of social service/financial support (Furstenberg, 1991).

Though we are cautioned against viewing the problem as "epidemic" (Furstenberg, Brooks-Gunn, & Morgan, 1987; Vinovskis, 1988), we are reminded by some (Hofferth, 1988) that it *is* endemic. Consequently, one does not want to discount the concern about adolescent childbearing. There is no question that, as a society, we are faced with the need to consider the best courses of action to alleviate the individual, familial, and societal strains created by adolescent childbearing. Adolescent childbearing is everywhere. There have been advocacy groups who have adopted this cause as a major focus of study and lobbying (e. g., Children's Defense Fund). Legislative activity resulting from this includes the establishment of the federal Office of Adolescent Pregnancy Programs (OAPP) in 1978 and the passage of the Adolescent Family Life Act in 1981 (Hofferth, 1988).

Most recently, the Family Support Act of 1988 provided specific direction for the educational and vocational lives of adolescent mothers.

Given these major efforts, what do we really know about the antecedents and outcomes of this life course and the effects of intervention felt by adolescent mothers? What is the accurate description of an adolescent mother's life course in terms of educational and economic outcomes? More important, is there *one* description of adolescent mothers or is there a range of diversity found within this group? What obstacles and/or assistance are adolescent mothers likely to experience in their transition to parenthood and adulthood?

Educational Outcomes

It is widely assumed that adolescent mothers, by the nature of the timing of childbearing, often find it necessary to interrupt or truncate their educations. This premise has been relatively unchallenged by the public over the years. Recently, some researchers have begun to challenge this presumption (Furstenberg, 1991; Furstenberg et al., 1987; Mott & Maxwell, 1981; Upchurch & McCarthy, 1989, 1990). For instance, Upchurch and MCarthy (1989) suggest that "institutional and societal change may have weakened the association between adolescent childbearing and high school dropout" (p. 199). The changes that the authors note are the enactment and implementation of Title IX of the Educational Amendment Act in 1972 and 1975, respectively; the changing marital patterns of pregnant adolescents; and the changing social norms regarding unwed mothers.

Title IX, though not specifically designed as adolescent parent legislation, served as a watershed to change the way schools served this population. Effective in 1975, the Act made it "illegal for schools receiving federal funds to expel students because of pregnancy or parenthood" (Upchurch & McCarthy, 1989, p. 199). It specified that schools could not discriminate against or exclude a student as a result of pregnancy, miscarriage, childbirth, or abortion (Adler, Bates, & Merdinger, 1985; Mott & Maxwell,1981; Upchurch & McCarthy, 1989). It did not, however, require schools to develop programs to serve these women. This legislation had a major impact on the public's awareness of adolescent pregnancy as a fact of life rather than an act to be punished. The options for pregnant adolescents, as a result, expanded to include both staying in school until completion or returning to school after the resolution of the pregnancy (either through birth, miscarriage, or abortion). Consequently, high school completion statistics post-1975 are quite different from those pre–Title IX (e.g., Upchurch & McCarthy, 1989). For instance, Upchurch and McCarthy (1989) indicate that 45% of those white women who were younger than 17 at the birth of their first child had completed 12 or more years of school in

1975, compared to 71% in this same group in 1986. There were racial differences apparent in these analyses, with 69% of young black mothers finishing school in 1975, compared with 76% in 1986, a much narrower gap. Overall, the authors considered high school graduation to be the norm in the 1986 sample.

It is almost impossible to consider these increases in high school completion rates in a discrete fashion. There are a number of concomitant factors that influence whether an adolescent mother completes high school. The first, and previously mentioned, factor is the availability of options. As stated, Title IX provided opportunities for adolescent mothers to complete their education. What other factors contribute to these mother's decisions to remain or return to school?

Grindstaff (1988) did a retrospective study of 30-year-olds who had been adolescent mothers. He found that if adolescent mothers married prior to the age of 20, 77% did not complete a high school education. He suggests that early marriage and early childbearing serve to keep women in an inferior position in society.

Mott and Marsiglio (1985) examined the National Longitudinal Survey of Work Experience of Youth (NLSY), a collection of retrospective and prospective information on a sample of U.S. adolescents and young adults. There were 6,288 young women first interviewed in 1979 and each year afterward. In 1983, Mott and Marsiglio (1985) tapped data from those women who were 20–26. By examining women in their early 20s, the researchers were able to avoid one of the pitfalls of such research by allowing for a time lag in which adolescent mothers might return to school to complete their educations. The authors also differentiated those women who gave birth before leaving school from those who conceived while in school but gave birth after leaving. Their conclusions suggest that childbearing for these two groups seriously limits their chances for finishing a secondary credential. The dropout rate for these two groups was 47% for those experiencing conception and then leaving school and 36% for those giving birth while still in school compared to 5% for women who do not have children by their early 20s (Mott & Marsiglio, 1985).

Furstenberg's (Furstenberg et al., 1987) longitudinal study of adolescent mothers has provided us with some of the most valuable insights into the life-course outcomes of adolescent mothers. The comprehensive data collection began with a group of 404 pregnant adolescents and 350 of their mothers in 1966, with a follow-up of 382 of the adolescent mothers 1 year after delivery, 363 adolescent mothers 3 years after delivery, 331 mothers 5 years after delivery, and 289 of the original sample in 1984 16 years after delivery. The educational attainment for the sample 5 years after delivery was 50% having completed high school. In 1984, a third of the sample had completed some postsecondary education.

There are risks in drawing conclusions about cause and effect of adolescent childbearing and limited educational attainment. A number of researchers (Furstenberg, 1991; McCluskey, Killarney, & Papini, 1983; Polit & Kahn, 1986; Upchurch & McCarthy, 1990) have raised questions about the self-selectivity of adolescent mothers in terms of other background variables. Upchurch and McCarthy (1990) propose a conceptual framework for predicting high school completion. Though the authors will be exploring the family background variables more thoroughly later in this chapter, it is important to acknowledge the "clumping" of particular characteristics such as poverty, low educational aspirations, and limited education of their parents. It is difficult to know whether those women who leave school when they become pregnant might have left school in any case. Were there family variables that predisposed them to school failure? It is difficult to "tease out" these factors. Furstenberg (1991) suggests the background characteristics for these young women prepregnancy are different from those of later childbearers. The adolescent mothers are likely to have grown up in poverty and instability, with academic and social problems. He suggests that perhaps we should not try to sort out these factors but view them as all of one developmental trajectory that leads to "at risk" adult status.

Economic Outcomes

It is logical that educational attainment affects income, occupational opportunities, and chances for employment (Hayes, 1987). Perhaps this is what Furstenberg et al. (1987) meant when they said: "Timing of marriage and childbearing is determined by a delicate interplay between individual decisions, based on personal and economic considerations, and prevailing social norms" (p. 5).

Also related to the economic history of adolescent mothers are the fertility patterns of this group. Mott (1986), drawing on the NLSY data, examined the relationship between age at birth of first child and subsequent births. His conclusions suggest that these patterns are not universal. For example, black women were likely to have a second birth sooner than white women were, with the elapsed time between births shorter for those who gave birth at a younger age. Hispanic women were likely to have a second child sooner, than either of the other two groups. Certainly, the fertility patterns influence the logistics of going back to school, receiving job training, and seeking and holding employment.

The literature regarding vocational choices and employment histories of adolescent mothers is scant. Furstenberg (1991) examined income levels, occupational choices, and dependence on public assistance in his Baltimore study. In 1967, 40% of his sample were employed; in 1984, 67%

were employed, with an additional 9% seeking employment. A third of his sample had incomes below $10,000; one quarter had incomes exceeding $25,000; another quarter had incomes between $15,000 and $24,999; the remainder had incomes between $10,000 and $15,000. Seventy percent of the sample questioned in 1984 replied that they had received public assistance at some time in the previous 12 years. Twenty-five percent had received public assistance during the preceding 12 months. Certainly, the women were not economically well-off. However, there were a number of subjects who were doing reasonably well.

In all cases, there is no discussion of the economic self-sufficiency of adolescent mothers that describes career-oriented individuals. Rather, the population seems to engage in survival employment. The literature could be expanded in this area in order to better describe the economic outcomes for adolescent mothers.

Need for an Accurate Assessment

To gain an accurate assessment of what happens educationally and economically to adolescent mothers, we need to consider the following:

1. There appear to be some historical confounds that distort our perceptions of trends in educational attainment (e.g., Title IX).
2. We are not in agreement regarding the indicators of success. Is it socioeconomic status (SES) or educational attainment or both?
3. Are we timing our data collection appropriately to allow for a lag effect in both educational attainment and economic self-sufficiency?
4. What is a reasonable comparison group? Nonpregnant teens? Later childbearers? Intragroup comparisons between adolescent mothers?
5. Do we have a clear enough perception of family variables and their relationship to these outcomes?
6. We need to explore factors connected with long-term resiliency of adolescent mothers.

FAMILY OF ORIGIN VARIABLES AND EDUCATIONAL/ECONOMIC OUTCOMES FOR ADOLESCENT MOTHERS

Implicit in our review of literature related to the educational and economic paths of women who became mothers as adolescents is the perspective that the environment of response to their pregnancy and motherhood affects their future lives. In a broader perspective, the authors think, like many writers and researchers (Bertalanffy, 1968; Hoffman, 1981; Minuchin, 1974) that individuals, in this case adolescent mothers, are a part of an interrelated system, e.g. families, that is mutually influential. However, for our review, rather than look at the mutual influences we looked predominantly at the educational and career paths of adolescent mothers relative to their family of origin.

Interestingly, there is not a wealth of research on the educational and career paths of adolescent mothers, and the subset of literature related to the relationship between educational and career development of adolescent mothers and their family of origin is indeed small. Instead, the dominant bodies of literature relating to adolescent mothers focus on the children born to adolescent mothers and on trying to explain why these young women became pregnant. It is as though research agendas have reflected the public sentiment that was seemingly sympathetic to the children of adolescent mothers but derisive of the mothers themselves. Research concerning adolescent mothers has often viewed them as instruments targeted for intervention as a way of improving the lives of their children. Few researchers have studied adolescent mothers from the perspective of improving *their* lives.

Yet studies that have investigated the relationship between family of origin variables and parenting attitudes and behaviors of adolescent mothers have helped to establish whether the environment of response to the adolescent mother mediates the decisions she makes. For example, Stevens (1988) found that African-American teens who sought assistance with child-rearing problems from extended family members were more skillful parents. Richardson, Barbour, and Bubenzer (1991) found that adolescent mothers indicated that their families of origin were important sources of child-rearing, emotional, and material support. These researchers also found that families of origin, although providing important support, can also be sources of interference for adolescent mothers. In both instances, support and/or interference, families of origin had an impact on the young mothers.

The importance of family members as a source of support for adolescent mothers was addressed in the research of Becerra and deAnda (1984). In their study of 39 Spanish-speaking Mexican-American adolescents, 43 English-speaking Mexican-American adolescents, and 40 white non-Hispanics, mothers were shown to be the major source of support for all adolescent mothers. In both English-speaking subgroups, over 80% of the adolescents indicated their mothers as major sources of support both during pregnancy and after the birth of their child. Only 52% of the Spanish-speaking adolescents reported that their mothers were major sources of support. The authors speculate that the reason for this difference may be that the Spanish-speaking adolescents' mothers lived in Mexico and thus at a significant geographic distance. These same three groups of adolescents indicated support from their fathers was often minimal. However, support from fathers varied by the age of the adolescent mothers and by the cultural subpopulation.

Younger adolescents (13–17 years) perceived their fathers to be less supportive than did older adolescents. White adolescents, both young and old, saw their fathers as least supportive (15% of younger adolescents, 35% of older adolescents). Hispanic adolescent mothers saw their fathers as more supportive than did comparable groups of white adolescent mothers.

Becerra and deAnda (1984) also found acculturation to be a factor explaining differences among these three groups of adolescent mothers. In general, adolescents across cultural groups reported that their parents were permissive in terms of allowing dating at an early age, permitting steady dating at an early age, and providing little enforcement of curfews. Although all environments were viewed as lax, adolescent mothers who spoke Spanish (less acculturated) were more likely to obey parents than were the two English-speaking groups.

The research reported above highlights the fact that families of origin are an influencing variable in the lives of adolescent mothers. The studies also reveal important differences in the interactive influences that families and culture have in the decision-making processes of adolescents. Finally, the studies are enlightening concerning the role mothers of adolescent mothers have as sources of influence in the lives of the young mothers. Yet none of the studies directly addressed the connection between family-of-origin influence and the adolescent mother's decision making with regard to educational attainment and gaining of economic security.

The most extensive research conducted with adolescent mothers is that of Furstenberg et al. (1987). Their longitudinal study of women, a primarily black sample, who were adolescent mothers questioned some myths that society has about the predictable course of their life path. They indicated, for example, that other researchers' failure to control for preexisting (before pregnancy) differences in adolescent mothers' lives may have led them to an overestimation of the effect of premature parenthood. Furstenberg et al. also cautioned that because we have not studied adolescent mothers over an extended period, they may have precluded a later-life "catch-up" in areas of education and economic security. Furstenberg and colleagues indicated that the quality of the adolescent's emotional relationship with her parents had no singular important effect on her long-term adjustment to early child-rearing. However, they also found family variables that were related to educational attainment and economic security outcomes for women who experienced premature motherhood. The educational attainment level of parents was a significant predictor of both educational attainment and economic security in later life. Family cultural issues also were significant variables related to later-life "success" for adolescent mothers in that Caucasians were more likely to achieve later-life economic success. Welfare experience as a child was an additional negative predictor of economic security in later life. Why education of parents and economic level of parents is related to later-life economic security for women who experienced adolescent motherhood is a matter of speculation. Furstenberg et al. (1987) pondered the relationships among parental education and income levels, the economic resources available to adolescent mothers, the networking connections available to them, social skills modeling by parents, the push to attend school, and the discouragement of utilizing welfare assistance that may be given to adolescent children who are experiencing motherhood.

In earlier work, Furstenberg and Crawford (1978) found that, among unmarried adolescent mothers, parents play a key role in determining whether young mothers continue or resume their education and obtain stable employment. Unmarried adolescent mothers who lived with their parents were more likely than those who did not enjoy such residency to depend more on parents for advice and support; receive more aid such as food, clothing, and child care; and, receiving such aid, to continue their educational and occupational careers. Thus, adolescent mothers who depend on their families for support are more likely to engage in educational and career opportunities. Furstenberg and Crawford tied this dependence at least partially to the economic situations of the families of origin. That is, mothers who could depend on financial assistance by living in their parent's home were more likely to engage in educational and work opportunities than were mothers who did not receive such assistance from their parents. Adolescent mothers who married or who established independent households were far less likely to resume educational pursuits and less likely to enter stable work environments.

A final study, which looked specifically at the connection between parent households and educational pursuits of adolescent mothers, was conducted by Young, Berkman, and Rehr (1975). The study built on the assumption that mother–daughter relationships are important determinants of decisions made by adolescent mothers and looked at the proposals of mothers in terms of their daughters' decisions about living arrangements, plans for the baby, education, and so on. In all instances mothers' views were significantly related to daughters' plans. For examples, when the mothers wanted their daughters to continue school, 81% of the daughters planned to do so. When the mothers believed their daughters should discontinue school, 18% of the girls agreed and 82% expressed uncertainty about their future educational plans. When mothers were un-certain as to whether their daughters should continue in school, 56% of the girls planned to discontinue, 22% were uncertain, and 22% expressed a desire to continue their education. The study involved black adolescent mothers and their mothers.

Results of these studies provide enlightenment on a number of is-sues surrounding the relationship of families or origin and the educa-tional and economic paths of adolescent mothers. Foremost, we are confronted with the lack of research about the well-being of adolescent mothers and about the connection between their well-being and the con-ditions of their families of origin. Few generalizations can be made about conditions existing in families of origin and the "success" adolescent mothers achieve in educational attainment and in gaining economic secu-rity. It does, however, appear that the educational attainment and eco-nomic conditions of parents is highly related to the ultimate educational attainment and career paths of women who experienced premature moth-erhood. It also appears that the mothers of these young mothers are highly influential in the decisions made by the adolescent mothers. Thus, it seems that families of origin could be a rich target of treatment and assistance if society desires to improve the futures of adolescent mothers.

However, additional research is need that looks at subpopulations of adolescent mothers and their families of origin. These subpopulations should be formed around cultural differences, socioeconomic circum-stances, cognitive and interpersonal abilities and the family dynamics pre-sent in families of origin as these differences relate to educational attainment and economic security. Such research will add to our informa-tion and knowledge base and help us to address the myths surrounding adolescent motherhood. Likewise, such findings would contribute to the development of programs, both intervention and prevention, that would help brighten the educational and economic horizons for adolescent mothers. The following section provides an overview of programs pres-ently available to adolescent mothers.

SCHOOL-BASED INTERVENTION PROGRAMS

In response to Title IX legislation, most school districts have developed policies and/or programs to enable pregnant adolescents to remain in school. The extent of these developments varies widely from one state to the next and, within states, from one district to the next. Neither the fed-eral government nor the states have assumed a leadership role in dealing with the problems confronted by school-age pregnant and parenting ado-lescents (Adler et al., 1985). In 1981, the Rand Corporation conducted a national study of schools' responses to the problem of teenage pregnancy and concluded that "schools neither seek nor want an active role in dealing with student pregnancy or parenthood" (Zellman, 1982, p. 20). Thus, in many districts the response consists merely of an antidiscrimination policy that theoretically allows pregnant adolescents to remain in school. However, implicit barriers such as discrimination by teachers and administrators, social stigmatization by peers, and restrictive attendance policies that do not allow for the number of absences often associated with pregnancy generally render such policies ineffective for supporting school attendance by pregnant adolescents.

When a special program is initiated within a school district, it is usually because of the persistence of a single individual. As a result, the quality of special programs is uneven across districts (Zellman, 1982). Generally, there is an underemphasis on traditional academics, with greater importance given to "relevant" studies such as information about pregnancy, child development, and parenthood. Zellman (1982) has delineated three types of school-based programs for adolescent pregnancy and parenthood: (1) inclusive curriculum programs (2) supplementary curriculum programs and (3) noncurricular programs.

Inclusive Curriculum Programs

These are alternative educational programs for pregnant and parenting adolescents that are physically and administratively separate from the regular school (Zellman, 1982). In some cases, programs are oriented toward the period of pregnancy; thus, postnatal enrollment is limited to one or two semesters. These inclusive curriculum programs provide education through a traditional high school curriculum that may be delivered through an individualized instruction approach (Holman & Arcus, 1987). In addition to continued education, these programs also provide any or all of the following: health education and medical services; counseling and social support services; classes in pregnancy, childbirth, and child care; remedial tutoring; infant day care; vocational work experience (Bennett & Bardon, 1980; Holman & Arcus, 1987; Rickel, 1989; Roosa & Vaughn, 1983).

Evaluations of the effectiveness of inclusive curriculum programs in promoting school completion and job attainment among adolescent parents are limited. Holman and Arcus (1987) cited an average completion rate of 65% for their Tupper Mini School program as evidence of its success.

A few authors have reported promising results of evaluative studies. Bennett and Bardon (1980) compared a group of 86 low-SES minority adolescent mothers who attended an inclusive curriculum program (Educational Services for School Age Parents [ESSP] to 30 adolescent mothers of the same SES and ethnic composition who attended schools in the same metropolitan area but with no program for pregnant adolescents. Their data indicated that the ESSP mothers made more prenatal visits to a maternity clinic and went on to complete more total years of schooling than did the control group mothers. Similarly, Roosa and Vaughn (1983) conducted a 2–4-year follow-up study of 15 adolescent mothers who had been enrolled in an alternative educational program. Their comparison group consisted of 24 adolescent mothers recruited through a health clinic or day care centers who had never been involved in a special educational program. Their results yielded statistically significant differences between the two groups in the number of years of education completed, the number graduating from high school, and the number enrolled in school at the time of the follow-up. In each case, the alternative school group scored higher than the comparison group. Roosa and Vaughn (1983) concluded that the alternative educational program had a significant impact on adolescent mothers' educational progress. However, the small sample size and the fact that all data were collected post hoc may limit these conclusions.

Supplementary Curriculum Programs

Supplementary curriculum programs for pregnant and parenting adolescents are those in which the women remain in regular classes and receive academic credit for supplementary courses in topics such as child care, parenting, and self-development. Individualized counseling and support may also be available to students enrolled in these programs (Zellman, 1982).

One example of a supplementary curriculum program that is available to students in the state of Ohio is GRADS (Graduation, Reality, and Dual-role Skills) (Ohio Department of Education, 1989). GRADS is offered through the vocational home economics programs of secondary schools throughout the state. The goals of GRADS are to keep pregnant and parenting students in school until graduation, to assist students in appreciating the importance of prenatal care, to teach students practical parenting and child development skills, to help students gain an orientation to work, and to enable students to set goals toward balancing work and family. GRADS students have opportunities to meet individually with the GRADS coordinator in their school, as well as attend class on a daily basis for academic credit.

Evaluative information on GRADS is limited. The Ohio Department of Education (1989) cites the fact that 85.4% of GRADS participants graduated from and/or reentered school, compared to a national retention rate of 40% for pregnant and parenting adolescents, as evidence of the program's success. However, GRADS is offered as an elective course, and not all pregnant or parenting adolescents choose to participate. The success of the program may depend upon personal characteristics of the students who choose to enroll, such as motivation, family support, self-esteem, and general academic ability.

Noncurricular Programs

Noncurriculum programs are school-based programs in which pregnant and parenting adolescents attend regular classes and have opportunities to receive services such as counseling, referral, and medical care at school (Zellman, 1982). However, no academic credit is available to students for participating in these support programs. The primary advantage of this type of program is that it allows the student to remain with her friends and teachers throughout her pregnancy while receiving specialized instruction on topics related to pregnancy and parenthood. Once again, however, one might expect only the most motivated, well-adjusted students to select participation in these programs, and therefore documenting that the program per se is responsible for higher rates of school success would be difficult.

McAfee and Geesey (1984) described an in-school program for pregnant adolescents that is an example of a noncurricular program. Students are referred to the program by physicians, local service agencies, school principals, guidance counselors, or nurses. The program consists of a series of biweekly 2-hour classes held in the high school building. The curriculum focuses on issues of relevance to pregnant adolescents such as nutrition, medical care, labor and delivery, infant care, and achieving a healthy mother-child relationship. McAfee & Geesey cite a financial savings to the school district of $35,502 and a dropout rate of only 9.5% among pregnant students in the district as evidence of the success of the program.

COMMUNITY-BASED PROGRAMS

Aside from school-based programming, another forum for delivering services to pregnant and parenting adolescents is the community. Programs developed on the local level to meet the needs of these adolescents fall into two categories: (1) comprehensive programs and (2) specialized-component programs. Examples of each type of community-based program is discussed below.

Comprehensive Programs

The comprehensive model of service delivery is a product of the 1960s, when it was first used as a response to adolescent childbearing. Based on the promise of a few early comprehensive programs, the Adolescent Pregnancy Act of 1978 (which was later replaced by Title XX of the Public Health Service Act) included a mandate that grantees of federal programming funds must include 10 core elements in their programs (Weatherly, Perlman, Levine, & Klerman, 1986). These 10 elements have since come to define comprehensive programs: (1) pregnancy testing; (2) maternity counseling and referral; (3) family planning; (4) primary and preventive health services, including prenatal and postnatal care; (5) nutrition information and counseling; (6) adoption counseling and referral; (7) education in sexuality and family life; (8) referral for screening and treatment of sexually transmitted diseases (9) pediatric care; and (10) educational and vocational services (Weatherly et al., 1986). Theoretically, the development of such comprehensive programs would be possible through the mobilization and coordination of existing health, educational, and social services. Harteker (1980) has referred to this as a "linkage approach."

A national study of 10 comprehensive programs identified numerous obstacles to developing and maintaining such programs. These include inadequate financial support, an insufficient health and social welfare infrastructure, negative public and political attitudes, and unproven intervention technology. As a result, comprehensive service programs for pregnant and parenting adolescents are less widely available than one might expect and are located primarily in urban areas, where a network of services already exists.

One comprehensive approach for which evaluative data are available is Project Redirection. Begun in 1980 under the direction of the Manpower Demonstration Research Corporation, Project Redirection was a large-scale (N = 300) comprehensive program designed to "redirect" the lives of disadvantaged adolescent mothers onto a path of economic self-sufficiency (Polit, 1989). The program was implemented in four cities across the United States and offered either a comprehensive array of services directly to participants or served as a broker to help adolescent mothers find these services within the community. Three distinctive features of Project Redirection were the use of mentors to provide role modeling and support for the adolescents, the development of Individual Participant Plans for each client, and the provision of peer-group sessions for social support and mutual problem solving (Polit, 1989).

Evaluations of program effectiveness within the first year showed promising results in that participants did better than the comparison group of matched nonparticipants in terms of school enrollment, employment experience, and avoidance of a repeat pregnancy. At a 2-year follow-up only those subgroups of Project Redirection participants who were school dropouts and were receiving AFDC (Aid to Families with Dependent Children) benefits at the time of initial enrollment showed gains, such that they were more likely to have obtained a diploma or equivalency certificate and to be employed (Polit, 1989).

Results of a 5-year evaluation indicated that although the program had negligible effects on educational outcomes for adolescent mothers, it had a positive impact on parenting skills and on long-term employment outcomes. Specifically, 5 years after Project Redirection, program participants were more likely to have ever held a paying job, had worked more hours per week, had higher average weekly earning, and were less dependent on AFDC (Polit, 1989). Thus, through the attainment of work-related skills, work experience, and self-confidence, participants in Project Redirection attained better economic outcomes in that they were better employed and more self-sufficient. These positive effects of the program were most notable for that subgroup of women who had been receiving AFDC at the time of entry into Project Redirection (Polit, 1989). Overall, it appears that a comprehensive community-based program that incorporates employment-related services is an effective approach to improving long-term economic outcomes for adolescent mothers.

Specialized-component Programs

In contrast to comprehensive programs that provide a wide array of services, specialized-component programs are community-based efforts to meet specific needs of pregnant and parenting adolescents. Once successful component programs are identified, one theoretically could link them together into a comprehensive program to build efficiency of programming. Based on the assumption that problems with child care are in large part responsible for the failure of many adolescent mothers to complete their educations, Campbell, Breitmayer, and Ramey (1986) undertook a longitudinal study of the effects of free educational day care for disadvantaged single adolescent mothers and their children. Fourteen low-income adolescent mothers received free educational day care for their children from birth to age 4, in addition to free transportation and medical care for the children. A 4 1/2-year follow-up evaluation revealed that, when compared to a group of 15 adolescent mothers who had not received the services, the program mothers were more likely to have completed high school and to have become self-supporting. Specifically, nearly three fourths of the mothers who received the free day care had completed high school and were no longer using AFDC, compared to less than one half of the non-day-care mothers. Thus, it appears that availability of infant day

care is an important factor in promoting positive educational and economic outcomes for adolescents mothers.

A direct approach to promoting school completion among low-income adolescent mothers is exemplified by the Learning, Earning and
Parenting (LEAP) program of the Ohio Department of Human Services.
LEAP is a program for pregnant and parenting adolescent women who
receive AFDC to encourage them to finish their high school educations. By
providing incentives and support to these adolescents, it is hoped that
they will eventually leave the public assistance system and be economically independent (Cuyahoga County Department of Human Services,
1990). Pregnant and/or parenting adolescents under 20 years of age who
are receiving AFDC and have not already received a high school diploma
or GED receive a one-time monetary bonus of $62 in their AFDC check for
registering for school. In addition, participants who meet school attendance requirements (fewer than seven absences per month) receive a
monthly $62 bonus. Likewise, those who fail to attend school are sanc-
tioned and lose $62 a month in AFDC benefits (Cuyahoga County Depart-
ment of Human Services, 1991). A LEAP case manager assists the
adolescent mother in securing necessary supports, such as child care and
transportation, to permit her to attend school. To date, outcome data are
not available to assess the effectiveness of this program for promoting
high school completion.

EVALUATION OF PROGRAMS

Based on this review of programs for pregnant and parenting adolescents,
it appears that many school-based programs have as their primary goal
the completion of a high school education, whereas community-based
programs generally adopt a broader perspective and recognize the diverse service needs of this population. Clearly, more systematic evaluation of program effectiveness is needed. This evaluation needs to
consider which specific program components are effective in meeting
which specific goals. In addition, in designing and evaluating programs,
antecedent factors need to be considered.

This need to examine preexisting characteristics of pregnant and
parenting adolescents points to the importance of recognizing diversity
within this population. One adolescent mother is not like all of the rest in
terms of a wide variety of characteristics, such as motivation to succeed,
self-concept, family support, and socioeconomic and cultural background. As a result, intervention that "works for one adolescent mother
may or may not be effective in meeting the needs of another.

Roosa (1986) has proposed three different classifications of adolescent mothers who drop out of school, each of which have different intervention needs. One group is adolescents for whom dropping out is a manifestation of subcultural norms and expectations combined with relatively little success in school. A second group of adolescent mothers are those who drop out of school in the first few months after the baby is born because of the lack of a support network (e.g., family support) to assist with child care, transportation, and financial needs. Finally, the third group of adolescent mother dropouts are those with high educational aspirations and strong support systems who become overwhelmed by a second pregnancy. Unfortunately, most of our intervention programs to date, particularly the school-based ones, are designed for those with high educational aspirations, an available social support system, and child care, and transportation (Roosa, 1986). Many adolescent mothers do not fit this profile. Thus, we need to recognize the diversity in the population of adolescent mothers and develop programming in response to these diverse needs.

KENT ADOLESCENT MOTHERS PROJECT

In 1987 the present authors began a study of the personal, family, and social context of adolescent motherhood. Forty-six women who were 19 or younger and had given birth to their first child within the year 1986 were recruited through public access birth records. During a series of two 2-hour in-home visits, each subject completed several structured interviews and self-report questionnaires that assessed personal characteristics (demographics, self-image, perceived parenting stress), family characteristics (family environment, family or origin relationships), and social factors (sources and levels of informal social support) of adolescent mothers. Four years later, in 1991, all 46 women were recontacted and invited to participate in a follow-up study. Eighteen of the original group eventually completed this second assessment. In this 4-year follow-up, subjects completed a mail survey, in which they indicated their educational attainment, employment and welfare status, residential independence, and psychosocial maturity.

Results of the follow-up support the notion of diversity in the life paths of adolescents mothers. Half of the women had had a second or third child during the 4 years after first giving birth. Half were single and never married at the time of the 4-year follow-up; the other 50% were either married or divorced. Educationally, one of three had completed high school or an equivalency diploma and an additional one half had completed some post–high school education. In terms of economic stability, at the time of the 4-year follow-up 60% of the adolescent mothers were employed, and 50% were receiving some form of public assistance. Just over half of the sample reported annual incomes under $10,000. Residentially, all of the women had their children living with them, and one of three were residing with their families of origin.

Data from the original assessment were used to examine what factors were predictive of educational and economic outcomes 4 years later. Those findings indicated that being enrolled in school during the first year after the baby's birth and experiencing lower levels of parenting stress during the first year were both associated with higher levels of overall educational attainment 4 years later. The total amount of education achieved was, in turn, predictive of employment status at the 4-year follow-up. Welfare dependency at the 4-year mark was predicted by lower self-image and less positive family functioning 4 years earlier. All of these findings support the notion that personal and family characteristics are important in determining the educational and economic outcomes of adolescent motherhood. Across all of the analyses of the follow-up data, the personal factors that consistently emerged as significant were perceived parenting stress and self-image. Family characteristics of most notable importance were intimacy, quality of the adolescent mother's relationship with her own mother, and coming from an achievement-oriented family. Overall, the data lend support to the importance of recognizing diversity within the population of adolescent mothers and of developing programming that is responsive to this diversity and considers the clients' personal and family backgrounds.

SUMMARY AND RECOMMENDATIONS

We know that there are widespread variations in what happens to the educational attainment, economic security dimensions, and career paths of women who experienced motherhood as adolescents. Some of these variations are partially explained by family of origin. For example, family economic security, educational status, and the strength of relationships between mothers and daughters are all related to outcomes for adolescent mothers. One suspects these same variables relate to success of adolescents in general. We also know that support through legislation and social policy has a significant impact in the lives of adolescent mothers. For example, Title IX of the Educational Amendment Act of 1972 seems to have had a positive impact on the educational attainment of these women. We also suspect that educational and training programs developed in response to the developmental and parenting needs of adolescent mothers have been helpful. Although evaluative data are limited, school-based programs appear to facilitate school attendance for adolescent mothers who desire it. Community-based efforts to provide child care, personal development, and employment-related skills may result in better educational and economic outcomes. In general, it appears that conditions that support adolescents development support the development of adolescent mothers. However, adolescent mothers have special needs for child care, additional economic support, health services, early knowledge and skills related to parenting, interpersonal and cross-generational skills training (exacerbated by the need for closer relationships with families of origin at a time when they are trying to differentiate from these families), and developing and keeping a self-vision amid the competition for attention of a child, peers, and parents, and intimate relationships. Thus, efforts should be made to accommodate the special circumstances related to adolescent motherhood so that more typical developmental processes can continue.

From the authors review and knowledge of the field, we think particular attention should be given to the following three areas: basic research related to adolescent mothers and their social networks, evaluation studies of both school-based and community based programs for these women, and development of social policy addressing the needs of pregnant and parenting adolescents.

Basic research should consider the individual, cultural, socioeconomic, and family and support network variations among adolescent mothers. Such research should seek to discover patterns of variation among adolescent mothers and the milieus that encourage personal, educational, and career development within these patterns. Studies of intervention programs need to focus on systematic evaluation in order to define what components of programs make a difference with which women. Such information would allow for more intentional educational interventions. Finally, we need to continue to develop social policy that recognizes the special conditions of adolescent mothers by providing economic and child care support, educational and career opportunities, and social and health services.

REFERENCES

Adler, E. S., Bates, M., & Merdinger, J. M. (1985). Educational policies and programs for teenage parents and pregnant teenagers. *Family Relations, 34,* 183–187.

Alan Guttmacher Institute (1976). *Eleven million teenagers.* New York: Author.

Becerra, R., & deAnda, D. (1984). Pregnancy and motherhood among Mexican American adolescents. *Health and Social Work, 9,* 106–123.

Bennett, V. C., & Bardon, J. I. (1980).The effects of a school program on teenage mothers and their children. *American Journal of Orthopsychiatry, 50,* 671–678.

Bertalanffy, L. von. (1968). *General systems theory: Foundation, development, applications.* New York: Braziller.

Campbell, F. A., Breitmayer, B., & Ramey, C. T. (1986). Disadvantaged single teenage mothers and their children: Consequences of free educational day care. *Family Relations, 35,* 63–68.

Cuyahoga County Department of Human Services. (1991). *Learning, earning and parenting.* (Available from Cuyahoga County Department of Human Services, 1641 Payne Avenue, Cleveland, OH 44114).

deAnda, D., & Becerra, R., (1984). Networks for adolescent mothers. *Social Casework, 65,* 172–181.

Furstenberg, F. F. (1991). As the pendulum swings: Teenage childbearing and social concern. *Family Relations, 40,* 127–138.

Furstenberg, F. F., Brooks-Gunn, J., & Morgan, S. P. (1987). *Adolescent mothers in later life.* Cambridge: Cambridge University Press.

Furstenberg, F. F., & Crawford, A. G. (1978). Family support: Helping teenage mothers to cope. *Family Planning Perspectives, 10,* 322–333.

Grindstaff, C. F. (1988). Adolescent marriage and childbearing: The long-term economic outcome, Canada in the 1980s. *Adolescence, 23*(89), 45–58.

Harteker, L. (1980). Meeting the needs of adolescent parents and their children: The linkage approach. *Children's Hospital National Medical Center Clinical Proceedings, 36,* 334–344.

Hayes, C. D. (Ed.). (1987). *Risking the future: Adolescent sexuality, pregnancy, and childbearing.* Washington, DC: National Academy Press.

Hofferth, S. L. (1988). Endemic, but not epidemic [Review of M. Vinovskis, *An "epidemic" of adolescent pregnancy?*] *Family Planning Perspectives, 20*(5), 247–248.

Hoffman, L. (1981). *Foundations of family therapy.* New York: Basic Books.

Holman, N., & Arcus, M. (1987). Helping adolescent mothers and their children: An integrated multi-agency approach. *Family Relations, 36,* 119–123.

McAfee, M. L., & Geesey, M. R. (1984). Meeting the needs of the teen-age pregnant student: An in-school program that works. *Journal of School Health, 54,* 350–352.

McCluskey, K. A., Killarney, J., & Papini, D. R. (1983). Adolescent pregnancy and parenthood: Implications for development. In E. J. Callahan & K. A. McCluskey (Eds.), *Life span developmental psychology: Nonnormative life events.* New York: Academic Press.

Minuchin, S. (1974). *Families and family therapy.* Cambridge, MA: Harvard University Press.

Moore, K. A. (Ed.). (1992, January). *Facts at a glance.* (Available from Child Trends, Inc., 2100 M Street, NW, Washington, DC 20037)

Mott, F. L. (1986). The pace of repeated childbearing among young American mothers. *Family Planning Perspectives, 18*(1), 5–7.

Mott, F. L., & Marsiglio, W. (1985). Early childbearing and completion of high school. *Family Planning Perspectives, 17*(5), 234–237.

Mott, F. L., & Maxwell, N. L. (1981). School-age mothers: 1968 and 1979. *Family Planning Perspectives, 13*(6), 287–292.

Ohio Department of Education. (1989). *GRADS*. (Available from Ohio Department of Education, Division of Vocational and Career Education, 65 South Front Street, Columbus, OH 43266–0308).

Polit, D. F. (1989). Effects of a comprehensive program for teenage parents: Five years after Project Redirection. *Family Planning Perspectives, 21,* 164–169.

Polit, D. F., & Kahn, J. R. (1986). Early subsequent pregnancy among economically disadvantaged teenage mothers. *American Journal of Public Health, 76*(2), 167–171.

Richardson, R. A., Barbour, N. B., & Bubenzer, D. L. (1991). Bittersweet connections: Informal social networks as sources of support and interference for adolescent mothers. *Family Relations, 40,* 430–434.

Rickel, A. U. (1989). *Teen pregnancy and parenting.* New York: Hemisphere Publishing.

Roosa, M. W. (1986). Adolescent mothers, school drop-outs and school based intervention programs. *Family Relations, 35,* 313–317.

Roosa, M. W., & Vaughn, L. (1983). Teen mothers enrolled in an alternative parenting program. *Urban Education, 18,* 348–360.

Stevens, J. H. (1988). Social support, locus of control, and parenting in three low-income groups of mothers: Black teenager, Black adults, and white adults. *Child Development, 59,* 635–642.

Upchurch, D. M., & McCarthy, J. (1989). Adolescent childbearing and high school completion in the 1980's: Have things changed? *Family Planning Perspectives, 21*(5), 199–202.

Upchurch, D. M., & McCarthy, J. (1990). The timing of a first birth and high school completion. *American Sociological Review, 55,* 224–234.

Vinovskis, M. (1988). *An "epidemic" of adolescent pregnancy? Some historical and policy considerations.* New York: Oxford University Press.

Weatherley, R. A., Perlman, S. B., Levine, M. H., & Klerman, L. V. (1986). Comprehensive programs for pregnant teenagers and teenage parents: How successful have they been? *Family Planning Perspectives, 18,* 73–78.

Young, A. T., Berkman, B., & Rehr, H. (1975). Parental influence on pregnant adolescents. *Social Work, 20,* 387–391.

Zellman, G. L. (1982). Public school programs for adolescent pregnancy and parenthood: An assessment. *Family Planning Perspectives, 14,* 15–21.

■ 9
Work, Family, and the Chicana: Power, Perception, and Equity

Elsa O. Valdez and Scott Coltrane

The recent swift and pervasive entry of mothers into waged work is arguably the most significant demographic trend of our time. In 1960, just 39% of U.S. women with school-age children were in the labor force. By 1988, that figure had climbed to over 72%. Although social commentators emphasize that current trends toward maternal employment are unprecedented, we must remember that women with children have always "worked." Mothers in the working class or from ethnic minorities have traditionally relied on wages for survival, and throughout history, mothers from all walks of life have been responsible for a wide range of activities that would classify as productive labor. What has changed is the site of that work, which has tended to shift from inside to outside the home, for at least a portion of the day. What has changed little, if at all, is that working mothers, regardless of class or race, still perform most of the unpaid labor that goes into maintaining a household and raising children.

In this chapter, we explore some of the reasons for, and results of, the unequal division of household labor in a small sample of Chicano families. In all of these families, mothers and fathers share the responsibility of earning money, although the men tend to earn substantially more than the women do. In all of the families, the men also share some of the domestic labor. These dual-earner couples undoubtedly share more child care and housework than most do, and we explore how differential access to resources and various cultural constraints produce patterns of household labor allocation that are markedly asymmetrical. We describe who does what around the house, paying particular attention to who notices when things need doing, who sets standards for performance, and who feels responsible when tasks are left undone. By exploring the details of home life for four different couples, we also speculate on some of the reasons for, and results of, unequal divisions of household labor. In particular, we examine the ways that waged work and home work interpenetrate, and we highlight how they affect men and women differently. Finally, we focus on some salient differences between families and identify some of the processes that appear to promote or discourage more equal divisions of labor.

THE SIGNIFICANCE OF HOUSEHOLD LABOR

Why are mundane topics like cleaning toilets and wiping noses worthy of serious scholarly inquiry? Although housework has long been studied within the field of home economics, it has generally been considered "women's work," and few academic disciplines have bothered to question the "naturalness" of women's performing it. Similarly, researchers studying child development and family socialization processes virtually ignored fathers as direct caretakers of children until the early 1970s. At that time, scholars in fields like sociology, anthropology, psychology, history, political science, family studies, and women's studies began to pay increased attention to the gender division of labor and the centrality of household labor to the perpetuation of male dominance.

Over the past two decades, feminist theorists have developed a variety of explanations for women's disadvantage relative to men. Men's limited domestic contributions have played an important role in many of these theories. For example, psychoanalytic theorists like Chodorow (1978) and Dinnerstein (1976) reformulated Freudian theory to suggest that men's lack of participation in child care maintains male dominance by reproducing men and women with different psychic structures and personalities. Marxist-feminist theorists like Hartmann (1981) and Eisenstein (1981) postulated dual systems of oppression for women under capitalist economies, suggesting that men's control of women's household and market labor are the material bases of "patriarchy." Most theorists have tended to grant causal priority to systems of economic stratification, with imbalances in marital power seen as stemming from women's lower earning capacity (e.g., Blumberg & Coleman, 1989). Such theories usually claim that the household division of labor is an important indicator of women's limited power, and most also assert that the allocation of domestic tasks is a central feature of gender stratification, though not its primary cause (Chafetz, 1988).

Other recent theoretical formulations have granted an even more central causal role to domestic divisions of labor. Rather than viewing household labor as simply a reflection of women's low status, these theories see household labor as a site for the production of gender and hence gender inequality. For instance, West and Zimmerman (1987) view gender as a routine, methodical, and recurring accomplishment that casts particular pursuits as expressions of masculine and feminine "natures." The everyday tasks of running a household and raising children provide numerous occasions for reaffirming one's gendered relation to the world. As people perform, or fail to perform, "appropriate" household tasks, they are actively creating and sustaining images of themselves as appropriately gendered individuals (Berk, 1985; Coltrane, 1989). According to this view, cultural conceptions of appropriate behaviors for men and women begin to change in response to the micropolitics of gender within each household. By focusing on the mundane realities of who takes out the trash, who plans the dinner menu, and who stays home from work to be with a sick child, we can explore potentials for change in structures of male dominance. By highlighting issues of power, perception, and equity in the domestic labor of dual-earner families, we can also understand how and why gender relations have appeared so impervious to change.

THE GENDER DIVISION OF LABOR

Before describing who does what in the 20 Chicano dual-earner families we interviewed for this study, we will briefly review what other studies have found. To begin with, there are two major shortcomings evident in the literature on household labor that are of concern here. First, most studies have included very few minority families, so our impressions of household task allocation, like most findings in social science, tend to reflect a white, middle-class bias. Second, most studies of household labor have contained a preponderance of couples who established patterns of housework and child care at least a decade or two ago. This is because many studies of household labor have used data collected in the 1970s or before and because studies using more recent data tend not to analyze data by age of respondents, so people who married 30 years ago are often lumped together with those who got married just last year. These two shortcomings leave us with a picture of household labor allocation that is racially specific and somewhat dated.

In general, past studies tell us that housework and child care are divided into separate spheres on the basis of gender. Women usually do most of the indoor work, especially cooking, laundry, cleaning house, doing dishes, and caring for young children. Men usually do most of the outdoor work, such as lawn care and car care, as well as making most household repairs and sometimes playing with older children (Berk, 1985; Coverman & Sheley, 1986; Hiller & Philiber, 1986; Kamo, 1988; Thompson & Walker, 1989; Vanek, 1974). What should be immediately evident from these lists of tasks is that women do virtually all of the repetitive and mundane housework and hence spend a significantly greater proportion of their time performing household labor than do men. Although studies have used different samples and different data collection techniques, virtually every study has concluded that wives do two to three times more of the total household labor than husbands do and four to five times more of the mundane housework (Berk, 1985; Pleck, 1983; Thompson & Walker, 1989).

In spite of the fact that more and more women and mothers became employed during the 1960s and 1970s, the pattern of women doing almost all of the housework persisted into the 1980s. In general, the most typical family response to women entering the labor force was for wives to reduce their contributions to housework somewhat while husbands continued to make the same contributions they had in the past. This has the effect of increasing men's proportionate share of household labor, even though their behavioral changes were negligible (Coverman & Sheley, 1986; Pleck, 1983). Images of men doing housework and child care became more plentiful during this period, but when men increased their contributions to household labor, it was usually by doing more of the "manly" chores, like taking out the trash, barbecuing, or mowing the lawn (Robinson, 1988). The rigid division of housework based on gender appeared so resistant to change in the late 1970s that one review of research called studies of change in men's housework "much ado about nothing" (Miller & Garrison, 1982, p. 242).

More recent time-budget data suggest that there is some change underway but that women still tend to do most of the work that it takes to run a household. Robinson (1988) reported that, between 1975 and 1985, women reduced the average amount of time they devoted to the tasks of cooking meals, meal cleanup, housecleaning, laundry, and ironing, by about 4 hours, from almost 20 hours per week to 16 hours per week. During the same period, men almost doubled their average time devoted to these household tasks, from 2 hours to 4 hours. Thus, although there is some tendency for men to begin assuming more responsibility for performing housework, we can see that they are contributing only a small percentage of the time devoted to tasks traditionally considered "women's work." Nevertheless, Robinson's findings show one subgroup where men are beginning to make somewhat larger contributions: since 1965, men with children have doubled the amount of time they spend doing housework (excluding direct child care), from about 4–5 hours per week to 9–10 hours per week. So although women and mothers continue to do much more than men and fathers do, there is some evidence that the gender gap in housework is beginning to narrow, especially for parents of young children.

Recent qualitative studies of family life reveal some of the stresses and strains associated with asymmetric divisions of family labor. Hochschild (1989) reported on how women handled the "second shift" that they must work after their paid jobs are over, concluding that women are deeply torn between the demands of work and family. She described how women tend to talk more intensely than men about being overtired, sick, and emotionally drained, and she labeled men's favored position in the family as the "leisure gap." Part of the reason for the leisure gap is that the tasks performed by women tend to be unrelenting and repetitive. Tasks such as shopping, cooking, cleaning, laundry, and child care repeated over and over in a never-ending cycle. In addition, wives and mothers typically act as household managers, assuming responsibility for planning and initiating most household chores and monitoring the emotional well-being of family members. Husbands, in turn, tend to remain in a "helper" role, even when they make significant contributions to routine household labor (Berk, 1985; Ehrensaft, 1987; Hochschild, 1989).

Women's household burdens can be especially overwhelming when they are also working outside the home, but it does not necessarily follow that wives and husbands would attempt to share most household tasks. Pleck (1983) reported that only about half of American husbands believed that men should do more housework and child care when their wives were employed. In general, studies also show that most women have relatively low expectations for assistance from their husbands. Only about one fifth to one third of survey respondents are likely to report that current divisions of domestic labor are "unfair" (Barnett & Baruch, 1987; Berk, 1985; Pleck, 1983; Thompson & Walker, 1989).

STRUGGLES OVER SHARING HOUSEWORK

What happens when couples attempt to share housework and child care? Although good studies are still rare, we are beginning to understand some of the complex realities of attempting to change taken-for-granted divisions of household labor. Most studies show that wives whose husbands share more household labor are more satisfied with marriage than are other wives (Staines & Libby, 1986). Wives who want help from husbands and receive it are less depressed than other wives (Ross, Mirowsky, &

Huber, 1983). Husbands' willingness to "help out" with family work tends to carry symbolic significance for wives that can enhance their psychological well-being and reaffirm the strength of the couple relationship (Kessler & McRae, 1982).

In contrast, other studies have found that when women demand help from their husbands, it puts added strains on the marital relationship (Barnett & Baruch, 1987; Crouter, Perry-Jenkins, Huston, & McHale, 1977). Many wives have difficulty pushing for an equitable division of labor if it means fighting with loved ones (Berheide, 1984). Some have found that sharing child care and housework is accompanied by increased marital conflict, although those involved do not always define this in negative terms (Kimball, 1988; Radin & Russell, 1983; Szinovacz, 1987). Some researchers have commented that wives who attempt to share domestic labor typically monitor its performance and are often forced to accept their husbands' lower standards (Coltrane, 1990; Lamb, Pleck, & Levine, 1986). Others have suggested that when wives criticize the quality of their husbands' domestic work they are protecting threatened territory in the only domain over which they have exercised control (LaRossa & LaRossa, 1981; Walker & Thompson, 1989).

This brief review highlights some of what researchers know about the division of household labor in dual-earner families and suggests what additional research needs to be done. Most of the qualitative research is based on samples of college-educated, dual-earner white couples with higher than average incomes, and the larger-scale survey research tends to contain too few people of color to make subgroup comparison. As a potential corrective, the authors looked at some of these issues in a select group of Chicano couples, also primarily well educated and with higher than average incomes but largely employed in white-color and working-class jobs. Our intent was to explore how this group of dual-earner husbands and wives talked about the sharing—lack of sharing—of housework and child care. On the following pages,we examine their accounts of who did what, how tasks were allocated, and how they felt about it.

Before presenting the interview results, however, we will briefly comment on some findings that pertain specifically to Chicano and other minority families. Most early social science research on minority families tends to focus on presumed deficiencies. For examples, Baca Zinn and Eitzen (1987) note that up until the late 1960s,

> Black and Hispanic families have been portrayed as disorganized due to distinctive cultural patterns that are passed down from generation to generation. According to this reasoning minority families were holdovers from the past. The Black family was transmitted from slavery while the

Chicano family was passed down from traditional Mexican society. (pp. 163–164)

Some contemporary social scientists continue to depict the Chicano family as rigidly patriarchal. "Machismo" is often emphasized to describe the destructive aspects of the Chicano family:

> Within the family, gender roles are well defined. Both mothers and daughters are expected to be protected and submissive and to dedicate themselves to caring for the males of the family. For the Mexican male, machismo, or the demonstration of physical and sexual prowess, is basic to self-respect. (Hess, Markson, & Stein, 1991; p. 273)

Some contemporary scholars would reject such stereotypes as misguided. For instance, Mirandé (1988) asserted that *machismo* implies respect, loyalty, responsibility, and generosity and noted that contemporary Chicano fathers now participate more actively in child care than in the past. Some recent research on marital interaction in Mexican-American families seems to support the notion that gender relations are more egalitarian than the traditional model assumes. Studies of marital decision making have found that Chicano couples tend to regard their decision-making as relatively shared and equal (Cromwell & Cromwell, 1978; Hawkes & Taylor, 1975; Ybarra, 1982). Most researchers agree, however, that marital roles are not truly egalitarian in dual-earner Mexican-American households (nor are they in dual-earner Anglo-American households) (Garcia-Bahne, 1977; Hartzler & Franco, 1985; Segura, 1984; Williams, 1988, 1990; Zavella, 1987). Because Mexican cultural ideals require the male to be honored and respected as the head of the family, Baca Zinn (1982) contends that Chicano families maintain a facade of patriarchy while mothers assume authority over day-to-day household activities. It has also been suggested that Mexican-American women, like their Anglo-American counterparts, exercise more marital decision-making power if they are employed outside the home (Baca Zinn, 1980; Ybarra, 1982).

The concept of "familism" has often been invoked to describe both traditional and contemporary Mexican-American families, with their higher-than-average birthrates and household size. Familism refers to "a constellation of values which give overriding importance to the family and the needs of the collective as opposed to individual and personal needs" (Bean, Curtis, & Marcum, 1977, p. 760). Chicano families are typically found to have the highest levels of extended familism, compared to blacks and Anglos of various class levels (Mindel, 1980). The impacts of familism on divisions of household labor and husband-wife relations in Chicano families appear to be mixed. At present, we have few studies that allow us to describe the most important social processes or to make predictions about the impacts of various factors on divisions of labor in dual-earner Chicano families.

METHODS

Data for this study were collected by conducting multiple in-depth interviews with 20 dual-income Chicano couples with at least one child. The term *Chicano* refers to respondents who are of Mexican descent. Participants were largely first- to fourth-generation Mexican Americans. Many social scientists lump Chicanos with undocumented workers, Mexican nationals, and other Hispanics, including Puerto Ricans, Cubans, and Latin Americans. This is misleading because, although Chicanos identify with their Mexican roots, their national social identity is a product of their being members of U.S. society (cf. Keefe & Padilla, 1987). Subject families were obtained through purposive snowball sampling techniques, and mothers and fathers were interviewed separately. All interviews were tape-recorded, and portions were later transcribed for coding into emergent categories.

Characteristics of the Sample

Respondents in the sample ranged in age from 25 to 43 years old. Ten of the respondents were married between 5 and 9 years; 14, between 10 and 14 years; and 16, between 15 and 16 years. Four couples had one child, nine had two children, five had three children, and two had four children. The ages of the children ranged from 1 to 14 years. Fifteen of the couples lived in suburban communities of the southwestern United States and five in semirural communities of the same region. Over 90% were Catholic. Twenty fathers and 15 mothers were employed full-time (40 hours or more per week), and 5 mothers were employed part-time (less than 30 hours per week). Respondents were relatively well educated: 15 husbands and 9 wives had at least a B.A. degree; 3 husbands and 7 wives had attended some college; and just 2 husbands and 4 wives had only high school diplomas.

Family incomes were also higher than the average for Chicano couples. Annual family income ranged from $26,000 to $79,000. Annual individual incomes also varied widely—from $4,000 to $48,000—but most of those at the low end were women. Of the 11 subjects who earned between $4,000 and $19,999, only 1 was a man. Of those who earned between $20,000 and $29,999, 7 were husbands and 7 were wives. And finally, of those who earned between $30,000 and $48,000, 12 were husbands and 3 were wives. Subjects tended to vary with respect to occupational prestige.

Five husbands and 6 wives were employed in working-class jobs, 11 husbands and eight wives had white-collar occupations (limited autonomy, modest wages, etc.), and 4 husbands and 6 wives had professional careers. Therefore, although these Chicano couples tended to be gainfully employed, they were more representative of lower-middle-class and working-class families.

Measures of Household Labor

Detailed data on housework and child care were obtained by having each individual sort stacks of index cards with various household and child care tasks listed on them. Husbands and wives separately indicated who performed each of 64 tasks during the previous 2 weeks: (1) wife always, (2) wife almost always, (3) husband and wife about equally, (4) husband almost always, (5) husband always. The 64 tasks were later grouped into six major areas: (1) housecleaning, (2) meal preparation and cleanup, (3) clothes care, (4) home maintenance and repairs, (5) finances and home management, and (6) child care. Subjects were also queried about who initiated various tasks, who set standards for their performance, and whether they felt that their domestic division of labor was fair.

FINDINGS

The results of the interviews and card sorts show that wives were responsible for almost all of the housecleaning, clothes care, and meal preparation/cleanup. Husbands were primarily responsible for home maintenance/repairs, whereas finances/home management tended to be shared. Child care was performed primarily by wives, but according to husbands, as many tasks were shared as were performed more often by wives. In and of themselves, these findings are not surprising. Similar to findings on dual-earner Anglo couples, this sample of dual-earner Chicano couples shared a few more child care tasks than others, but divisions of household labor still conformed to traditional expectations.

Table 9.1 presents wives' and husbands' perceptions of who most often performs the 64 household tasks. For housecleaing, wives tended to rate themselves as doing most of the vacuuming, mopping, sweeping, dusting, cleaning sinks, cleaning toilets, cleaning tubs, making beds, picking up toys, tidying the living room, hanging up clothes, and spring cleaning. Wives listed only cleaning the porch and washing windows as shared, and they indicated that husbands most often took out the trash. Husbands also listed trash as their chore but rated more tasks as equally shared than as being done by the wives.

TABLE 9.1 Who Performs the Task? Wives' and Husbands' Perceptions of Domestic Task Performance

Wife's Perception			Husband's Perception		
Wife More	Both Equally	Husband More	Wife More	Both Equally	Husband More
House cleaning					
Vacuum	Clean porch	Take out trash	Mop	Clean porch	Take out trash
Mop	Wash windows		Sweep	Wash windows	
Sweep			Dust	Vacuum	
Dust			Clean toilets	Clean sinks	
Clean sinks			Making beds	Clean tub	
Clean Toilets			Hang up clothes	Pick up toys	
Make Beds				Tidy living room	
Pick up toys				Spring cleaning	
Meal Preparation					
Plan Menus	Put food away		Plan menus	Put food away	
Prepare breakfast			Prepare breakfast	Prepare lunch	
Prepare lunch			Cook dinner	Make snacks	
Cook dinner			Bake	Put away dishes	
Make snacks			Wash dishes	Wipe kitchen counters	
Bake			Grocery shopping		
Wash dishes					
Put dishes away					
Wipe kitchen counters					
Grocery shopping					
Clothes care					
Laundry	Ironing		Laundry	Ironing	
Hand laundry			Hand laundry	Shoe care	

Item	Wife's Perception			Husband's Perception		
	Wife More	Both Equally	Husband More	Wife More	Both Equally	Husband More
Clothes care (cont'd)						
Shoe care	Shoe care					
Sewing	Sewing			Sewing		
Buying clothes	Buying clothes			Buying clothes		
Home maintenance and repairs						
Redecorating		Redecorating			Redecorating	
General yardwork		General yardwork				General yardwork
Watering lawn		Watering lawn				Watering lawn
Mowing lawn		Mowing lawn				Mowing lawn
Gardening		Gardening				Gardening
Interior painting		Interior painting				Interior painting
Exterior painting		Exterior painting				Exterior painting
Cleaning rain gutters		Cleaning rain gutters			Cleaning rain gutters	
House repairs			House repairs			House repairs
Car maintenance			Car maintenance			Car maintenance
Car repairs			Car repairs			Car repairs
Washing car			Washing car			Washing car
Finances and home management						
Running errands	Running errands				Running errands	
Paying bills	Paying bills			Paying bills		
Contacting relatives/friends				Contacting relatives/friends		
Preparing taxes		Preparing taxes			Preparing taxes	
Making investments		Making investments			Making investments	
Handling investments		Handling investments				
Handling insurance					Handling insurance	
Deciding major purchases		Deciding major purchases			Deciding major purchases	
Planning couple dates		Planning couple dates				

continued

TABLE 9.1 (cont.)

	Wife's Perception			Husband's Perception		
	Wife More	Both Equally	Husband More	Wife More	Both Equally	Husband More
Finances and home management (cont.)						
Contacting relatives/friends		Contacting relatives/friends				
Planning couple dates					Planning couple dates	
Child care						
Putting children to bed	Putting children to bed				Putting children to bed	
Awakening children	Awakening children			Awakening children		
Helping children dress	Helping children dress			Helping children dress		
Helping children bathe	Helping children bathe			Helping children bathe		
Driving children	Driving children				Driving children	
Supervising children		Supervising children			Supervising children	
Disciplining children		Disciplining children			Disciplining children	
Playing with children		Playing with children			Playing with children	
Planning outings with children		Planning outings with children			Planning outings with children	
Taking child to doctor	Taking child to doctor			Taking child to doctor		
Caring for sick child	Caring for sick child			Caring for sick child		
Arranging baby-sitting	Arranging baby-sitting			Arranging baby-sitting		

A similar pattern was evident for meal preparation and cleanup. Wives listed all tasks in this area as being performed by themselves, with the exception of putting food away, which was listed as shared. Husbands again placed almost half of the tasks in the shared column, with many of the less time-consuming tasks rated as performed by husbands and wives about equally. Such tasks included putting food way, preparing lunch, making snacks, putting dishes away, and wiping kitchen counters. Both husbands and wives indicated that wives were primarily responsible for planning menus, preparing breakfast, cooking dinner, baking, washing dishes, and shopping for groceries.

The discrepancies between spousal accounts were much smaller in the area of clothes care, primarily because both husbands and wives agreed that wives did almost all of it. Wives were rated as performing the laundry, the hand laundry, the sewing, and the purchase of clothes. In an unexpected finding, both husbands and wives listed ironing as shared activity. Husbands also rated shoe care as being performed equally by the two spouses.

The same general trend observed above was also evident for child care. Here both spouses listed more tasks as shared than they did for housework, but husbands listed as many tasks in the equal column as in the wife's column. In contrast, wives listed only supervising, disciplining, playing with, and planning outings with the children as shared activities. Husbands said that putting children to bed and driving them places were also shared activities. Bodily care aspects of child rearing, including getting children up in the morning, monitoring bathing, helping them dress, taking them to the doctor, tending them when sick, and arranging for baby-sitters were all listed by both spouses as the province of the wife.

For tasks traditionally considered "manly" activities, similar discrepancies were evident between spousal reports. Wives listed 7 of 12 home maintenance and repair tasks as performed equally by both spouses and one—redecorating—as performed principally by themselves. Husbands, in contrast, listed only redecorating and cleaning gutters as shared, with all other tasks listed as being performed principally by themselves.

In the area of finances and home management, both spouses listed six of eight tasks as shared and put two in the wife's domain. Both spouses listed paying bills as being primarily the wife's task. Wives saw themselves as running errands more often, whereas husbands considered errands to be an equally shared activity. Whereas wives indicated that spouses shared phoning and writing relatives and friends, husbands saw wives as being primarily responsible for such social contact.

These results suggest that, at least for perceptions of household labor, husbands and wives are living in different worlds. In general, wives think they have sole or primary responsibility for many more housework and child care tasks than their husbands give them credit for. Husbands tend to rate many of the frequently performed housework and child care tasks of short duration as shared, whereas their wives rate these same tasks as performed principally by themselves. Similarly, some of the more frequently performed tasks of yard and home care are perceived by wives as shared but by husbands as mostly performed by themselves. The authors will consider some of the reasons for and implications of these differences in perception after we present findings from interviews with some representative families.

FOUR CASE STUDIES

On the basis of the couples' reported divisions of labor, their accounts of task allocation procedures, their perceptions of equity, and their gender ideology, we sorted the 20 couples into four categories: traditional, semitraditional, transitional, and nontraditional (cf. Hochschild 1989). Although all of the couples are somewhat nontraditional in that both spouses are employed, our typology is based on the performance and perception of household labor, particularly the more mundane aspects of housework and child care. On the following pages, we describe one exemplary couple from each of the four types.

Traditional Division of Labor

Jorge and Gabriella Garcia

The most striking first impression when you walk into this couple's home is how immaculate and pleasing to the eye the home appears. During the interview, Gabriella acknowledged that she takes great pride in her role as a homemaker and readily accepts responsibility for managing the household. She commented, "I have the say-so on the running of the house, and I also decide on the children's activities." Gabriella, 28 years old, has been married to Jorge, 37, for 6 years. They have two children, a son 5 years old and a daughter 4 years old. Both Catholics, she grew up in Mexico, and he was raised in the southwestern United States. Although Gabriella has a college degree, she feels that her current job as a teacher's aide is ideal for her. She is able to work 20 hours per week at a neighborhood school and is home by the time her own children get home from school. She earns only $6,000 per year but justifies the low salary by the fact that the job fits so well with her family schedule. Jorge's administrative job at a major university allows them to live comfortably, he earns $48,000 annually.

Gabriella described the division of labor in their household as very traditional. She said she does most of the cleaning, cooking, clothes care, and child care tasks, and Jorge takes care of yard work, home repairs, finances, and home management. Her major complaints are that her husband doesn't notice things and that he creates more work for her:

> The worst part about housework and child care is the amount of nagging I have to do to get Jorge to help. For example, say I just cleaned the house; Jorge will leave the newspaper scattered all over the place or he will leave wet towels on the bathroom floor.

Jorge's perception of housework and child care reflects more sharing than Gabriella reports. For example, he admitted that Gabriella does most of the cleaning and clothes care, but he also gave her credit for handling the finances and home management. He perceived his contributions to be substantially larger than she thought they were, as he indicated that cooking, child care, and home maintenance were largely shared.

When asked whether there had been any negotiation over who would do what chores, Jorge responded, "I don't think a set decision was made; it was a necessity." Gabriella's response was similar: "It just evolved that way; we never really talked about it." Jorge's provider role was taken for granted, but occasionally Gabriella would voice some muted resentment. For example, she commented that she gets discouraged and upset when he tells her that she should not be working because the children are so small. Additionally, Gabriella mentioned in passing that she was sometimes bothered by the fact that she has not been able to further her career or work overtime because it interfered with the family's schedule.

When queried about how they felt about appropriate roles for men and women, this couple gave some contradictory responses. For instance, when asked if he thought fathers could provide the kind of nurturance that mothers do, Jorge said, "I'd say no, but it is necessary for both to provide qualitatively different nurturing." Casting men's and women's natures as essentially different might lead Jorge to ignore social processes that narrow women's opportunities. Nevertheless, he acknowledged that women are disadvantaged in our society relative to men: "Usually assumptions are made about what women can and cannot do, which leads to differing expectations, opportunities, and life choices."

Gabriella admitted that their division of labor was unfair, but she did not expect it to change. In contrast, Jorge commented that he expected it to change because they had "no choice." He reproaches her for working while the kids are still young, and she ends up in a job that allows her to serve her family first. Her "perfect" job, however, pays so little that she may never feel justified in demanding more housework from him. For his part, Jorge tends to see substantial sharing already and predicts more in the future. Somehow, this is not the type of sharing that satisfies Gabriella, but she continues to place what she perceives as her family's needs above her own.

Almost half of the couples we interviewed fit the traditional pattern exemplified by Jorge and Gabriella. Wives in these families performed virtually all housework and child care, and both spouses tended to accept this as "natural." The wife's commitment to outside employment was generally limited, and her income was generally considered "extra" money. The husband's few domestic contributions were seen as "helping out," and he tended to take much more credit for his contributions than his wife was willing to grant him. The husbands in these families failed to see most of the details of running the household, but because they were not "supposed" to be responsible for such tasks, they were rarely challenged by wives or anyone else to redefine housework as their responsibility.

Semitraditional Division of Labor

Octavio and Olivia Obregon

Octavio and Olivia Obregon both grew up in a small desert community and have never ventured far from home. This is not to imply that they are naive or ignorant but rather that they seem to be very content living in an area where everyone knows each other. The have not been tempted by big city life, and for this family, it appears that there is very little disagreement over family work. Walking through their modest home, one notices that it looks lived-in but clean. Olivia admitted that housework is not a high priority for her, commenting that she does just enough to make it look decent, especially the living room. For the most part, however, she spends as little time on housework as she can "get away with." She prefers to spend her time doing things with her children, going to yard sales on the weekend, or visiting her mother.

Thirty-eight-year-old Olivia and 36-year-old Octavio have been married for 15 years and have two boys, aged 9 and 11. Octavio works as a mechanic for a local business and usually puts in between 50 and 60 hours each week at his job. He also belongs to the National Guard, and several times a year he travels to various cities for training sessions. According to Octavio, this is similar to going on a vacation for him because he gets away for a few days and enjoys the break from the same old routine. Olivia reported that Octavio's reserve stints are also a break for her. With Octavio gone, she doesn't feel she has to cook regular meals, especially, she says, because her sons don't seem to mind.

As a teacher's aide, Olivia works about 30 hours a week and earns $8,000. Both spouses reported that family work was moderately segregated. Olivia said she performs most of the cleaning and cooking and that clothes care, home maintenance/repairs, finance/home management, and child care were mostly shared. In contrast, Octavio reported that Olivia takes care of cooking, finances/home management, and clothes care. He rated housecleaning and child care tasks as about evenly split between her responsibility and shared; home maintenance/repairs, split between his responsibility and shared. In spite of spending so much time away from the house, both Octavio and Olivia commented that he spent considerable time with his sons. Octavio said, "I don't hang around with friends after work, so I can come home and spend time with my boys." Olivia also mentioned that when Octavio is around she has more freedom to do what she wants because Octavio keeps the boys occupied so that they don't get "bored."

When it comes to deciding how housework should be done, Olivia said that she makes a schedule that shows what needs to be done for the week. According to Olivia, "Octavio helps out, but I say what needs to be done." Octavio's version of their allocation procedures mirrored hers, though he was careful to specify that he had some discretion over which requests he would follow: "She tells me and then I decide what needs to be done, I do most of it." Both spouses indicated that decisions regarding the children were shared. For example, Olivia said, "In school, if they don't do what they are supposed to do, I let Octavio know, and we decide which privileges to take away."

Although Octavio is very involved with his children and helps Olivia with some of the housework, he has a rather traditional view of women's status. For instance, when asked if he thought women were disadvantaged in society, he remarked:

> No. I'm okay as long as women stay out of my affairs. Like today, I was at work doing what I'm supposed to be doing and the payroll secretary started getting smart about my job duties and I pretty much had to tell her to stay out of my business.

In contrast to his views on women and equal rights, he noted that fathers can provide the same kind of nurturance that mothers do. In addition, he said housework should be shared so that husbands and wives can have more time for each other.

The unique feature of this family is the husband's willingness to perform some nontraditional tasks to better the couple's relationship and his willingness and eagerness to spend some time with his sons. According to their accounts of the situation. Octavio was motivated to spend time with his children because he had lost his own parents at a young age and because he had few close friends. For Olivia, her husband's participation in child care afforded her a measure of freedom to do things for herself. Nevertheless, she shared Octavio's expectation that "proper" meals be placed before him, and only when he was away on reserve training did she allow herself to "slack off."

Semitraditional couples like Octavio and Olivia tended to describe themselves as being open to new roles as they adjusted to the daily realities of living in a dual-earner family with young children. Many of the fathers spent considerable time with their children, particularly if they were at least of school age and especially if they were boys. Although the men tended to do a few more household tasks as well, their contributions were still seen as "helping" their wives. Interesting, many of the men and women in these families saw the domestic division of labor as unfair. This was perhaps because most of the women also worked 40-hour jobs in addition to assuming most of the household chores.

Transitional Division of Labor

Miguel and Maria Marroquín

Miguel and Maria Marroquín have a rather unique work situation in that they are both employed full-time for the same firm as engineering technicians, and they have comparable annual salaries of $27,000. The Marroquíns are a close-knit family, and their free time is spent on family activities that are centered around their 7-year-old son. Miguel is 35 years old; Maria, 36. Both grew up in the Southwest, and they have been married for 13 years.

When questioned about their division of household labor, both Miguel and Maria reported that it was not rigidly segregated. However, like the Garcias and Obergons, they had different ideas of how much was shared and how much was performed by them individually. According to Maria, cleaning, cooking, and clothes care were primarily her responsibility; home maintenance/repairs where largely handled by Miguel; and finances/home management and child care were mostly shared. In contrast, Miguel said that Maria does most of the cooking and clothes care tasks; he takes care of the cleaning and home maintenance/repairs, and both take care of the finances/home management and child care. Like Jorge and Octavio, Miguel gives himself more credit for performing tasks that are traditional and repetitive than his wife does. When Miguel was asked whether he felt that the division of tasks was fair, he replied, "Probably not; I think I do more of the dirtier tasks." In striking contrast,

Maria had previously stated during her interview that "generally, I initiate things that need to be done, but Miguel won't clean the toilets."

According to this couple's accounts, Miguel sees child care as a more important part of his life than Maria does. For instance he commented that "I tend to think of myself as the more involved parent, and people seem to have noticed that too. I think its the worry-wart tendency. I tend to worry more about things than she does." Maria also noted Miguel's willingness to help with child care but saw public acknowledgment of his involvement in a different light: "My husband gets more praise than me, but this is because most men do not help out with child care and housework and so it gets noticed more." With reference to housework, Miguel said, "Maria has high standards for cleanliness, and I tend to acknowledge you can't always get it done."

Like Octavio in the semitraditional family, Miguel's intense focus on child care was discussed in terms of his childhood experiences. His parents divorced when he was young, and his mother had to go to work in a factory. He talked about his own work/family conflicts in light of his desire to "be in touch" with his son's life:

> It's hard to figure how I felt about my mother working. She seemed to take more of an interest in keeping the house immaculate. When she went to work, we ate a lot of TV dinners and visited my grandparents in a convalescent hospital. Being a father is something I want to do right. There was a lot of noninvolvement from my Dad—not intentional though. I want to be in touch with my son's life. I need to spend more time learning my job, but it's hard to do it because I want to spend time with my son.

Maria, on the other hand, grew up with two involved parents and still sees them frequently—at least several times a week when they lived a few miles away. She commented that being a mother was a very important part of her life, but she appeared less dependent on her parental role for self-esteem than Miguel did and had much more frequent contact with kin and friends. Although Maria reported that many of her friends though she was lucky to have a husband who shared family work with her, she tended to render his actions accountable by seeing them as what men should do: "In our situation, a caring husband has made it much easier for me. I wish more men were like that. They are not less of a man if they share. A real man should share. He is losing out if he does not participate." Note that, unlike mothers in traditional families, Maria did not take primary responsibility for facilitating father-child interaction because her husband was doing it on his own. Although she was less compelled to be the total homemaker than were wives in semitraditional couples, she still ended up doing most of the cleaning, cooking, and clothes care. In his view, however, most tasks were shared.

The few transitional couples seemed to be engaged in a subtle battle over the definition of the situation. For her, the important focus was some minimal levels of cleanliness and his inability to notice what "obviously" needed doing. For him, the focus was on her "high" standards and his "realistic" assessment of what could get done. For Miguel, an intense focus on child care and a desire to "do it right" or "be in touch" are balanced by her commitment to career and valued social contacts. What we thus see in the transitional couples is a convergence of some of the work/family conflicts for husbands and wives. Concerns that were once experienced only by mothers are now surfacing for fathers in the child-centered dual-earner families. Some of the worry about child well-being and individual career advancement is now shared between husband and wife.

In transitional families, however, wives still end up doing about two thirds of the housework. She notices it; he doesn't. She sees the disparity in task performance; he basks in admiration for being such a wonderful father. In general, the couples in this category are in a state of flux. More and more issues about family work and appropriate behavior become open for negotiation, and resentment is fairly common. As mothers acknowledge their individual needs by pursuing careers, fathers nurture themselves by developing an emotional rapport with their children. Few report that the changes they are going through are easy, and most do not claim to have found a solution that satisfies both of them. They do agree, however, that what they are attempting is superior to a traditional approach. They also tend to frame their understanding of what they are doing in terms of benefits to children, and they emphasize the beauty of two parents having full and caring relationships with the children.

Nontraditional Division of Labor

Carlos and Cristina Cadena

In contrast to the other families, Carlos and Cristina Cadena appear to have set clear guidelines about the distribution of child care and house work early in the relationship. This is reflected in Cristina's comment about why they decided to share: "When we started thinking about having children, I did not want to stay home and be a traditional wife, and to survive I knew I had to let Carlos know this." Carlos and Cristina have two children, ages 10 and 12. Carlos is a 38-year-old self-employed general contractor who earns $30,000 per year. Cristina is 37 years old and works full-time as an executive director for a nonprofit agency, earning

$37,000 per year. Not only did Carlos and Cristina report that they shared more tasks than did the other couples, but they tended to agree on who did what or even to overestimate the partner's contributions. For instance, both agreed that activities associated with cleaning, cooking, clothes care, and child care were shared. Cristina said Carlos took care of most of the household maintenance/repairs, whereas he said that they were shared equally. Both agreed that finances/home management was Cristina's responsibility.

When asked about who decides how housework should be done, Cristina replied, "I initiated a system several years ago—like for who cleans a specific room—but generally, I have to do the reminding." Carlos agreed that Cristina decides what needs to be done about child care and housework. Cristina asserted that her career and child care were about equally important to her. She commented that she felt "lucky" because, unlike most women, she had been able to work and advance up the career ladder and to combine that with motherhood without feeling guilty. She feels she received considerable respect from family and friends because of her career and is therefore somewhat exempt from sanctions that those in her social network might apply to less successful women.

Carlos remembers that when Cristina first started earning more money, it was rather difficult for him to accept this situation because he had always felt that the man should be the main breadwinner. However, when he went back to school he was exposed to new ideas and began to accept more flexible gender roles. Additionally, when he realized that two solid incomes meant they could purchase nice things for the home and family, he began to feel less concerned about who made more money. When interviewed, Carlos and Cristina were remodeling their spacious home situated on several acres of land.

Carlos and Cristina are the only couple from our sample in which the wife earned more than the husband. They are also unique in that Cristina did not hesitate to let Carlos know from the beginning that she wanted to combine a career with a family. Although Carlos resisted in the beginning, when he saw the benefits of combining two incomes with family life, he began to accept more responsibility for child care and housework. Only one other couple in the 20 we interviewed could be classified as having a truly shared division of household labor. In that case as well, the wife enjoyed a well-paying job and was willing to negotiate to lessen her burden at home. Although agreement was not complete in that couple, they too had relatively similar perceptions of who did what around the house. With more equal performance of household tasks, we assume that husbands "see" more of what goes on with housework and child care and are thus more likely to agree with wives about who does what.

Discussion

What is particularly intriguing about our general findings is the lack of agreement between spouses. Wives would repeatedly list a housework or child care task as being performed principally by themselves, whereas husbands would list the task as shared. This pattern was especially likely for frequently performed tasks of short duration that are stereotypically performed by one gender.

The authors speculate that two cognitive processes are at work. First, vivid events are easier to recall and secondly, people tend to overestimate their own contributions. We agree with Nesbett and Ross (1980) who suggest that vivid and rare events are more likely to be recalled than events that are everyday and commonplace. What could be more common than wiping the kitchen counter or putting away the dishes for the hundredth time this month? Thus, mundane housework activities are probably not likely to be precisely attended to, stored, or retrieved. This cognitive bias leads to possibilities for overestimating one's own contributions to these routine everyday tasks. As Thompson and Kelley (1981) point out, memory distortions or miscalculations can often be ego-enhancing. In general, the direction of error, if we can so label the lack of fit between husbands' and wives' perceptions of household labor, can often be ego-enhancing. That is, people tend to overestimate their own contributions to these short repetitive tasks that appear insignificant.

In our sample, husbands believed they had nontraditional family roles because they were "seeing" more sharing than their wives were. These differences in perception were further conditioned by two important factors: gender ideology and perceptions of equity. Most husbands viewed themselves as nontraditional and open to new conceptions of appropriate roles for men and women. This probably encouraged the men to overestimate their housework contributions and thus bring their behavioral reports inline with their egalitarian ideology. For wives, on the other hand, it was probably not so easy to ignore the realities of the household division of labor, in spite of wishing it were otherwise. In their case, an intimate familiarity with the mundane details of every aspect of running a household probably made these activities vivid, and their salience may have been enhanced by the lack of time available to accomplish them. This may have counteracted any tendency they might have had to romanticize by claiming that their egalitarian ideals were actually being enacted in everyday household labor.

Although husbands were significantly more likely than wives to rate household tasks as shared, both spouses were likely to claim that existing divisions of labor were unfair. Thirteen wives and 12 husbands indicated that current divisions of labor were not fair. One possible explanation is that even though the men tended to put more household task cards in their own stacks, when they had finished sorting, it was obvious that the wife's stacks were much taller. This perception, coupled with an ideology that things "should" be shared, probably encouraged husbands to acknowledge the unfairness of their current domestic task allocations.

For traditional, semitraditional, and some transitional couples, overestimating the contributions that one's spouse makes to household labor was rare, but it did occur for the task of maintaining social contacts. The one task that men listed as performed by wives more often than the wives themselves did was writing or phoning relatives and friends. The role of "kin-keeper" has been perceived as the wife's obligation in the familistic tradition of Chicano couples, and this overestimation may reflect the husband's belief in the appropriateness of the traditional arrangement. Another interesting finding is that one of the only stereotypically "women's" tasks that was consistently ranked as shared was ironing. This may also reflect the husband's concern for presenting a proper image to the outside world, and he might be motivated to iron his best shirts or children's nicest clothes in order to show his stature in the community. Ironing is also a task that some of the men reported that they could do while watching sporting events on television.

In a famous passage, the sociologist Jesse Bernard (1972) asserted that every marital union contains two marriages—"his" and "hers." What we found from our interviews, observations, and survey techniques was that most of the husbands and wives did indeed live in separate worlds. She saw the mundane reality of daily housework as an ever-present burden that she had to shoulder herself or delegate to someone else. Although many wives did not expect the current division of labor to change, they did acknowledge its asymmetry. The men, on the other hand, tended to minimize the asymmetry by seeing many of the short, repetitive tasks associated with housekeeping as shared activities.

This difference in perception corresponds to the common complaint from wives: he just doesn't see when things need doing or take responsibility for initiating the important details of housekeeping. This "not seeing" serves to perpetuate the men's favored positions within their families. Even in the transitional or nontraditional families, most wives remained in control of setting schedules and generating lists for domestic chores. This also enabled men to underestimate their wives' contributions and to escape the full range of tensions and strains that come with having full responsibility for the "second shift." Not seeing what needed to be done and not seeing the extent of their wives' contributions to household labor protected male privilege.

Nevertheless, some shifts were noticeable in the changing terrain of work/family responsibilities. Many child care tasks were shared, and fathers uniformly spent more time in direct interaction with their children than their own fathers had done with them. In the more traditional families, the wives still exercised control over all child care and facilitated father-child interaction. In other families, however, the fathers themselves were initiating and sustaining regular contact with their children. In some cases, the fathers' commitments to spending more time with their children created work/family conflicts that have been associated only with mothers. At least some child care tasks were shared in every family, and a few families divided responsibility for the children approximately equally. Because of a traditional emphasis on children's well-being and family solidarity in Chicano families and because of a general cultural shift toward acceptance of hands-on fathering, this may be one of the first areas in which we will see widespread sharing in Chicano households. The other aspect of sharing confirmed by this study was in the area of family decision making, where both spouses reported that things like finances and major purchases were jointly discussed and agreed on.

One of the power dynamics that underlies the division of labor in these families is the relative earning power of each spouse. In three fourths of the families, the husband earned substantially more than the wife did. In three families, the husbands made only slightly more money than the wives did, and two families, wives earned at least as much as their husbands did. Significantly, it was among these income-balanced couples that we found the most equal divisions of labor. We are not suggesting a simple or straightforward exchange of market resources for domestic services, but the resource/power differentials we observed do help us to understand why some wives were willing to push a little harder for change in the division of household labor. Only when wives explicitly took the initiative to shift some of the housework burden to husbands did the men begin to assume significant responsibility for the day-to-day operation of the household.

Although our small nonrandom sample limits our conclusions, we find support for power/resource models of household labor allocation. Wives earning less money, working fewer hours, holding less prestigious jobs, having less education, or being much younger than their husbands were the most likely to feel responsible for all of the housework and child care. Wives with less power had less choice about paying attention to dirty floors, dirty clothes, or hungry children. Husbands generally had more resources and power and, backed by gender stereotypes, were able to avoid seeing the little things that needed doing around the house. The men's inattention helped sustain the belief that household labor was shared.

REFERENCES

Baca Zinn, M. (1980). Employment and education of Mexican American Women: The interplay of modernity and ethnicity in eight families. *Harvard Education Review, 50*, 47–62.

Baca Zinn, M. (1982, Summer). Qualitative methods in family research: A look inside the Chicano families. *California Sociologist*, pp. 58–79.

Baca Zinn, M., & Eitzen, D. (1987). *Diversity in American families.* New York: Harper and Row.

Barnett, R. C., & Baruch, G. K. (1987). Determinants of fathers' participation in family work. *Journal of Marriage and the Family, 49*, 29–40.

Bean, F. D., Curtis, R. L., Jr., & Marcum, J. P. (1977). Familism and marital satisfaction among Mexican Americans: the effects of family size, wife's labor force participation, and conjugal power. *Journal of Marriage and the Family, 39*, 759–767.

Berheide, C. (1984). Women's work in the home: Seems like old times. *Marriage and Family Review, 7*, 37–55.

Berk, S. F. (1985). *The gender factory: The apportionment of work in American households.* New York: Plenum.

Bernard, J. (1972). *The future of marriage.* New York: World.

Blumberg, R. L. & Coleman, M. T. (1989). A theoretical look at the gender balance of power in the American culture. *Journal of Family Issues, 10*(2), 225–250.

Chafetz, J. S. (1988). The gender division of labor and the reproduction of female disadvantage. *Journal of Family Issues, 9*(1), 108–131.

Chodorow, N. J. (1978). *The reproduction of mothering: Psychoanalysis and the sociology of gender.* Berkeley: University of California Press.

Coltrane, S. (1989). Household labor and the routine production of gender. *Social Problems, 36*, 473–490.

Coltrane, S. (1990). Birth timing and the division of labor in dual-earner families. *Journal of Family Issues, 11*(2), 157–181.

Coverman, S. & Sheley, J. (1986). Change in men's housework and child-care time, 1965–1975. *Journal of Marriage and the Family, 48*, 413–422.

Cromwell, V., & Cromwell, R. (1978). Perceived dominance in decision-making and conflict resolution among black and Chicano couples. *Journal of Marriage and the Family, 40*, 749–759.

Crouter, A. Perry-Jenkins, M., Huston, T., & McHale, S. (1977). Processes underlying father involvement in dual-earner and single-earner families. *Developmental Psychology, 23*, 431–440.

Dinnerstein, D. (1976). *The mermaid and the minotaur.* New York: Harper and Row.

Ehrensaft, D. (1987). *Parenting together.* New York: Free Press.

Eisenstein, Z. (1981). *The radical future of feminism.* New York: Longman.

Garcia-Bahne, B. (1977). La Chicana and the Chicano family. In R. Sanchez (Ed.), *Essays on la mujer*, (pp. 30–47). Los Angeles: UCLA Press.

Hartmann, H. (1981). The family as the locus of gender, class, and political struggle. *Signs, 6*, 366–394.

Hartzler, K. & Franco, J. N. (1985). Ethnicity, division of household tasks and equity in marital roles: A comparison of Anglo and Mexican American couples. *Hispanic Journal of Behavioral Sciences, 7*(4), 333–344.

Hawkes, G. R., & Taylor, M., (1975). Power structure in Mexican and Mexican-American farm labor families. *Journal of Marriage and the Family, 37*, 807–811.

Hess, B., & Markson, E. W., & Stein, P. S. (1991). *Sociology.* New York: Macmillan.

Hiller, D. V., & Philiber, W. W. (1986). The division of labor in contemporary marriage: Expectations, perceptions, and performance. *Social Problems, 33,* 191–201.

Hochschild, A. (1989). *The second shift: Working parents and the revolution at home.* New York: Viking.

Kamo, Y. (1988). Determinants of household labor: Resources, power, and ideology. *Journal of Family Issues, 9,* 177–200.

Keefe, S. E., & Padilla, A. M. (1987). *Chicano ethnicity.* Albuquerque: University of New Mexico Press.

Kessler, R. & McCrae, J. (1982). The effects of wives' employment on the mental health of married men and women. *American Sociological Review, 47,* 216–227.

Kimball, G. (1988). *50–50 parenting: Sharing family rewards and responsibilities.* Lexington, MA: Lexington Books.

Lamb, M. E., Pleck, J. H., & Levine, J. A. (1986). Effects of paternal involvement of fathers and mothers. In *Marriage and Family Review, 9: 67–83.*

LaRossa, R., & LaRossa, M. (1981). *Transition to parenthood.* Beverly Hills, CA: Sage.

Miller, J., & Garrison, H. H. (1982). Sex roles: The division of labor at home and in the workplace. *Annual Review of Sociology, 8,* 237–262.

Mindel, C. H. (1980). Extended familism among urban Mexican-Americans, Anglos and blacks. *Hispanic Journal of Behavioral Sciences, 2,* 21–34.

Mirandé, A. (1988). Chicano fathers: Traditional perceptions and current realities. In P. Bronstein and C. Cowan (Eds.), *Fatherhood today: Men's changing role in the family* (pp. 3–28). New York: Wiley.

Nisbett, R., & Ross, L. (1980). *Human inference: Strategies and shortcomings of social judgment.* Englewood Cliffs, NJ: Prentice-Hall.

Pleck, J. H. (1983). Husband's paid work and family roles: Current research issues. In H. Lopata & J. Pleck (Eds.), *Research in the interweave of social roles* (pp. 251–333). Greenwich, CT: Jai Press.

Radin, N., & Russell, G. (1983). Increased father participation and child development outcomes. In M. Lamb & A. Sagi (Eds.), *Fatherhood and family policy* (pp. 191–218). Hillsdale, NJ: Erlbaum.

Robinson, J. (1988). Who's doing the housework. *American Demographics, 10,* 24–28, 63.

Ross, C. & Mirowsky, J. (1987), August. *Children, child care, and parents' psychological well-being.* Paper presented at the annual meeting of the American Sociological Association, New York.

Ross, C., Mirowsky, J., & Huber, J. (1983). Marriage patterns and depression. *American Sociological Review, 48,* 809–823.

Segura, D. (1984). Labor market stratification: The Chicana experience. *Berkeley Journal of Sociology, 29,* 57–91.

Staines, G. L., & Libby P. L. (1986). Men and women in role relationships. In R. D.

Ashmore & F. K. DelBoca (Eds.), *The social psychology of female-male relations: A critical analysis of central concepts* (pp. 211–258). New York: Academic Press.

Szinovacz, M. (1987). Family power. In M. B. Sussman & S. K. Steinmetz (Eds.), *Handbook of marriage and the family* (pp. 651–693). New York: Plenum.

Thompson, L. & Walker, A. J. (1989).Gender in families. *Journal of Marriage and the Family*, 51: 845–871.

Thompson, S. C. & Kelly, H. H. (1981). Judgment of responsibility for activities in close relationships: *Journal of Personality and Social Psychology*, 41, 469–477.

Vanek, J. (1974). Time spent in housework. *Scientific American*, 231, 118–120.

West, C., & Zimmerman, D. H. (1987). Doing gender. *Gender and Society, 1*, 125–151.

Williams, N. (1988). Role making among married Mexican American women: Issues of class and ethnicity. *Journal of Applied Behavioral Science, 24*(2): 203–217.

Williams, N. (1990). *The Mexican American family: Tradition and change*. New York: General Hall.

Ybarra, L. (1982). When wives work: The impact on the Chicano family. *Journal of marriage and the Family, 44*, 169–178.

Zavella, P. (1987). *Women's work and Chicano families: Cannery workers of the Santa Clara Valley*. Ithaca, NY: Cornell University Press.

■ 10
Employment among African-American Mothers in Dual-Earner Families: Antecedents and Consequences for Family Life and Child Development

Vonnie C. McLoyd

Historically, African-American mothers have been exempt from the role of economic provider with far less frequency than Anglo-American mother have.[1] Rarely afforded the luxury of motherhood or housewifery as full-time, female "occupations," theirs is history marked by high rates of productive labor outside the home, combined with domestic and child care responsibilities (Collins, 1987). Until the early 1950s, black married mothers were in paid employment at double the rate of white married mothers (Beckett, 1976). Race differences in mothers' rates of employment grew smaller during the subsequent decades as a result of the unprecedented entry of white mothers into the labor force, the lower rates of labor force participation among never married black mothers (compared to their white counterparts), and the increased concentration of never married black mothers as a proportion of all black mothers (Jones, 1986; Malveaux, 1985; Sweet & Bumpass, 1987). By 1991, black mothers with

*The author gratefully acknowledges the generous and able assistance of Eve Trager, Sheba Shakir, and Tony White in the preparation of this chapter.

children under 18 years of age had a labor force participation rate of 66.1%, compared to a rate of 66.9% for white mothers (U.S. Bureau of Labor Statistics, 1992).

Although the racial gap in mothers' overall labor force participation rate has closed, this development is far from the whole story. Three points in particular warrant mention. First, race differences continue to exist in the occupational distribution of women. Black women are over-represented in less lucrative occupations. Compared to white women, they are more likely to be employed in service occupations (27% vs. 16.1% in 1989) and less likely to be employed in managerial and professional occupations (18.8% vs. 27.4% in 1989) (U.S. Bureau of the Census, 1991a). Second, black women typically are more than twice as likely as white women to be unemployed, that is, seeking but unable to find employment. In 1989, the unemployment rate for white women was 4.5% but 11.4% for black women (U.S. Bureau of the Census, 1991b). Recent survey data also indicate that rates of job displacement are higher, duration of unemployment is longer, and rates of reemployment are lower among black women, compared to their white counterparts (Kletzer, 1991).

Third, substantial race differences in rates of maternal employment are evident when married mothers are distinguished from single mothers. In 1991, 76.5% of black wives with children under 18 were in the labor force, compared to 66.2% for comparable white wives. As has been true for decades, the race differential is largest among those with preschool children. In 1991, the employment rates for black wives and white wives with children under 6 years were 71.5% and 57.5%, respectively. However, among wives with children between 14 and 17 years of age, the rates for blacks and whites were virtually identical (73.2% vs. 74.5%, respectively) (U.S. Bureau of the Census, 1991b; U.S. Bureau of Labor Statistics, 1992). These patterns of maternal employment reflect the tendency of black married mothers to work continuously, regardless of the presence of preschool children, in contrast to the tendency of a substantial proportion of white mothers to withdraw from the labor force when they have preschool children and return to the labor force when the youngest child enters school or when the children are older (Beckett, 1976; Blau & Robins, 1989; Eccles & Hoffman, 1984).

The race disparity in single mothers' labor force participation is opposite that for married mothers. That is, black single mothers have a lower rate of employment than their white counterparts (in 1991, 59.6% vs. 69.8%, respectively) (U.S. Bureau of Labor Statistics, 1992). This is partly due to the fact that black single mothers are younger and less well educated than their white counterparts; hence, they often have not acquired the skill and experience necessary to hold many of today's better-paying jobs. Also contributing to this disparity is the tendency of black single mothers to have more children under 18 and to never marry. Never married mothers tend to have lower rates of employment than formerly married mothers (Johnson & Waldman, 1983). Traditionally, race disparities in the employment rates of single mothers have been greatest among never married mothers. However, patterns of employment rates among single mothers may be in a state of transition because in 1991 the race disparity was greatest among formerly married mothers (i.e., widows and divorcees) (Jones, 1986; U.S. Bureau of Labor Statistics, 1992). Also worthy of note is the fact that among black mothers, those who are married have higher labor force participation rates than those who are single, whereas among whites, the reverse is true (Tienda & Glass, 1985; U.S. Bureau of Labor Statistics, 1992). These observations should not obscure the fact that, contrary to popular perception, *within* each marital status category, including the *never married* category, the majority of black mothers with children under 18 are currently in the labor force (U.S. Bureau of Labor Statistics, 1992).

This chapter presents an integrative summary of what is known about employment among black married mothers, highlighting both recent research and critical gaps in our knowledge base. It focuses attention on the confluence of factors that have contributed to the tendency of black married mothers to work in disproportionate numbers, compared to white married mothers, and considers the impact of maternal employment in black dual-earner families on mothers' psychological functioning, family life, and children's development. Significant gaps exist in research-based knowledge about these issues, and they are noted and necessarily reflected in this review. Stimulated in large part by the controversial "black matriarchy" thesis popularized by Moynihan (1965), the decade of the 1970s witnessed a burgeoning of research on the antecedents and consequences of employment among black wives. This trend, however, was short-lived. The decade of the 1980s was marked by an impressive growth in research studies on the family lives of black Americans and a discernible shift away from the stereotypic negative focus of black family studies (Demos, 1990; Taylor, Chatters, Tucker & Lewis, 1990), but remarkably few of these studies explored the work-family nexus or basic issues of family and child functioning as they relate to parental work. To the extent that these issues were set apart for empirical study, investigations tended to focus on groups distinguished by relatively low rates of labor force participation (e.g., adolescent mothers, mothers on welfare) and family-related factors acting as a deterrent to this employment pattern (e.g., household composition, availability of day care). This neglect, noted by other scholars as well (Spitze, 1988), is all the more perplexing given the continued prominence of paid employment in the lives of black mothers and the recent explosion of research on psychological functioning and family relations among white women who occupy multiple roles (e.g., Barnett & Baruch, 1985; Baruch & Barnett, 1986; Hoffman, 1989; Kandel, Davies, & Raveis, 1985; Spitze, 1988; Thompson & Walker, 1989).

The chapter is divided into five sections. The first section presents a historical overview of black women's labor force participation. With the discussion of historical forces as a backdrop and anchor, we examine in the second section interlocking and more proximal antecedents of the higher rates of maternal employment among blacks, including economic pressure, role modeling, direct training, and cultural norms. Attention is also given to the psychological variables that mediate the link between these factors and maternal employment. The third section focuses on the impact of black mothers' employment, as well as unemployment, on psychological functioning. The fourth section examines links between maternal employment and various domains of familial relations, including marital relations, division of household labor, and family role strain. Finally, the influence of maternal employment on black children's development is discussed.

A TRADITION OF PRODUCTIVE LABOR: HISTORICAL INFLUENCES

Intense participation in productive labor is a common thread that runs throughout the history of black women and mothers, with the collective experience of each historical epoch apparently reinforcing the economic role that existed in a prior period. Because of space limitations, only brief comment about each of these periods is possible.

Pre-Diaspora

Women in West Africa, an area where a considerable amount of the North American slave trading occurred, played important economic functions as traders in village markets and as administrators in political and economic affairs. Most notable were the women of the Akan-Ashanti tribes of Ghana, the Dahomeans, the Yoruba of western Nigeria, and the Bini of eastern Nigeria. Some became independently wealthy as a result of their entrepreneurial endeavors (Herskovits, 1958; Ladner, 1971). West African women often did field work as well, assuming primary responsibility for tilling (but not clearing) the soil and cultivating the crops. It is difficult to generalize further about their role in agriculture because those captured for the North American slave trade came from different hoe-culture economies. For example, men and women of the Ibo tribe worked together in planting, weeding, and harvesting, whereas among the Yoruba, women only helped with the harvest (Jones, 1985).

Slavery

Because the sexual division of labor varied among tribes, it has proved impossible to ascertain the effect of West African culture on slaves' perceptions of women's agricultural work (Jones, 1985). What is certain, however, is that slave women did double duty, tending their children, cooking, sewing, and cleaning house, all after putting in a full day of labor for the master. Daily household maintenance tasks were completed either very early in the morning, before the start of the "regular" workday on the plantation, or at night, after other family members had gone to sleep (Dill, 1988; Jones, 1985). Black men were not the main providers or authority figures in slave families and were systematically deprived of the responsibilities and privileges of normative masculine roles in American culture. The practice of selling away fathers left mothers as the prime authority in households, and even when males were present, slave masters all but negated their role as fathers and husbands. Women who bore large numbers of children were accorded high status because of the children's financial value, but they were equal to men in the oppression and burdens of labor they suffered during slavery (Davis, 1981; Staples, 1970). Female slaves were subjected not only to whippings and mutilations by white men but to rape as well. Davis (1981) has argued convincingly that the institutionalized pattern of rape during slavery was not simply an expression of white men's sexual urges but a weapon of domination and repression intended to extinguish slave women's will to resist the institution of slavery and to demoralize slave men.

Postslavery

After emancipation, the sexual division of labor among blacks sharpened along traditional lines. Evoking bitter criticism and complaints from white employers, freed wives of ablebodied husbands greatly reduced their participation in field labor and devoted more time to child rearing and domestic duties. Many black husbands, wishing to protect their wives from the abuses of the slave system, were unrelenting and vehement in their refusal to allow their wives to work as field hands and servants for white families (Gutman, 1976; Jones, 1985). That married women with children had lower levels of paid employment than those of single women, married women without children, and women with children but without resident husbands is borne out by census data. For example, an 1866 Freedmen's Bureau census of the occupations of over 500 ex-slave women in a single county of Virginia indicated that 47% of the married women with children listed occupations, compared to 74% of women in all other statuses (Gutman, 1976). Overall, three of four women listed occupations, virtually all servants and washerwomen. Many black wives continued to work in the fields, as they had done during slavery, but in accordance to the needs and priorities established by their own families rather than in response to the demands of a slave master. Seasonal changes partly governed wives' involvement in field labor. At planting and harvesting time, they joined their husbands and children in agricultural labor; at other times, some wives supplemented family income by hiring out to white planters to pick cotton for a daily wage. In areas where black husbands could find additional work during the year—for example, in mines, in mills, and on rice plantations—black wives and children were left to tend crops (Jones, 1985).

For the most part, black women who did not toil in the fields were forced to work as domestic servants and laundresses, occupations that bore the stamp of slavery (Davis, 1981). Data from the 1890 census indicate that more than a million of the 2.7 million black girls and women over the age of 10 worked for wages: 38.7% in agriculture, 30.8% in household domestic service, 15.6% in laundry service, and 2.8% in manufacturing. It would be several decades before black women escaped domestic service in significant numbers (Davis, 1981). (By 1960, the proportion of black women in household domestic service had dropped to about 35% and between 1960 and 1981, most moved out of domestic service and into clerical jobs [Malveaux, 1985]).

By the end of the 19th century, 9 of 10 blacks lived in the South, and 80% of these resided in rural areas, primarily in the cotton belt. In 1910, 90% of all southern blacks who made their living from the soil worked as tenants, sharecroppers, or contract laborers, the lowest positions in the economic hierarchy. Not owning their own equipment and unable to market their crop independently of the landlord, most barely eked out enough in cotton to pay for rent, food, and supplies. The dire economic situation associated with tenant farming rendered black women's productive labor essential to the family's survival. Cotton cultivation and harvesting were so labor-intensive and crucial to the family's well-being that they typically laid claim on the labor of every ablebodied person in the household, including wives, taking priority over all but the most vital household chores (Jones, 1985). In addition to domestic responsibilities and field work, many black wives in rural areas engaged in petty moneymaking activities (e.g., selling eggs, vegetables, milk). During the 1890s and early 1900s, rural white wives and mothers were exempted from neither grinding poverty nor wage labor, but the racial caste system rendered both circumstances far less probable for them than for their black counterparts (Dill, 1988; Jones, 1985).

This racial disparity in wage labor was even more evident in urban areas, where black women, unlike their sharecropping counterparts, relied almost exclusively on wage labor to support their families and supplement their husbands' incomes. In the early 1900s, 50% to 70% of all adult black females in the largest southern cities were gainfully employed at least part of the year, working primarily as domestic servants and laundresses. Urban married black women had a labor force participation rate five times that of white wives, and urban single black women were three times more likely to be employed than were comparable white women (Jones, 1985).

The Great Migration

Seeking relief from the oppressive sharecropping system, low wages, disfranchisement, Jim Crow Laws, and a plague of boll weevils destroying cotton crops, 2 million blacks left the South and moved to cities in the industrial Northeast and Midwest between 1900 and 1930 (Jones, 1985). It was a bittersweet experience, for although blacks earned higher wages, and could vote and participate in politics, and their children had expanded opportunities for schooling, they were not to escape the racial caste system that relegated them to the lowest rungs of the occupational and social hierarchy. In the manufacturing and industry sectors where most traditionally male jobs were located, employers preferred white foreign-born immigrants to blacks, the latter accorded employment opportunities only after the supply of immigrant labor lessened. Black women, systemically excluded from the sales and clerical sectors and desperate for income, resorted to domestic work. Especially because of the sporadic and chronically low wages of black men and hence the need for supplementary breadwinners in the household, the job discrimination against black wives and mothers was a crucial factor in inhibiting the upward mobility of their families. After World War I, almost two thirds of all gainfully employed black women in the North worked as servants and laundresses, excluding those who worked in commercial laundries. Black women constituted more than one fifth of all domestics in New York and Chicago and over one half in Philadelphia. In 1920, fully 90% of all black women living in Pittsburgh made their living as day workers (private household workers who return to their own homes at night), washerwomen, or live-in servants. Their labor force participation rate continued to exceed that of white women, hovering between 50% and 60% (Jones, 1985).

A phenomenon of particular interest during this time was the tendency of black wives to work at rates far exceeding those of immigrant wives of roughly the same socioeconomic class. Few foreign-born wives in northern cities took jobs outside the home, except those in New England mill towns. For example, census data indicate that in 1920, only 10% of immigrant wives in the Northeast and Midwest were gainfully employed

(Gutman, 1976; Jones, 1985). Pleck (1978) has speculated at length about the reasons for the differential that existed between Italian-American and African-American wives in particular. Her arguments are reviewed here briefly because the cultural factors she highlights continue to be implicated in the employment patterns of contemporary black married mothers. Pleck concedes that being of the same socioeconomic class during the 1920s did not necessarily equate African-American and Italian-American families materially. Although men in both groups suffered low wages and chronic unemployment, African-American men were much less likely to have jobs in skilled trades with opportunities for advancement (Gutman, 1976; Pleck, 1978). But even taking these economic differences into account, argues Pleck, there appear to be residual race differences in women's rates of labor force participation, traceable to the slave experience and its impact on husband-wife relations, patterns of child rearing, and parental attitudes toward children's education. First, according to Pleck, African-American wives respected their ability to assist the family as a result of laboring in the fields and caring for their family in their husbands' absence. Realizing their instrumental competence, they felt a responsibility to secure paid employment to help ameliorate the family's financial problems. Italian-American wives, on the other hand, perhaps did not define a higher standard of living as a family goal, or if they did, they may have believed that it was the responsibility of the husband and older children. Second, Pleck contends, because slave women were accustomed to having elderly black nurses and older children care for their young and typically trained their children to be independent and self-reliant at an early age, they did not equate good parenting with being home with their children. Italian-American wives, in contrast, believed in close supervision—a properly raised Italian child was never left alone—a view that precluded maternal employment outside the home. Finally, according to Pleck, African Americans placed much greater emphasis than did Italian Americans on a child's schooling as a means of meeting long-term family needs. Consequently, African Americans set aside their reluctance to engage in paid labor, often working extra hours to help educate their children. The virulent racial discrimination in the marketplace fostered a strong belief in education among African Americans and, at the same time, increased school attendance among African-American children by making it difficult for them to secure employment.

It is impossible to specify with any degree of precision the potency of the historical experiences reviewed here as determinants of the higher rate of labor force participation among contemporary black married mothers. However, the systematic racism and oppression experienced by blacks during these periods of history arguably operate as distal antecedents through two mechanisms: (1) their creation and maintenance of economic deprivation, a condition that typically pushes wives and mothers into the labor force, and (2) their encouragement of child socialization practices that render black females less traditional in their sex-role ideology and more disposed to assuming wage-earning responsibilities along with maternal and marital roles. The next section of this chapter examines these and other factors as proximal antecendents of employment among contemporary black wives with children.

PROXIMAL ANTECEDENTS OF RACE DIFFERENCES FOR MARRIED MOTHERS IN RATES OF EMPLOYMENT

Economic Need

Black wives with dependent children are more likely to work than are their white counterparts, partly because their economic disadvantage forces them to do so. Their hourly earnings and the hourly earning of their husbands are relatively lower than those of comparable white workers. Although it is true that black women have recently achieved income parity with white women (e.g., the annual income of black women rose from 62% of white women's income in 1960 to 98% of white women's income in 1989), it is also the case that this income parity was achieved because black women worked longer hours and had longer job tenure than did comparable white females. At every educational level, black women are more likely than white women to work full-time, full-year, and when they work part-time or at multiple jobs, it is more likely for the purpose of meeting regular household expenses than is the case for white women. In short, although the racial gap in women's annual earnings has closed, the gap in hourly earnings has not (Farley & Allen, 1987; Stinson, 1990; U.S. Bureau of the Census, 1991b). Viewed in this light, the assertion that black women have achieved economic equality with white women clearly is an overstatement (Malveaux, 1985).

The racial disparity in earnings among men, much greater than the one among women, is a major contributor to race differences in wives' labor force participation. Except when the husband's earnings are extremely low, the probability that a wife works increases with a decrease in the husband's earnings. This relation holds within levels of educational and family status (Sweet & Bumpass, 1987). In accord with this relation is an abundance of evidence that the increased rate of employment among black women is partly due to the unstable and depressed earnings of black husbands and ex-husbands. Black men typically experience unemployment at more than double the rate of white men at each level of education.

For example, in 1989, the unemployment rate for college-educated black men aged 25 to 64 was about three times the rate for white men (5.6% vs. 1.8%, respectively) (Meisenheimer, 1990).

Moreover, black men have been less able than white men to translate their educational achievements into more desirable occupations and greater remuneration. They earn less than white men do at each level of education (Gary, 1981; Geschwender & Carroll-Seguin, 1990; Meisenheimer, 1990). The racial gap in the median income of men aged 25 and over has consistently narrowed between 1960 and the present, but it continues to be substantial (Allen & Farley, 1986). In 1989, the median earnings of black men who were high school graduates and worked full-time, year-round, was 77% of the median earnings of comparable white men, whereas the black male/white male earnings ratio for those with 4 or more years of college was 76% (U.S. Bureau of the Census, 1991). The earnings gap among college-educated men is partly attributable to race differences in men's occupational distribution. Population survey data for 1989 indicate that college-educated black men are considerably less likely than their white counterparts to work in managerial and professional fields (53% vs. 66%, respectively) and more likely to work in lower-paying occupations that typically do not require a college degree (e.g., clerical work, other forms of administrative support, service, operators) (31% vs. 14%, respectively) (Meisenheimer, 1990). However, occupational differences do not fully account for the earnings gap because black men earn less than do their white counterparts even when working in the same occupation (Gary, 1981). Other factors that may contribute to race differences in men's earnings within educational level and within occupation are amount of training received on the job, local labor market factors, size and financial strength of employers, racial discrimination, and job performance (Meisenheimer, 1990).

It is clear that husband's depressed and unstable wages have forced black women to work in disproportionate numbers, compared to white women, but it is also the case that employment status among black wives is less sensitive than that of white wives to husbands' present income (Landry & Jendrek, 1978; Sweet, 1973). This may reflect two factors. First, black husbands' incomes are more likely to be below the income threshold that must be reached before this factor acts as a deterrent to wives' employment (Landry & Jendrek, 1978). Second, in their decision making with respect to employment and their families' economic fortunes, black wives may adopt a defensive, long-term perspective. Despite relatively high levels of current income garnered by their husbands, black wives may maintain a strong attachment to the labor force as a buffer against the greater instability and smaller lifetime accrual of their husbands' earnings (Beckett & Smith, 1981).

As a consequence of the depressed and unstable earnings of black men, the earnings of black wives, compared to those of their white counterparts, are and have been far more consequential to their families' economic well-being. This is documented by three overlapping types of evidence. First, the earnings of black wives constitute a much greater percentage of total family income than is the case among whites (Geschwender & Carroll-Seguin, 1990). In 1984, black wives contributed 35% to total family income, compared to 25% contributed by white wives (Tienda & Jensen, 1988). Second, the earnings of black wives result in a relatively greater improvement in the family's standard of living, compared to the earnings of white wives. For example, in 1987, the labor force participation of black wives improved median family income by 98% (from $16,822 to $33,333) compared to a 50% improvement associated with the labor force participation of white wives (from $27,394 to $41,023) (Geschwender & Carroll-Seguin, 1990). Third, the earnings of black wives are more crucial as a hedge against poverty than are the earnings of white wives. In 1984, 45% of black families would have been poor if only the husband worked, but if both husband and wife worked, this percentage dropped to 29%. Among white families, 33% would have been poor if only the husband worked, compared to 25% if both husband and wife worked (Tienda & Jensen, 1988). This is consistent with evidence from longitudinal research that drops in the work hours of wives in two-parent households are much more likely to push black children into poverty than is the case for white children (Duncan & Rodgers, 1988).

Collectively, these data indicate that whereas working wives make a difference in the economic well-being of all families, they clearly make a far greater difference for black families than for white families. The narrowing of the gap during the past two decades in the incomes of two-parent black families and two-parent white families is largely a function of the race differences in patterns of wives' participation in the paid labor force. In that sense, the claim that blacks have made considerable progress toward achieving economic equality with whites is grossly exaggerated (Geschwender & Carroll-Seguin, 1990). To the extent that two-parent black families are able to achieve a standard of living comparable to that of two-parent white families, it is largely because black wives are more likely to work and work full-time than are white wives (Geschwender & Carroll-Seguin, 1990). This reality is not lost on black college women about to enter the labor force. They expect to have family incomes comparable to those of whites, but they are far more likely than white women to expect to achieve this parity by working continuously following childbirth (Granrose & Cunningham, 1988).

Because of increased financial need, perhaps in combination with cultural factors, black wives' labor force participation is much less constrained by family factors than is white wives'. In particular, preference of the husband for the wife to remain at home and presence of preschool-age children (under 6 years of age) in the family deter black wives' labor force participation to a much lesser extent, if at all, than that of their white counterparts (Bell, 1974; Landry & Jendrek, 1978; Lehrer & Nerlove, 1986). Black wives whose husbands prefer that they stay home or are neutral about their wives working, as well as black wives with preschool-age children, have markedly higher rates of full-time employment than do comparable white wives. Race differences in the influence of young children on the labor force participation rates of married women do not appear to be accounted for by differences in work intensity, flexibility of working hours, marital instability, or availability of child care services from relatives and friends (Landry & Jendrek, 1978).

Some evidence exists that black married mothers *who are already in the labor force* are more likely than are comparable white mothers to rely on relatives for child care (Lehrer & Kawasaki, 1985), but most studies report no relation between race and child care arrangements after appropriate controls are introduced (Duncan & Hill, 1977; Lehrer, 1983). Moreover, there is no evidence that increased availability of child care services from relatives accounts for black wives' higher rates of *entry* into the labor force. A related question posed in recent investigations is whether nonnuclear adults in the household facilitate young mothers' labor force participation by providing child care and relieving domestic burdens. Living in an extended household, a circumstance more likely to characterize black women than white women (Floge, 1989; Wilson, 1989), enhances labor forces participation among single but not married mothers (Tienda & Glass, 1985). Indeed, in their analyses of population survey data, Tienda and Glass (1985) found that an increase in the number of nonnuclear adults in the household actually operated to depress the propensity of married mothers to enter the labor market. The proportion of nonnuclear adults who were female, employed, or over 70 years old bore no relation to rates of employment among married mothers. More recent evidence suggests that even among young single mothers it is the presence of *employed kin* in the household, rather than *nonemployed kin available to provide child care*, that predicts entry into the labor force (Parish, Hao, & Hogan, 1991).

Increased economic need contributes to but does not fully account for the higher rate of labor force participation among black married mothers. Currently, as in the past, race differences in married mothers' employment rates persist even after controlling for current income and husband's income (Mott & Shapiro [1978, cited in Granrose & Cunningham, 1988; Pleck, 1978; Sweet & Bumpass, 1987). Of course, this does not conclusively eliminate economic need as an antecedent because analysis of current income does not take into account instability of wages. In any case, it is likely that several social factors, such as role modeling, direct training, and social norms, contribute to black wives' increased tendency to assume wage-earning responsibilities along with their roles as mothers. Each of these processes is discussed in the next section. Although presented as such, these processes cannot be seen as independent of economic factors because, to some unknown extent, they clearly are adaptations to a history of economic oppression.

Role Modeling

Exposure to a working mother during childhood and adolescence predicts both intention to work during adulthood among female adolescents (Granrose & Cunningham, 1988; Macke & Mott, 1980) and actual employment among young mothers (Parish et al., 1991). Black children receive more exposure than do white children to mothers who work outside the home and to fathers who help with household tasks and child care (Beckett & Smith, 1981; Ericksen, Yancey, & Ericksen, 1979; Maret & Finlay, 1984; Ross, 1987). These findings, taken together, lend strong support to the view that higher labor force participation rates among black married mothers and increased supportiveness of maternal employment by their husbands are partly due to increased exposure during childhood and adolescence to working mothers and, in general, to less traditional or rigidly sex-stereotyped role models (Harrison, 1989; Reid, 1982).

Modeling also appears to be implicated in daughters' career orientations and aspirations to work in nontraditional jobs (Burlew, 1982; Lamb, 1982). Black women and men who hold doctorates in social and biological science tend to have educated mothers who were employed during their childhood (Reid & Robinson, 1985). These findings are reminiscent of Epstein's (1973) seminal study of black women who achieved occupational success in prestigious male-dominated professions. A consistent theme in these women's recollections was of a vital, instrumental mother who skillfully combined the mother–worker roles and offered a model of adult women different from that espoused in white culture. Only four of the mothers of these 30 women had never worked (one of the "nonworking" mothers had 13 children), and many of the 26 employed mothers were professionals or semiprofessionals.

Data also indicate that black female college students are more likely to choose a nontraditional major (pre-med, physical sciences, pre-law, engineering) rather than a traditional major (e.g., teaching, nursing, social work) if their mothers have been or are employed in nontraditional jobs (Burlew, 1982). Experience during childhood with stereotypically male tasks (e.g., tinkering with or repairing mechanical objects, building mechanical or electrical kits) can also increase women's proclivity toward nontraditional jobs. Both black mothers and white mothers employed in low-wage, traditionally female, clerical and administrative jobs express greater willingness to switch to higher-paying but physically demanding, traditionally male blue-collar jobs if, as children, they had greater exposure to tasks and experiences typically reserved for boys (Padavic, 1991).

Positive modeling effects of maternal employment, however, are not always found. Indeed, there is some suggestion that black girls have a weaker work orientation if their mothers hold highly undesirable jobs. Macke and Morgan (1978) found that 12th-grade black girls whose mothers worked in low-status, mostly domestic jobs were less likely to plan to work as adults than were black girls whose mothers did not work. This decreased tendency to emulate the mother is most likely mediated by the dissatisfaction mothers expressed about their jobs and the resulting desire of daughters to avoid the psychological, physiological, and social costs of employment exacted from their mothers.

Direct Training

The legacy of economic racism and discrimination casts a long and pervasive shadow on the family socialization of black children. It has effectively rendered full-time mothering a luxury beyond the reach of most black women. Black parents appear to do several things to prepare their daughters for this reality, among them (1) sending recurrent messages to daughters about the value of being economically independent and, conversely, the economic, psychological, and interpersonal hazards of being dependent on a man (Ladner, 1971; Schulz, 1969); (2) teaching and rewarding daughters for behavioral and psychological dispositions such as maturity, accelerated autonomy, and instrumental competence that are compatible with the provider role (Bartz & Levine, 1978; Baumrind, 1972); and (3) minimizing, but certainly not eliminating, differences in their treatment of sons versus daughters, relative to white parents (Lewis, 1978). Data from empirical studies confirm that black parents of preschools and elementary school children, compared to their white counterparts, are more likely to press for developmental acceleration of instrumental skills in their children, are less accepting of children's casual use of time (Bartz & Levine, 1978), and, among those with daughters, are more discouraging of infantile behavior (Baumrind, 1972).

Normative Approval of Maternal Employment

Compared to white women, black women expect and receive greater approval of paid employment, at least from some of their significant others. A recent study by Granrose and Cunningham (1988) found that black women were more likely than white women to believe that their mothers would approve of their decision to work shortly after childbirth. However, no race differences were found in the overall level of perceived normative approval or in women's perceptions of approval from their fathers, husbands, or friends. Subjective norms about work have been found to predict the work intentions of both black and white women (Granrose & Cunningham, 1988).

The evidence is even stronger that black men are more likely than white men to encourage, support, and approve of mothers' and wives' employment (Axelson, 1970; Beckett, 1976; Landrey & Jendrek, 1978; Scanzoni, 1975). Data published during the 1970s consistently indicated that middle-class and working-class black men, compared to their white counterparts, viewed women's employment more positively and endorsed more strongly the right of wives to have their own careers (Axelson, 1970; Beckett, 1976; Landrey & Jendrek, 1978). Furthermore, race differences persist when men are asked about women's employment, specifically with reference to the needs and behaviors of other family members. Black men express less support for the view that wives' occupational interests and aspirations should be secondary to the interests of husbands and children. They are more likely than white men to believe that husbands should make compromises and accommodations in the interest of the special needs of working wives (e.g., staying at home with a sick child, having a smaller family, being amenable to the wife's absence from home overnight because of work requirements) (Scanzoni, 1975). Support for women's employment may give way to normative pressures for women to work—specifically, the tendency to view women's employment as a responsibility. Given black husbands' more favorable attitude toward wives' employment, it is not surprising that they espouse this view more strongly than do white husbands. In fact, both black husbands and wives are more likely than their white counterparts to endorse the idea that ablebodied wives, mothers, and women in general should be expected to work (Huber & Spitze, 1981). This finding is in keeping with Pleck's (1978) hypothesis that black women have traditionally felt a greater responsibility than do white women to contribute to the family's income. Their sense of agency, nurtured by the independence training and experience as productive laborers, appears to both kindle this psychological disposition and enhance their ability to act on it.

Race differences also have been found to exist in men's beliefs about the effects of maternal employment on children and in their perception of their wives' ability to manage multiple roles. Research published during the 1970s indicated that black husbands, compared to white husbands, were less likely to believe that wives' employment would have a detrimental effect on school-age children. Furthermore, they consistently rated their wives higher in management (e.g., ability to organize things, manage households, handle a number of responsibilities) and in intellectual and caregiving abilities (e.g., taking care of and understanding children) (Alexson, 1970; Scanzoni, 1975). Research is needed to determine if these race differences in husbands' attitudes continue to exist or if they have been attenuated or obliterated by social and economic changes since the 1970s.

As intimated earlier, race differences in men's level of approval of women's and mothers' employment probably reflect, in part, differences in childhood experiences. Working mothers and wives, for example, traditionally have been no less salient as models in the lives of black boys than of black girls. These differences in men's attitudes probably also reflect the influence of wives' attitudes, as well as differences in the importance of wives' earnings to the family's economic well-being. In view of these considerations, it is not surprising that race differences in men's attitudes about women's employment parallel those found among women themselves. The next section addresses the latter issue.

Role Modeling, Direct Training, and Normative Support: Links to Race

Role models, direct training, and normative support influence work intentions and work efforts partly through their impact on expectancies and attitudes about work, sex-role attitudes, and behavioral orientations and self-perceptions associated with masculine and feminine roles (e.g., independence, assertiveness, instrumental competence, expressiveness). In keeping with this view is evidence that black women and white women differ in each of these domains.

Expectations and Attitudes about Work

Adolescent females' expectancies of paid employment in the future have been found to predict their labor force participation as adults (Macke & Morgan, 1978). By the time the typical black female reaches late adolescence, she is extraordinarily well primed for assuming a provider role and expects to combine it with the obligations associated with the maternal and marital roles (Collins, 1987; Macke & Morgan, 1978; Thomas, 1986). This was true long before the women's liberation movement of the 1970s (Ladner, 1971). In Malson's (1983) qualitative study of urban black women, for example, virtually all of the women said that when they were growing up they expected as adults to have jobs or careers as well as children, and very few envisioned life as a mother who did not work outside the home. Likewise, when asked about their future work plans, black girls in high school are more likely than their white counterparts to "plan to work all the time" and less likely to "plan to work after children have entered grade school" (Macke & Morgan, 1978). As college students, they report a stronger desire to maintain job contact, earn their own money, and advance their career following childbirth, compared to their white counterparts. They also are more likely than white female college students to anticipate boredom as a consequence of not working (Granrose & Cunningham, 1988).

Perhaps it is because the expectancy of employment is so well established during childhood and because models of working mothers and wives are so commonplace that black women tend to view employment as compatible with maternal and marital roles and express high levels of confidence in their ability to fulfill these three roles simultaneously and successfully (Beckett, 1976). Several studies confirm that black women, compared to white women, are less wedded to a traditional maternal role ideology (e.g., belief that a working mother is unable to establish as warm and secure a relationship with her children as is a mother who does not work, feeling that a preschool child is likely to suffer if the mother works) and have greater confidence in their ability to manage domestic tasks, have adequate time for their children, and raise secure, well-disciplined children while employed (Granrose & Cunningham, 1988; Macke & Morgan, 1978; Mednick & Puryear, 1975; Scanzoni, 1975). It is not surprising, then, that they are less likely than white women to anticipate feeling guilty if they work during the first 3 years after the birth of their first child (Granrose & Cunningham, 1988; Mednick & Puryear, 1975). Indeed, among employed black women, being a good provider is typically seen as a critical marker of successful motherhood (Myer, 1975).

The prospect of combining work and marital roles also appears less daunting to black women. Black women are less likely than white women to view their employment as interfering with the quantity and quality of interaction with their husbands (Granrose & Cunningham, 1988). In another interesting and related line of work, researchers have found that black women preparing for traditionally male-dominance fields (e.g., engineering, physical science, economics, pre-med, pre-law) do not think they are any less likely to marry than are their counterparts preparing for stereotypically female occupations (e.g., teaching, social work, nursing). Both groups anticipate a lifetime of work and express little worry about combining work and marriage (Burlew, 1982; Mednick & Puryear, 1975).

The centrality of work in the lives of black women appears to persist into old age. Elderly black women are less likely to retire than are white women, despite being eligible to receive a pension (Belgrave, 1988), and the personal narratives of those who are retired depict work as a life continuity that dominated their childhood and adulthood. Moreover, even in old age, the meaning and context of leisure are inextricably linked with work and helping others (Allen & Chin-Sang, 1990).

Sex-Role Attitudes and Behavioral Orientations/Self-Perceptions

Because of the paucity of relevant data, it is not possible, except in rare cases, to directly link parental socialization practices during the early years to developmental outcomes in black girls or to race differences in females' behavior and attitudes. Black girls do not appear to differ from white girls in their self-perceptions of competence and expressiveness nor in the extent to which their self-descriptions cohere with sex-role stereotypes (Romer & Cherry, 1980). Neither are they generally evaluated as being more competent than white girls. However, under certain child-rearing circumstances, black girls are rated as more independent and resistive than white girls (Baumrind, 1972). Furthermore, during the grade school years, they register higher occupational aspirations than do white girls and black boys (Dorr & Lesser, 1980), less sex-stereotyped perceptions of appropriate occupational roles for others, and more androgynous attitudes toward female behaviors than do white girls (Kleinke & Nicholson, 1979; Reid, 1982). Consistent with evidence that black parents make fewer gender distinctions in their socialization practices (Lewis, 1978), female-male differences in reported expressiveness have been found to be smaller among black adolescents than white adolescents (Balkwell, Balswick, & Balkwell, 1978). Similarly, black children perceive fewer differences in expressiveness between male and female sex roles than do white children (Romer & Cherry, 1980). Increased egalitarianism in children's sex-role attitudes is perhaps the most consistently demonstrated effect of maternal employment (Bloom-Feshbach, Bloom-Feshbach, & Heller, 1982),—an effect that has been demonstrated for black (Brookins, 1985) as well as white children (Gold & Andres, 1978; Marantz & Mansfield, 1977; Miller, 1975). Increased achievement among black girls has also been found to be associated with nontraditional sex-role training (Carr & Mednick, 1988).

Race differences among women varying widely in age and level of education echo some of the findings from studies of children. For example, black women perceive themselves as more responsible, instrumental (e.g., active, competitive, task-capable), and expressive (e.g., nurturant, supportive) than do white women (Scanzoni, 1975; Turner & Turner, 1982), and they are more likely than white women to identify themselves as androgynous (Binion, 1990). The pattern of race differences found among both girls and women is consistent with the contention that black married mothers' higher rate of employment is partially attributable to their less traditional and more flexible sex-role attitudes. Of course, these attitudes could also be reinforced, if not engendered, by the experience of employment. In addition to explaining higher rates of employment among black married mothers, these psychological factors may partially account for recent evidence from a study by Padavic (1991) of greater willingness among black mothers than white mothers to switch from low-wage, traditionally female clerical and administrative jobs to higher-paying but physically demanding, traditionally male blue-collar jobs that require rotating shift work. Race differences in economic need cannot be completely ruled out as an explanation for this finding because although personal income was controlled, family income was not. This limitation notwithstanding, it is certainly plausible that differences in sex-role attitudes and self-perceptions also contributed to black women's greater willingness to make the switch.

There is a peculiar and apparently discordant finding in an otherwise impressively consistent pattern of race differences in women's sex-role attitudes. Specifically, compared to white women, black women espouse a more traditional ideology about the marital role, *although support for such an ideology is relatively low among both groups*. Black women are more accepting of a submissive role vis-a-vis men (e.g., refrain from being too competitive with men, keeping the peace rather than showing a man he is wrong) and less resistant to the notion that marriage is the bedrock of women's identity (Binion, 1990; Gackenbach, 1978; Gump, 1975). Data also indicate that they are more likely to believe that wives should put the interests of husbands and children ahead of their own and that husbands should be head of the family and the major breadwinners (Scanzoni, 1975). Collectively, these findings suggest that black women's sex-role identity is a complex one, incorporating what appear to be contradictory ideology, behavior, and self-perceptions. Binion (1990) proposes that this uneasy coexistence is the product of competing demands. On the one hand, black women need to work; hence, androgynous behavior and dispositions that bolster survival and success in the marketplace have considerable functional value. On the other hand, they desire acceptance from black men and others within their domestic networks, receipt of which is often conditional on maintaining traditional marital beliefs and behavior. Moreover, it is very likely that black women's ideological dilemmas have been intensified by exposure to the contradictory assertions of the women's liberation movement and the black power movement (Gump, 1975). The latter movement has adopted a patriarchal ideology that decrees a self-effacing, submissive role for black women, exemplified by deferring to, supporting, and standing behind black men. This ideology, as well as black women's propensity to espouse it in the context of marriage, no doubt reflects sensitivity to the stigma of the popular matriarch image traditionally borne by black women (Gump, 1975; Staples, 1970).

EFFECTS OF EMPLOYMENT STATUS ON PSYCHOLOGICAL AND PHYSICAL WELL-BEING

Employment Versus Nonemployment

Warr and Parry's (1982) review of existing studies of white American and European samples led them to conclude that rarely is paid employment among mothers with children significantly related to psychological well-being, but when it is, the association is positive. A growing number of well-controlled studies report significant mental and physical health differences in favor of employed versus nonemployed women (Baruch, Biener, & Barnett, 1987), but it is not clear whether the preponderance of evidence indicates positive psychological effects among mothers. Unfortunately, investigations of this issue in samples of black mothers are rare and yield conflicting findings. In some studies of black mothers, paid employment predicts more positive physical and psychological well-being (Coleman, Antonucci, Adelman, & Crohan, 1987; Reskin & Coverman, 1985; Thompson & Ensminger, 1989), whereas in others it is unrelated to physical or psychological well-being or negatively associated with satisfaction with family life (Broman, 1991; Brown & Gary, 1988; Hauenstein, Kasl, & Harburg, 1977). Several factors may account for the discrepant findings. Researchers often fail to discriminate between homemakers (i.e., nonemployed and out of the labor market) and unemployed mothers (i.e., mothers seeking but unable to find work), collapsing them into a single group. This distinction is crucial because homemakers and unemployed mothers are likely to differ considerably in level of satisfaction with their current situation. When employed mothers have been compared to homemakers, no differences in psychological or physical well-being have been found (Brown & Gary, 1988; Hauenstein et al., 1977).

Perhaps the most serious limitation evident in many of these studies is failure to take account of family (e.g., presence of young children in the home, age of youngest child in household, division of household labor), job (e.g., work hours), and individual factors (e.g., desire to work, job satisfaction) that might moderate the psychological impact of productive labor. Paid employment may afford women many benefits that enhance mental health, including stimulation, self-esteem, adult contacts, and relief from housework and child care responsibilities (Hoffman, 1989). Additionally, when combined with other roles (e.g., wife, mother), it may render women less susceptible to the adverse effects of stressful life events Kandel, et al., 1985; Malley & Stewart, 1988). At the same time, work can be the source of a number of conditions (e.g., time pressure, work overload, and need for, but inability to find, adequate and convenient child care) that undermine mental health and attenuate or neutralize the psychological benefits of paid employment.

That a wide array of factors influence the psychological impact of paid employment is documented by a growing number of studies. A few are cited here for illustrative purposes. Data from white dual-earner families indicate that wives' satisfaction with their work and husbands' help with child care but not household chores modifies the impact of paid employment on wives' mental health. Kessler and McRae (1982) found a significant psychological benefit of employment only among those women who are very satisfied with their jobs (compared to those who were satisfied, neutral, dissatisfied, or very dissatisfied); whereas among those who are dissatisfied with their jobs, employment was associated with greater psychological distress (Kessler & McRae, 1982). In addition, employed women had improved mental health only if their husbands spent equal time or more time on child care than did their wives. Other research indicates that black mothers report greater ambivalence about working and presumably experience fewer psychological benefits of paid employment if their children are inadequately supervised in their absence of if they perceive their children to be low in self-reliance (Woods, 1972).

Virtually no studies have assessed the role of job satisfaction or contextual factors in moderating or mediating the psychological effects of paid employment on black women's well-being, although a few have examined the psychological effects of job stressors and the antecedents or correlates of job satisfaction. For example, black women and men who perceive themselves as having been barred from job assignments for racial reasons experience higher levels of fatigue and emotional depletion than those who do not hold such perceptions (Johnson, 1989). There is some evidence of greater job satisfaction among black women who have a positive attitude about maternal employment and whose husbands approve of the wife's employment (Andrisani, 1978), but in other research, neither husband's approval (Harrison & Minor, 1978) nor presence of a preschool child in the home (Andrisani, 1978) is found to be related to black women's job satisfaction. In light of the complexities in the research discussed above, it is unlikely that paid employment is uniform in its effects on the psychological and physical well-being of black mothers. There is an acute need for carefully designed studies of the family and job conditions that moderate the psychological impact of paid employment on black mothers.

Given the race differences, discussed earlier, in women's sex-role ideology, wives' attitudes about work, and wives' relative contributions to their family's economic well-being, paid employment might be expected to affect black women and white women differently. To date, there is no evidence that the psychological effects of paid employment differ as a function of race (Reskin & Coverman, 1985) although black women have been reported to experience greater job dissatisfaction than do white women (Andrisani, 1978). Furthermore, black women's psychological response to paid work appears to be equivalent to the response of black men, a finding that is incompatible with the view that the role of paid worker is less central to women than to men (Reskin & Coverman, 1985). Some data suggest that employed black wives experience less satisfaction with their life than do employed black husbands, but this probably reflects gender differences in household labor, rather than differences in the psychological importance of work (Beckett & Smith, 1981; Broman, 1991; Ericksen et al., 1979; Maret & Finlay, 1984). In any case, more research is needed for an adequate determination of whether and under what conditions black women respond differently to paid employment than do white women or black men.

Employment Versus Unemployment

In recent years, researchers have shown a burgeoning interest in the psychological and social impact of unemployment among women and mothers (Broman, Hamilton, & Hoffman, 1990; Brown & Gary, 1985, 1988; Donovan, Jaffe, & Pirie, 1987; Ensminger & Celentano, 1990; Hawton, Fagg, & Simkin, 1988; Perrucci & Targ, 1988; Retherford, Hildreth, & Goldsmith, 1989; Romero, Castro, Cervantes, 1988; Rosen, 1987; Schlozman, 1979; Shamir, 1985; Taylor, 1988; Thompson & Ensminger, 1989). A few of these studies have focused on black women, and like those focusing on white and Latino women, they typically find that unemployment and job loss are associated with increased psychological distress. For example, longitudinal data from Thompson and Ensminger's (1989) unique study of approximately 800 black mothers indicated that those who had been laid off, lost a job, or stopped working in the past year reported more intense feelings of sadness than those who had not experienced job loss. Likewise, Brown and Gary's (1988) community-based survey found that unemployed black women experienced a greater number of depressive symptoms than did their employed counterparts across all demographic and sociocultural characteristics. In a recent study of black mothers by McLoyd, Jayaretne, and Ceballo (in preparation), both current unemployment and job interruption during the past 2 years predicted higher levels of depression. Among the factors found to buffer adverse psychological effects of unemployment among black women and men are higher levels of religiosity, greater perceived social support, increased satisfaction with social support, shorter duration of unemployment, and higher income. Neither marital status nor the presence of children in the household appear to have a modifying effect (Barbarin, in press; Brown & Gary, 1985, 1988).

Accompanying researchers' growing interest in the psychological and social impact of unemployment among women is a keen interest in sex differences in the impact of unemployment. The emergence of the latter research focus is largely in response to the widespread notions that work is less central in the lives and self-concepts of women than of men and that women faced with unemployment, unlike their male counterparts, have alternative roles (i.e., wife, mother) to which they can turn for psychological compensations. Few studies yield data that support these notions. Existing evidence, albeit sparse, suggests that unemployment is no less distressing psychologically for black women than for black men (Brown & Gary, 1985). Likewise, most studies of nonblack or racially diverse samples find no evidence of gender differences in reactions to unemployment (Ensminger & Celentano, 1990; Perrucci & Targ, 1988; Taylor, 1988). Even when gender differences are found, they appear to derive principally from differences in the economic consequences of unemployment, not differences in commitment or availability of alternative roles (Shamir, 1985). Wives' wages tend to constitute a smaller proportion of family income than do husbands' wages (Tienda & Jensen, 1988); hence, their unemployment tends to have less deleterious effects on the family's financial state than does husbands' unemployment. In Shamir's (1985) study of a highly educated sample of Israelis, unemployment among husbands had stronger effects on depressive affect, anxiety, and morale in men than did unemployment among wives, but these differences disappeared when the effects of financial state were controlled. The one exception to this general pattern comes from the large-scale study by Broman et al. (1990) of a racially diverse sample of unemployed autoworkers, the focus of which was family relations rather than psychological functioning per se. These researchers found that financial strain, which was predicted by unemployment, resulted in more spousal conflict if the unemployed worker was male rather than female. Belief that men should be the major source of support in their families may account for this difference.

Surprisingly, the sex-role attitudes of unemployed workers do not appear to modify the psychological impact of unemployment. However, research suggests that the sex-role attitudes of significant others can foster nonsupportive behavior that undermines unemployed women's psychological well-being. For example, many of the unemployed women in Ratcliff and Bogdan's (1988) study, especially those who were married, complained that their husbands, relatives, and friends questioned the value of women's paid work and hence were indifferent to their plight. Distress in response to unemployment was greatest among those women who had a strong commitment to working but perceived their social networks as unsupportive of this commitment.

Research assessing the influence of race on an individual's response to unemployment has been confined to males. Psychological impairment following job loss is more pronounced among black men than white men, apparently because of fewer financial assets, longer periods of unemployment, and, consequently, an increased tendency to define job loss as a crisis (Buss & Redburn, 1983). For similar reasons, we might expect the psychological effects of unemployment to be more severe among black married mothers than their white counterparts. Relatedly, increased need and desire to work, factors that distinguish black married mothers from white married mothers, may predict elevated psychological distress in response to failure to find employment. Such a relation has been documented in samples of Australian youth and white and Latino women (Feather & Davenport, 1981; Ratcliff & Bogdan, 1988; Romero et al., 1988). Female workers as a whole withdraw from the labor force more quickly than do male workers in response to economic downturns. However, this tendency is much more pronounced among white women than among black and other minority women, the latter responding in a manner similar to that of male workers. In short, black and minority women are more likely than their white counterparts to continue to seek employment in spite of their initial failure to find jobs, reflecting their greater commitment and need to work (Stevans, Register, & Grimes, 1985). The latter may bode greater ill for their psychological response to unemployment.

EMPLOYMENT AND FAMILY RELATIONS

Marital Relations

Not much is known about how maternal employment conditions affect marital relations among blacks, and the sparse research findings that do exist need to be replicated. Full-time employment among black wives has been linked to diminished satisfaction with communication and understanding between spouses and, among those who are highly educated, with reduced satisfaction with leisuretime companionship and sexual relations (Scanzoni, 1975). These indicators of marital quality are probably effects, rather than causes, of full-time employment of the wife, reflecting the fact that spouses in dual-earner families simply have less time available for intimacy. Further research is needed to determine the robustness of these relations.

An especially fertile but underdeveloped area of inquiry concerns the processes through which certain work-related attitudes and experiences affect the quality of blacks' marital relations. The few existing studies have yielded some intriguing findings that warrant replication and elaboration. For example, feelings of competition and resentment between spouses engendered by the husband's perception that black women face fewer barriers to career advancement than do black men appear to undermine marital happiness among dual-career black couples, as does racial discrimination, lack of racial/ethnic diversity, and social isolation in the workplace (Cazenave, 1983; Thomas, 1990).

Perceived racism in the workplace and its effects on marital relations among black couples have been investigated more extensively by Johnson (1989) in a pathbreaking study of a sample of black police officers, about half of whom were women. The direct and indirect effects on marital relations (e.g., satisfying communication with spouse, receipt and expression of emotional support, enjoyable sex life) of three types of perceived job stressors were assessed, namely, being judged by the actions of other officers because of race, being penalized more than other officers because of race, and being barred from certain assignments because of race. The latter two stressors had significantly negative, direct effects on the quality of marital relations that, in turn, increased the degree to which couples had considered divorce. With respect to indirect effects, being judged by the actions of other black officers had an especially potent and negative impact on marital interaction, mediated through an increased tendency to behave callously and impersonally. In addition, being barred from assignments because of race adversely influenced marital relations by increasing feelings of fatigue and emotional depletion and increasing officers' desire to quit their job. In subsequent analyses of data from a comparable sample of white police officers, desire to quit the job was more predictive of marital discord among blacks than whites, apparently because it constituted a more serious economic threat as a result of the reduced job opportunities available to blacks (Johnson, 1989).

Another job-related factor of particular interest in relation to marital relations among blacks is shift work. Blacks are more likely than whites to work night, evening, and variable shifts, perhaps because of their relative lack of opportunity for day jobs and because the extra pay often attached to non-day shifts is more critical for them, given their relatively low income (Hedges & Sekscenski, 1979; Presser, 1987; White & Keith, 1990). It is also noteworthy that shift workers generally hold lower-status and non-white-collar jobs and have lower incomes, more irregular hours, and lower job satisfaction (White & Keith, 1990). White and Keith (1990), in a longitudinal study of a nationalism random sample, found strong evidence of negative effect of shift work on marital happiness, happiness with sexual relations with the spouse, and parental relations, even after introducing controls for objective job characteristics and a number of additional variables. Moreover, through its negative impact on marital quality, shift work significantly increased the probability of divorce two years later. This effect was not modified by whether it was the husband or the wife who did the shift work. Although the sample included blacks, no subgroup analyses by race were reported. High priority should be given to determining if race conditions the effect of shift work on marital relations and the processes that mediate these differences.

Division of Household Labor

Whether employed or not, black wives, like their white counterparts, assume primary responsibility for domestic chores (e.g., grocery shopping, cooking, washing clothes) and caring for children (Beckett & Smith, 1981; Broman, 1988, 1991; Ericksen et al., 1979; Malson, 1983). Employment among black married mothers results in only a slight decrease in the amount of time they spend on housework and a slight decrease in the proportion of domestic chores they perform (Beckett & Smith, 1981; Broman, 1991; Maret & Finlay, 1984). Findings are inconsistent regarding whether it results in a decrement in the amount of time they spend in child care, perhaps because this outcome is heavily dependent on the child's age (Beckett & Smith, 1981; Maret & Finlay, 1984).

Several studies have identified factors other than gender that influence employed couples' division of household labor. In reviewing these studies, it is important to bear in mind that none of the factors examined, including wife's employment, wife's wage level, race, time availability, and ideology, is a more potent determinant than gender of amount and allocation of housework and child care (Thompson & Walker, 1989). Husbands of black women are somewhat more likely to share in household tasks and spend a larger amount of time on these tasks if their wives work full-time than if their wives are not employed. Nevertheless, the actual amount of time they spend on such chores is remarkably small (Beckett & Smith, 1981; Ericksen et al., 1979; Malson, 1983). In Beckett and Smith's (1981) study of two-parent families in the national Panel Study of Income Dynamics, all of whom had at least one child under 12 years of age, husbands of black employed wives spent a median of 5.9 hours per week performing household tasks and 6.8 hours per week in child care. Comparable figures for black husbands of nonemployed wives were 3.9 and 4.9 hours, respectively. The median number of hours employed black wives spent performing household tasks and child care was 21.3 and 9.8, respectively. As these data illustrate, the disparity between husband and wife is much greater for time spent in housework than for time spent in child care, a finding also reported in studies of dual-earner white families (Beckett & Smith, 1981). It is also of interest that husbands of black employed women spend less time on domestic chores as their income increases and that black employed wives share more home responsibilities as their relative economic contribution in the household increases (Ericksen et al., 1979; Farkas, 1976; Maret & Finlay, 1984). Although these findings suggest that economic power reduces domestic responsibility, the preponderance of evidence from studies of both black and white couples indicates that this relation is very weak (Thompson & Walker, 1989).

In view of the discrepancy between spouses in the amount of household labor performed and the fact that husbands' estimates of their level of participation in household work generally are higher than wives' estimates of the husbands' contribution (Douglas & Wind, 1978; Geerken & Gove, 1983; Thomas, 1990), it is not difficult to understand why dual-career black couples view inequitable division of household labor as a major problem (Thomas, 1990).

Black employed wives devote slightly less time to housework and report lower levels of domestic responsibility than do their white counterparts and hence may find household responsibilities somewhat less burdensome (Beckett & Smith, 1981; Maret & Finlay, 1984). In addition, their husbands spend a little more time on household tasks and child care than do white husbands (Beckett & Smith, 1981; Frakas, 1976; Ross, 1987). The latter finding is not always replicated, however (Huber & Spitze, 1981), and there is some suggestion from a recent study of shift work and child care that young black fathers in dual-earner families may be *less willing* than comparable white fathers to care for their preschool-age children during hours when they are at home but their wives are working (Presser, 1988). Further research is needed to determine if reported race differences in husbands' level of involvement in household labor are driven by ideology, pragmatics, relative contribution of wives' wages to household income, or a combination of factors. Despite evidence that black husbands are more likely than white husbands to perform domestic chores, assist in child care, and endorse the notion that husbands should make compromises and accommodations in the interest of the certain special needs of working wives (e.g., staying at home with a sick child, having a smaller family, being amenable to the wife's absence from home overnight because of work requirements), they do not appear to differ from their white counterparts in attitudes about sharing equally in household chores and child care if the wife works (Scanzoni, 1975). Hence, the role of ideology about role obligations in predicting husbands' participation in domestic work is uncertain.

Another possibility that has been investigated empirically is that black husbands' greater involvement in household labor is due to race differences in the work patterns of wives and hence to pragmatic considerations. As noted previously, black women are more likely than white women to work night, evening, and variable shifts (Hedges & Sekscenski, 1979; Presser, 1987). Such work patterns and the essentiality of family tasks may combine to compel husbands to perform household chores and child care (Thompson & Walker, 1989). Research that directly addresses this issue is lacking, but there is some indirect evidence that changes in husbands' contributions to household labor occur primarily on pragmatic rather than ideological grounds. In their study of a national probability sample of husbands and wives, Huber and Spitze (1981) found that husbands' contributions to household labor were more strongly predicted by wives' current employment status than by wives' earnings or attachment to the labor force over time. This finding was seen as consistent with a pragmatic interpretation of husbands' participation in household labor, on the grounds that ideology about role obligations is most likely to develop gradually and cumulatively in response to wives' work attachment over time. If changes in ideology undergird husbands' involvement in household labor, Huber and Spitze reasoned, wives' work attachment over time should affect husbands' household labor more than would wives' work attachment over time. It should also affect husband's household labor more than would wives' current employment status. Their finding were in the opposite direction, leading them to conclude that husbands of working wives assist with child care and domestic tasks primarily to enable the household to continue to function, not because of some fundamental change in their ideology about role obligations and responsibilities.

Note should also be made of the fact that both single and married black mothers receive significant amounts of assistance in household tasks and child care from their older children (Kotlowitz, 1991; Malson, 1983). However, the author is unaware of any investigations of the relation between maternal employment status and black children's participation in family chores. Studies of the effect of mother's employment on children's contributions to household labor in white, two-parent families report mixed findings. Some find no relation (Geerken & Gove, 1983; Peters & Haldeman, 1987), whereas others indicate that employed mothers shift a portion of their chores to their children rather than to their husbands, and second, that their children perform more chores and spend more time on chores than do children whose mothers are nonemployed (Goodnow, 1988; Medrich, Roizen, Rubin, & Buckley, 1982). Still others report that girls, but not boys, in full-time dual-earner families do more household chores than do their counterparts in families where only the father is employed (Benin & Edwards, 1990).

What is now needed are research investigations that resolve these discrepancies, examine the relation between maternal employment and black children's participation in household chores, and identify factors that moderate and mediate this relation. Black employed mothers may have lower levels of home responsibility than white employed mothers have (Beckett & Smith, 1981; Maret & Finlay, 1984) because their households are larger, and therefore more individuals are available to perform household chores. It could also be due to increased domestic labor by both husbands and children, controlling for household size (Beckett & Smith, 1981; Farkas, 1976; Ross, 1987). Data from the National Survey of Children indicate that neither children's overall development of practical skills nor their experience in performing certain domestic tasks without anyone's help (e.g., washing dishes, baby-sitting, shopping at a store, cooking a meal for the family) is related to race when family and socioeconomic characteristics are controlled. However, black children aged 7 to 11 are more likely than their white counterparts to have ironed clothes and changed sheets on a bed, but it is not clear what factors account for these differences (Zill & Peterson, 1982). Research that frames black children's household labor within the context of maternal employment and documents its psychological significance would be especially valuable.

Family Role Strain: Antecedents and Consequences

A surfeit of role obligations and a deficit in the amount of time needed to fulfill role obligations can engender role strain. Role strain can emanate from role overload (i.e., having so many demands related to one's role[s] that satisfactory performance is undetermined) or role conflict (i.e., competing demands from two or more roles so that adequate performance of one role jeopardizes adequate performance of the other[s]) (Barnett & Baruch, 1985). Although black women tend to view employment, marriage, and motherhood as compatible (Malson, 1983), this psychological orientation does not immunize them against role strain and its psychological effects. Indeed, small-scale interview studies report that family role strain is a problem for a sizable minority of employed black mothers, as indicated by the difficulty they experience in arranging time for mother–child interaction, completing household chores, and meeting appointments (Katz & Piotrkowski, 1983; Thomas, 1990). Even more telling, national survey data from dual-earner couples indicate that the majority of mothers who are employed full-time or more, desire to work fewer hours in order to have more time with their families, even if it means having less money. Predictably, this desire increases with an increase in perceived work–family interference (Moen & Dempster-McCalin, 1987). What follows is a brief discussion of family and job factors associated with increases in family role strain among black mothers, the coping strategies black mothers use when confronted with family role strain, and factors that appear to mitigate role strain.

Family Factors

One obvious contributor to family role strain among employed wives is husbands' markedly low levels of involvement in household labor and the resulting tendency of employed wives to do "double duty" (Beckett & Smith, 1981; Broman, 1988, 1991; Ericksen et al., 1979; Malson, 1983). Black employed wives are almost twice as likely as black employed husbands to say they feel overworked, a factor that predicts significantly lower levels of family life satisfaction. In general, black employed spouses who do most of the housework, irrespective of gender, report lower levels of satisfaction with their family life (Broman, 1988).

Family role strain increases among black, married, employed mothers as the number of children in the household increases but appears to be unrelated to the age of the youngest child in the household (Katz & Piotrkowski, 1983; Lewis, 1988, 1989). These findings are corroborated by Moen and Dempster-McClain's (1987) national study of dual-earner couples, in which neither age of the youngest child nor the number of children in the home predicted employed mothers' desire to work fewer hours in order to spend more time with their families. Role strain among black employed mothers is also unrelated to marital status (single vs. married) (Katz & Piotrkowski, 1983; Lewis, 1988, 1989), perhaps indicating that husbands' assistance in housework and child care is so modest, as discussed above, as to be ineffective in relieving wives' role strain. Another possibility is that single mothers receive assistance in meeting family demands from boyfriends, relatives, or children equivalent to that received by married mothers from their husbands.

Job Factors

We know appallingly little about how various characteristics and stressors of jobs held by black mothers influence family role strain. Existing research is not only sparse but conflicting. In Katz and Piotrkowski's (1983) study of black mothers who worked at least 20 hours per week, family role strain was unaffected by number of hours worked but increased with a decrease in job autonomy and an increase in job demands. The picture presented by Moen and Dempster-McClain's (1987) study of dual-earner couples appears to be at odds with these findings. These researchers found that mothers' desire for a reduced work week was a strong positive correlate of perceived work-family interference, and although this desire was predicted by an increase in the number of hours mothers worked, it was unrelated to mothers' occupational status, shift work, flex time, or job autonomy.

Strategies Used to Cope with Role Strain

Employed black women are less happy and less satisfied with their lives if they feel they lack adequate resources to comply with role demands and/or if they experience higher levels of strain in meeting their obligations as mother, housekeeper, worker, and partner (Crohan, Antonucci, Adelmann, & Coleman, 1989; Harrison, Bowman, & Beale, 1985). Because role strain contributes to psychological distress, it is of interest to know what strategies black employed mothers use to handle role strain and how effective these strategies are in relieving distress.

Three different types of coping behavior have been identified: (1) structural role redefinition, in which the individual attempts to modify external demands by negotiating and altering the expectations of others regarding her performance (e.g., working fewer hours at one's place of employment); (2) personal role redefinition, whereby the individual attempts to reduce role conflict by making changes in her attitudes, perception, and behavior without modifying the expectations, perceptions, or behavior of role senders (e.g., establishing priorities, partitioning roles, ignoring role demands, eliminating role-related tasks); and (3) reactive role behavior, in which the individual attempts to resolve role conflict by improving the quality of her role performance (e.g., planning, scheduling, working longer hours). Of the three coping strategies, personal role definition is considered the most healthy, reactive role behavior, the least healthy (Hall, 1972).

Black employed mothers' choice of coping strategy is influenced by type of interrole conflict and marital status. Essentially, when marital role demands conflict with the demands of either the maternal or worker role, black women typically seek to renegotiate the husband's expectations (structural role redefinition), whereas they tend to deal with conflict between maternal and worker roles by making internal changes in attitude and perceptions (personal role redefinition) (Harrison & Minor, 1978, 1982). They are least likely to deal with conflict between marital and maternal roles by trying to improve the quality of their role performance (reactive role behavior). In general, black employed wives with children give priority to maternal role demands over marital or worker obligations or completion of household chores. Further support for this conclusion comes from Katz and Piotrkowski's (1983) study of employed black mothers, in which number of hours worked predicted difficulty in completing household chores but was unrelated to difficulty in arranging time for mother-child interaction or meeting appointments. This allocation of time in favor of meeting children's needs is in keeping with evidence that black women's expectancy of failure in the mother role is a more potent predictor of unhappiness than the perception of general role overload (Harrison et al., 1985).

When confronted with maternal-worker conflict, single black mothers tend to adopt less healthy coping strategies than do their married counterparts. Although black married mothers typically attempt to deal with this conflict by modifying their attitudes and perceptions (personal role redefinition), black single mothers usually respond by trying to improve the quality of their role performance (reactive role behavior) (Harrison & Minor, 1982; McAdoo, 1986). That they do so may stem from the lack of viable alternative responses to role strain. Employment is their primary and, in most cases, sole source of economic support (Johnson & Waldman, 1983), and their children, overall, are less likely than children in two-parent households to have consistent, alternative caregivers to whom they can turn for satisfaction of their emotional and physical needs. Neither of these factors puts single mothers in a strong position to negotiate with role senders, ignore role demands, eliminate role-related tasks, or modify their own cognitive schemas.

Mitigating Factors

Assessments of the effects of choice of coping strategy on the psychological well-being of employed black mothers experiencing role strain have produced mixed results (Harrison & Minor, 1978, 1982; McAdoo, 1986). Structural role redefinition has sometimes been found to be more predictive of reduced psychological distress than personal role redefinition or reactive role behavior. This is consistent with Hall's (1972) claim that altering external demands on one's behavior is the healthiest choice of coping strategies, perhaps because it is more effective in reducing role conflict. However, structural role redefinition is not consistently associated with increased psychological well-being, and in any case, data are too sparse to draw firm conclusions.

Recent attention has been given to the mitigating effects of other cognitive and environmental factors on role strain. Strong religious beliefs have been found to buffer the adverse effects of interrole strain on the psychological well-being of employed African-American mothers. Moreover, such beliefs appear to be even more potent as a buffer than extended family bonds and para-kin friendships (Harrison et al., 1985). Other research on intrarole strain among black women indicates that the availability of someone to help with children reduces household maintenance strain, whereas *receipt of support* from the husband or partner (but not marital status per se), availability of kin in the same county or state as the respondent (but not the same neighborhood, city, or out of state), and fewer minor children in the household reduce parental role strain (Lewis, 1988, 1989).

EFFECTS OF MATERNAL EMPLOYMENT ON AFRICAN-AMERICAN CHILDREN

Black children under the age of 6 and living in a two-parent household are more likely to have a mother who works full-time than are their white counterparts (52% vs. 29%). However, if they live in a female-headed household, they are less likely than white children to have a mother who works full-time (37% vs. 49%) (Sweet & Bumpass, 1987). In this section, we examine research on the impact of maternal employment on black children's intellectual and socioemotional development. It will be recalled that findings documenting the influence of maternal employment on black children's sex-role attitudes were reviewed in an earlier section.

Maternal employment has been hypothesized to influence children's development through its impact on a range of factors, including the quantity and quality of parent–child interaction, the extent and quality of nonparental care, and the economic well-being of the family (Hoffman, 1989). Because it increases the amount of time the mother is away from home and often heightens feelings of role strain, the mother's employment may reduce both the quantity and quality of time she spends with the child—outcomes that may impede the child's intellectual and socioemotional development (Belsky & Eggebeen, 1991; Desai, Chase-Lansdale, & Michael, 1989). Negative outcomes are thought to be even more probable if nonparental care exceeds 20 hours per week in the child's first year of life or is less stimulating, responsive, and of markedly lower quality than that which the mother typically provides (Belsky, 1988; Desai et al., 1989). On the other hand, maternal employment increases the family's material resources, and this may afford the child greater access to goods and services that facilitate positive development. Under certain circumstances it may also enhance mothers' life satisfaction, which in turn may promote nurturant, sensitive, and involved parenting (Hoffman, 1989).

Consideration of these issues has led some researchers to predict that maternal employment is more likely to have adverse effects on children in high-socioeconomic-status (SES) families than on children in low-SES families. The quality of alternative care, *as compared to the quality of the mother's care*, it is argued, is likely to be lower within affluent families, given the high levels of education of mothers in such families, whereas it may be equivalent, if not higher, within lower-income families because mothers in these families tend to have low levels of education. In addition, the added earnings of a highly educated married mother are thought to make less of a positive difference in the overall material resources of the family than the added earnings of a poorly educated, low-income mother, the latter often making the difference between whether a family falls into or escapes poverty (Desai et al., 1989). As we have seen, however, the relative contribution of wives' earnings to family income is substantially greater among blacks than whites (Geshwender & Carroll-Seguin, 1990); hence, social class differences in the impact of maternal employment on children's development might be attenuated within black families, compared to white families. Unfortunately, this hypothesis has not been tested in existing studies.

Predictions about the differential impact of maternal employment as a function of socioeconomic status could be extended to family structure (single-parent vs. two-parent) in view of the strong correlation between the two. Given single mothers' high risk of poverty, anxiety, and depression and the punitive and inconsistent parenting engendered by these factors (Guttentag, Salasin, & Belled, 1980; McLoyd, 1990), it is especially plausible that maternal employment may be more advantageous to the child than routinely staying home with a single mother (Vandell, 1991).

Although evidence regarding the impact of maternal employment on black children's intellectual and socioemotional functioning is limited, a predominant pattern of findings is discernible. There are a few exceptions to this generalization (Cherry & Eaton, 1977), but maternal employment appears more likely to have salutary effects on black children if they are from single-parent or poor families than if they are from two-parent families. Whereas among poor or single-parent families, maternal employment tends to be either positively related or unrelated to preschool and elementary school children's cognitive and socioemotional functioning, there is evidence of negative effects among children from two-parent or more affluent families, a pattern consistent with the argument presented above.

In Milne, Myers, Rosenthal, and Ginsburg's (1986) study of a nationally representative sample of elementary school children (grades 1 through 6), the effects of maternal employment were mixed and primarily nonsignificant among black children living in two-parent families. However, among black children living in female-headed households, reading and math achievement increased significantly with an increase in the average number of hours the mother worked per week in the previous year, after controlling for mother's education, family income, number of children, and a variety of other demographic variables. Likewise, in Kriesberg's (1970) study of a sample of poor black and poor white children, maternal employment predicted higher grades but only if the children were living in a female-headed household. Woods (1972) also found positive correlations between maternal employment and children's intellectual functioning, school achievement, and social adjustment in a study of black fifth-graders and their mothers. In addition, social adjustment was higher among those black children whose mothers were more satisfied with their work. The mothers in this study were primarily upper lower class and working class, and although their marital status was not specified, it is likely that a significant number of them were single. Vandell and Ramanan's (1990) investigation of a sample of lower-class, ethnic-minority 61/2–8-year-olds, many of whom had adolescent single mothers, also found a link between maternal employment early in the child's life and improved academic functioning, after controlling for concurrent maternal employment and self-selection factors.

Low-income children from primarily two-parent families have also been found to have higher cognitive functioning if their mothers work. In Rieber and Womack's (1967) study of black, white, and Latino Head Start children, over half of the children in the highest quartile of the Peabody Picture Vocabulary test had mothers who worked, whereas only 25% of those in the lowest quartile had working mothers. Other studies find no relation between maternal employment and children's intellectual functioning within low income families but a negative relation within high-income families. Analyses of data by Desai et al. (1989) from a racially diverse sample of 4-year-olds in the National Longitudinal Survey of Youth indicated that full-time, continuous maternal employment (all 4 years of the child's life) was unrelated to intellectual functioning among children from low-income families but predicted lower intellectual functioning among boys from high-income families.

This pattern of findings must be qualified on several counts. Four points, in particular, warrant careful consideration. First, evidence of differential effects of maternal employment in favor of children from low-income or single-parent families, rather than children from high-income or two-parent families, is contradicted by other research. At least one study found just the opposite pattern. Specifically, Cherry and Eaton (1977) reported that maternal employment during the child's first 3 years of life was associated with higher cognitive functioning among black children living in two-parent but not female-headed households. Family structure was only one of several SES-related factors controlled (separately, not simultaneously) in their numerous comparisons of children of employed and nonemployed mothers (others included maternal age, per capita income, parity), the overwhelming majority were in favor of children of employed mothers. Other researchers have reported negative effects of maternal employment without regard to social class or poverty status. Using data from the racially diverse National Longitudinal Survey of Youth, Belsky and Eggebeen (1991) found that 4–6-year-old children whose mothers returned to work on a full-time basis prior to their second year of life were less socioemotionally adjusted (more behavior problems, less secure attachment, less compliance) than similarly aged children whose mothers did not work during the child's first or second year of life. This effect was not moderated by race, poverty status, maternal education, or children's age or gender.

Second, salutary effects of maternal employment in female-headed black families, when found, appear to be limited to elementary school students. Using data from a nationally representative sample of high school sophomores and seniors, Milne et al. (1986) found that the effects on reading and math achievement of both full-time and part-time employment were primarily negative and significant for black children living in female-headed households and primarily negative and nonsignificant for black children living in two-parent households. Milne et al., however, stress the need to interpret these findings with caution because there were so few black students whose mothers had never worked, particularly in the sample of single-parent families. If, in fact, maternal employment in the context of single parenthood does result in lower achievement and less positive socioemotional functioning among high school students, it may do so by undermining maternal supervision and monitoring precisely when they are most needed. Adolescence is accompanied by increased temptations, hazards, and peer influences. Among both black and white young mothers, kin assistance with child care and supervision diminishes rapidly as mothers grow older, largely due to increased distance from kin (Parish et al., 1991). This may adversely affect the mother's ability to provide adequate supervision of her now older children, especially if she is single. Deviance has been found to be lower among both black and white adolescents living in one-parent extended households (one-parent family sharing residence with extended family members) than among those living in mother-only households, even after controlling for income differences. Increased supervision and parental control and decreased adolescent autonomy in decision making may be implicated in the reduction of deviance (Dornbusch et al., 1985). The effects of maternal employment on achievement among children living in female-headed households may be mediated through similar processes.

Third, the studies reviewed here vary considerably in quality, and this may account for some of the discrepancy among findings. Many fail to control for known selection factors, reporting simple bivariate correlations between maternal employment and children's behaviors or controlling one selection factor for a particular comparison but ignoring a host of others (e.g., Cherry & Eaton, 1977; Rieber & Womack, 1967; Woods, 1972). The methodological problems that plague research on maternal employment have been discussed at length by other scholars and hence need not be repeated here (Heyns, 1982; Heyns & Catsambis, 1986; Hoffman, 1984a, 1984b; Milne et al., 1986). Suffice it to say that, compared to black non-employed mothers, black employed mothers, on average, have fewer children, are older, more educated, more likely to be married, and more likely to be middle class (U. S. Bureau of the Census, 1991b; U.S. Bureau of Labor Statistics, 1992). A number of these selective factors are themselves strong predictors of intellectual and school achievement. Consequently, it is possible that certain correlates of maternal employment, not maternal employment per se, accounts for differences in the behavior of children whose mothers do and do not work outside the home. Controls for such selective factors must be introduced in order to estimate the unique effects of maternal employment. For example, Heyns (1982) found that when income was controlled, the positive effects of maternal employment on cognitive achievement among fifth- and sixth-grade black children was greatly reduced and barely significant.

It must also be acknowledged that, in some cases, maternal employment may be partly a consequence, rather than a cause, of children's achievement and adjustment. Mothers may assign children domestic responsibilities and enter or remain in the labor force, partly because the child is well adjusted socially and performing adequately in school. Woods's (1972) study, in particular, is strongly suggestive of this possibility. Longitudinal research is needed to evaluate this hypothesis adequately.

Finally, none of the studies reviewed here identifies the mechanisms by which maternal employment impacts on black children's functioning. In most cases, researchers have ignored this important question; in others, their efforts have yielded few significant findings. Milne et al. (1986), for example, were unsuccessful in identifying intervening variables that mediated the positive effect of maternal employment on black elementary school children from female-headed households, despite examination of a wide range of variables (e.g., family income, number of children, parents' educational expectations, number of books in home, maternal help with homework). Fortunately, however, notable progress is being made on this front. Instead of focusing solely on child outcomes and relying on inference to explain these outcomes, researchers have begun to give more attention to mediational processes and their reliable measurement. For example, MacEwen and Barling (1991) recently demonstrated that mothers' experiences of employment are more predictive of children's behavior than mothers' employment status. They found that high interrole conflict and low job satisfaction among employed mothers predicted increased immaturity, conduct disorders, and anxiety/withdrawal in children. These relations were mediated by mothers' personal strain (i.e., cognitive difficulties and negative mood) and parenting behavior (i.e., punishment and rejection). In another line of work, Menaghan and Parcel (1991) found that occupational complexity of mothers' work positively affected the home environments that mothers provided for their children. Conceptual and methodological advances of this sort need to be extended to the study of maternal employment effects in black families. Research is needed that explores job-related factors (e.g., job characteristics, job satisfaction), economic factors, family characteristics, and household functioning for their impact on black mothers' psychological functioning, child-rearing goals, and parenting behavior. Increased understanding of these contextual factors, in turn, may help illuminate the conditions under which maternal employment has positive or negative effects on black children's development and the pathways by which such effects are produced.

NOTE

1. The terms "black" and "African American" are used interchangeably in this chapter, as are the terms "white" and "Anglo American."

REFERENCES

Allen, K. R., & Chin-Snag, V. (1990). A lifetime of work: The context and meanings of leisure for aging black women. *Gerontologist, 30*, 734–740.

Allen, W. R., & Farley, R. (1986). The shifting social and economic tides of black America, 1950–1980. *Annual Review of Sociology, 12*, 277–306.

Andrisani, P. J. (1978). Job satisfaction among working women. *Journal of Women in Culture and Society, 3*, 588–607.

Axelson, L. J. (1970). The working wife: Differences in perception among Negro and white males. *Journal of Marriage and the Family, 30*, 457–464.

Balkwell, C., Balswick, J., & Balkwell, J. W. (1978). On black and white family patterns in America: Their impact on the expressive aspect of sex-role socialization. *Journal of Marriage and the Family, 40*, 743–747.

Barbarin, O. (in press). Coping by blacks with joblessness: Relationships among stress, attributions, and mental health outcomes. In J. Jackson & P. Bowman (Eds.), *Coping with stress in black America.*

Barnett, R. C., & Baruch, G. K. (1985). Women's involvement in multiple roles and psychological distress. *Journal of Social and Personality Psychology, 49*, 135–145.

Bartz, K., & Levine, E. (1978). Childrearing by black parents: A description and comparison to Anglo and Chicano parents. *Journal of Marriage and the Family, 40*, 709–719.

Baruch, G. K., & Barnett, R. C. (1986). Consequences of fathers' participation in family work: Parents' role strain and well-being. *Journal of Personality and Social Psychology, 51*, 983–992.

Baruch, G. K., Biener, L., & Barnett, R. C. (1987). Women and gender in research on work and family stress. *American Psychologist, 42*, 130–136.

Baumrind, D. (1972). An exploratory study of socialization effects on black children: Some black-white comparisons. *Child Development, 43*, 261–267.

Beckett, J. O. (1976). Working wives: A racial comparison. *Social Work, 21* 463–471.

Beckett, J. O., & Smith, A. D. (1981). Work and family roles: Egalitarian marriage in black and white families. *Social Service Review, 55*, 314–326.

Belgrave, L. L. (1988). The effects of race differences in work history, work attitudes, economic resources, and health on women's retirement. *Research on Aging, 10*, 383–398.

Bell, D. (1974). Why participation rates of black and white wives differ. *Journal of Human Resources, 9*, 465–479.

Belsky, J. (1988). The effects of infant day care reconsidered. *Early Childhood Research Quarterly, 3*, 235–272.

Belsky, J., & Eggebeen, D. (1991). Early and extensive maternal employment and young children's socioemotional development: Children of the National Longitudinal Survey of Youth. *Journal of Marriage and the Family, 53*, 1083–1098.

Benin, M. H., & Edwards, D. A. (1990). Adolescents' chores: The difference between dual- and single-earner families. *Journal of Marriage and the Family, 52*, 361–373.

Binion, V. J. (1990). Psychological androgyny: A black female perspective. *Sex Roles, 22*, 487–507.

Blau, D. M., & Robins, P. K. (1989). Fertility, employment, and child-care costs. *Demography, 26*, 287–299.

Bloom-Feshbach, S., Bloom-Feshbach, J., & Heller, K. (1982). Work, family, and children's perceptions of the world. In S. Kamerman & C. Hayes (Eds.), *Families that work: children in a changing world* (pp. 268–307). Washington, DC: National Academy Press.

Broman, C. L. (1988). Household work and family life satisfaction of blacks. *Journal of marriage and the Family, 50*, 743–748.

Broman, C. L. (1991). Gender, work-family roles, and psychological well-being of blacks. *Journal of Marriage and the Family, 53*, 509–520.

Broman, C. L., Hamilton, V. L., & Hoffman, W. S. (1990). Unemployment and its effects on families: Evidence from a plant closing study. *American Journal of Community Psychology, 18*, 643–659.

Brookins, G. K. (1985). Black children's sex role ideologies and occupational choices in families of employed mothers. In M. Spencer, G. K. Brookins, & W. Allen (Eds.), *Beginning: The social and affective development of black children* (pp. 257–271). Hillsdale, NJ: Erlbaum.

Brown, D. R., & Gary, L. E. (1985). Predictors of depressive symptoms among unemployed black adults. *Journal of Sociology and Social Welfare, 12*, 736–754.

Brown, D. R. & Gary, L.E. (1988). Unemployment and psychological distress among black American women. *Sociological Focus, 21*, 209–221.

Burlew, A. K. (1982). The experiences of black females in traditional and nontraditional professions. *Psychology of Women Quarterly, 6*, 312–326.

Buss, T., & Redburn, F. S. (1983). *Mass unemployment: Plant closings and community mental health.* Beverly Hills, CA: Sage.

Carr, P. G., & Mednick, M. T. (1988). Sex role socialization and the development of achievement motivation in black preschool children. *Sex Roles, 18,* 169–180.

Cazenave, N. A. (1983). Black male-black female relationships: The perceptions of 155 middle-class black men. *Family Relations, 32,* 341–350.

Cherry, F. F., & Eaton, E. L. (1977). Physical and cognitive development in children of low-income mothers working in the child's early years. *Child Development, 48,* 158–166.

Coleman, L. M., Antonucci, T. C., Adelmann, P. K., & Crohan, S. E. (1987). Social roles in the lives of middle-aged and older black women. *Journal of Marriage and the Family, 49,* 761–771.

Collins, P. H. (1987). The meaning of motherhood in black culture and black mother/daughter relationships. *Sage, 4,* 3–10.

Crohan, S. E., Antonucci, T. C., Adelmann, K., & Coleman, L. M. (1989). Job characteristics and well-being at midlife. *Psychology of Women Quarterly, 13,* 223–235.

Davis, A. (1981). *Women, race, and class.* New York: Random House.

Demos, V. (1990). Black family studies and the issue of distorion: A trend analysis. *Journal of Marriage and the Family, 52,* 603–612.

Desai, S., Chase-Lansdale, P. L., & Michael, R. T. (1989). Mother or market? Effects of maternal employment on the intellectual ability of 4-year-old children. *Demography, 26,* 545–561.

Dill, T. B. (1988). Our mothers' grief: Racial ethnic women and the maintenance of families. *Journal of Family History, 13,* 415–431.

Dovovan, R., Jaffe, N., & Pirie, V. M. (1987). Unemployment among low-income women: An exploratory study. *Social Work, 32,* 301–305.

Dornbusch, S., Carlsmith, J., Bushwall, S., Ritter, P., Leiderman, H., Hastorf, A., & Gross, R. (1985). Single parents, extended households, and the control of adolescents. *Child Development, 56,* 326–341.

Dorr, A., & Lesser, G. S. (1980). Career awareness in young children. In M. Grewe-Partsch & G. J. Robinson (Eds.), *Women, communciation and careers* (pp. 36–75). New York: K. G. Saur.

Douglas, S. P., & Wind, Y. (1978). Examining family role and authority patterns: Two methodological issues. *Journal of Marriage and the Family, 40,* 35–47.

Duncan, G., & Hill, C. R. (1977). The child care mode choice of working mothers. In G. Duncan & J. N. Morgan (Eds.), *Five thousand American families: Patterns of economic progress* (Vol. 3, pp. 379–388). Ann Arbor, MI: Institute for Social Research.

Duncan, G., & Rodgers, W. (1988). Longitudinal aspects of childhood poverty. *Journal of Marriage and the Family, 50,* 1007–1021.

Eccles, J., & Hoffman, L. (1984). Sex roles, socialization, and occupational behavior. In H. W. Stevenson & A. Siegel (Eds.), *Child development research and social policy* (pp. 367–420). Chicago: University of Chicago Press.

Ensminger, M. E., & Celentano, D. D. (1990). Gender differences in the effect of unemployment on psychological distress. *Social Science Medicine, 30,* 469–477.

Epstein, C. F. (1973). Positive effects of the multiple negative: Explaining the success of black professional women. *American Journal of Sociology, 78,* 912–935.

Ericksen, J. A., Yancey, W. L., & Ericksen, E. P. (1979). The division of family roles. *Journal of Marriage and the Family, 41,* 301–313.

Farkas, G. (1976). Education, wage rates, and the division of labor between husband and wife. *Journal of Marriage and the Family, 38,* 473–483.

Farely, R. & Allen, W. R. (1987). *The color line and the quality of life in America.* New York: Russell Sage Foundation.

Feather, N. T., & Davenport, P. R. (1981). Unemployment and depressive affect: A motivational and attributional analysis. *Journal of Personality and Social Psychology, 41,* 422–436.

Floge, L. (1989). Changing household structure, child-care availability, and employment among mothers of preschool children. *Journal of Marriage and the Family, 51,* 51–63.

Gackenbach, J. (1978). The effect of race, sex, and career goal differences on sex role attitudes at home and at work. *Journal of Vocational Behavior, 12,* 93–101.

Gary, L. E. (1981). A social profile. In L. E. Gary (Eds.), *Black men* (pp. 21–45). Beverly Hills, CA: Sage.

Geerken, M., & Gove, W. R. (1983). *At home and at work: The family's allocation of labor.* Beverly Hills, CA: Sage.

Geschwender, J. A., & Carroll-Seguin, R. (1990). Exploding the myth of African-American progress. *Signs: Journal of Women in Culture and Society, 15,* 285–299.

Gold, D., & Andres, D. (1978). Relations between maternal employment and development of nursery school children. *Canadian Journal of Behavioral Science, 10,* 116–129.

Goodnow, J. (1988). Children's household work: Its nature and functions. *Psychological Bulletin, 103,* 5–26.

Granrose, C. S., & Cunningham, E. A. (1988). Post partum work intentions among black and white college women. *Career Development Quarterly, 37,* 149–164.

Gump, J. P. (1975). Comparative analysis of black women's and white women's sex-role attitudes. *Journal of Consulting and Clinical Psychology, 43,* 858–863.

Gutman, H. (1976). *The black family in slavery and freedom, 1750–1925.* New York: Pantheon Books.

Guttentag, M., Salasin, S., & Belle, D. (1980). *The mental health of women.* New York: Academic Press.

Hall, D. T. (1972). A model of coping with role conflict: The role behavior of college educated women. *Administrative Science Quarterly, 4,* 471–486.

Harrison, A. O. (1989). Black working women. In R. L. Jones (Eds.), *Black adult development and aging.* Berkeley, CA: Cobb & Henry.

Harrison, A. O., Bowman, P. J., & Beale, R. L. (1985). Role strain, coping resources, and psychological well-being among black working mothers. In A. Boykin (Eds.), *Empirical research in black psychology* (pp. 21–28). Washington, DC: National Institute of Mental Health.

Harrison, A. O., & Minor, J. H. (1978). Interrole conflict, coping strategies, and satisfaction among black working wives. *Journal of Marriage and the Family, 40,* 799–805.

Harrison, A. O., & Minor, J. H. (1982). Interrole conflict, coping strategies, and role satisfaction among single and married employed mothers. *Psychology of Women Quarterly, 6,* 354–360.

Hauenstein, L. S., Kasl, S. V., & Harburg (1977). Work status, work satisfaction, and blood pressure among married black and white women. *Psychology of Women Quarterly, 1,* 334–349.

Hawton, K., Fagg, J., & Simkin, S. (1988). Female unemployment and attempted suicide. *British Journal of Psychiatry, 152,* 632–637.

Hedges, J. N., & Sekscenski, E. S. (1979). Workers on late shifts in a changing economy. *Monthly Labor Review, 102,* 14–22.

Herskovits, M. (1958). *The myth of the Negro past.* Boston: Beacon Press.

Heyns, B. (1982). The influence of parent's work on children's school achievement. In S. Kamerman & C. Hayes (Eds.), *Families that work: Children in a changing world* (pp. 229–267). Washington, DC: National Academy Press.

Heyns, B., & Catsambis, S. (1986). Mother's employment and children's achievement: A critique. *Sociology of Education, 59,* 140–151.

Hoffman, L. W. (1984a). Maternal employment and the young child. In M. Perlmutter (Ed.), *Parent-child interaction and parent-child relations in child development.* The Minnesota Symposia on Child Psychology (Vol. 17, pp. 101–128). Hillsdale, NJ: Erlbaum.

Hoffman, L. W. (1984b). Work, family, and the socialization of the child. In R. Parke, R. Emde, H. McAdoo, & G. Sackett (Eds.), *The family: Review of child development research* (Vol. 7, pp. 223–282). Chicago: University of Chicago Press.

Hoffman, L. W. (1989). Effects of maternal employment in the two-parent family. *American Psychologists, 44,* 283–292.

Huber, J., & Spitze, G. (1981). Wives' employment, household behaviors, and sex-role attitudes. *Social Forces, 60,* 150–169.

Johnson, B. L., & Waldman, E. (1983). Most women who maintain families receive poor labor market returns. *Monthly Labor Review, 106,* 30–34.

Johnson, L. B. (1989).The employed black: The dynamics of work-family tension. *Review of Black Political Economy, 17,* 69–85.

Jones, B. A. (1986). Black women and labor force participation: An analysis of sluggish growth rates. In M. Simms & J. Malveaux (Eds.), *Slipping through the cracks: the status of black women* (pp. 11–31). New Brunswick, NJ: Transaction Books.

Jones, J. (1985). *Labor of love, labor of sorrow.* New York: Basic Books.

Kandel, D. B., Davies, M., & Raveis, V. H. (1985). The stressfulness of daily social roles for women: Marital, occupational and household roles. *Journal of Health and Social Behavior, 26,* 64–78.

Katz, M. H., & Piotrokowski, C. S. (1983). Correlates of family role strain among employed black women. *Family Relations, 32,* 331–339.

Kessler, R. C., & McRae, J. A. (1982). The effect of wives' employment on the mental health of married men and women. *American Sociological Review, 47,* 216–227.

Kleinke, C. L., & Nicholson, T. A. (1979). Black and white children's awareness of de facto race and sex differences. *Developmental Psychology, 15,* 84–86.

Kletzer, L. G. (1991). Job displacement, 1979–1986: How blacks fared relative to whites. *Monthly Labor Review, 114,* 17–25.

Kotlowitz, A. (1991). *There are no children here.* New York: Doubleday.

Kriesberg, L. (1970). *Mothers in poverty: A study of fatherless families.* Chicago: Aldine.

Ladner, J. (1971). *Tomorrow's tomorrow: The black woman.* Garden City, NY: Anchor Books.

Lamb, M. E. (1982). Maternal employment and child development: A review. In M. E. Lamb (Ed.), *Nontraditional families: Parenting and child development* (pp. 45–69). Hillsdale, NJ: Lawrence Erlbaum.

Landry, B., & Jendrek, M. P. (1978). The employment of wives in middle-class black families. *Journal of Marriage and the Family, 40,* 787–797.

Lehrer, E. L. (1983). Determinants of child care mode choice: An economic perspective. *Social Science Research, 12,* 69–80.

Lehrer, E. L., & Kawasaki, S. (1985). Childcare arrangements and fertility: An analysis of two-earner households. *Demography, 22,* 499–513.

Lehrer, E., & Nerlove, M. (1986). Female labor force behavior and fertility in the United States. *Annual Review of Sociology, 12,* 181–204.

Lewis, D. K. (1978). The black family: Socialization and sex roles. In R. Staples (Ed..), *The black family: Essays and studies* (pp. 215–226). Belmont, CA: Wadsworth.

Lewis, E. A. (1988). Role strengths and strains of African-American mothers. *Journal of Primary Prevention, 9,* 77–91.

Lewis, E. A. (1989). Role strain in African-American women: The efficacy of support networks. *Journal of Black Studies, 20,* 155–169.

MacEwen, K. E., & Barling, J. (1991). Effects of maternal employment experiences on children's behavior via mood, cognitive difficulties, and parenting behavior. *Journal of Marriage and the Family, 53,* 635–644.

Macke, A. S., & Morgan, W. R. (1978). Maternal employment, race, and work orientation of high school girls. *Social Forces, 57,* 187–204.

Macke, A. S., & Mott, F. L. (1980). The impact of maternal characteristics and significant life events on the work orientation of adolescent women: A longitudinal look. *Research in Labor Economics, 3,* 129–146.

Malley, J. E., & Stewart, A. J. (1988). Women's work and family roles: Sources of stress and sources of strength. In S. Fisher & J. Reason (Eds.), *Handbook of life stress, cognition and health.* New York: John Wiley.

Malson, M. R. (1983). Black women's sex roles: The social context for a new ideology. *Journal of Social Issues, 39,* 101–113.

Malveaux, J. (1985). The economic interests of black and white women: Are they similar? *Review of Black Political Economy, 15,* 5–27.

Marantz, S. A., & Mansfield, A. F. (1977). Maternal employment and the development of sex-role stereotyping in five-to eleven-year-old girls. *Child Development, 48,* 668–673.

Maret, E., & Finlay, B. (1984). The distribution of household labor among women in dual-earner families. *Journal of Marriage and the Family, 46,* 357–364.

McAdoo, H. P. (1986). Strategies used by black single mothers against stress. In M. Simms & J. Malveaux (Eds.), *Slipping through the cracks: The status of black women* (pp. 153–166). New Brunswick, NJ: Transaction Books.

McLoyd, V. C. (1990). The impact of economic hardship on black families and children: Psychological distress, parenting, and socioemotional development. *Child Development, 61,* 311–346.

McLoyd, V. C., Jayaratne, T., & Ceballo, R. (in preparation). The effects of maternal unemployment and work interruption on African American adolescents: Mechanisms of influence.

Mednick, M. T. S., & Puryear, G. (1975). Motivation and personality factors related to career goals of black college women. *Journal of Social and Behavioral Science, 21,* 1–30.

Medrich, E. A., Roizen, J., Rubin, V., & Buckley, S. (1982). *The serious business of growing up: A study of children's lives outside school.* Berkeley: University of California Press.

Meisenheimer, J. R. (1990). Black college graduates in the labor market, 1979 and 1989. *Monthly Labor Review, 113,* 13–21.

Menaghan, E. G., & Parcel, T. L. (1991). Determining children's home environments: The impact of maternal characteristics and current occupational and family conditions. *Journal of Marriage and the Family, 53,* 417–431.

Miller, S. M. (1975). Effects of maternal employment on sex-role perception, interests and self-esteem in kindergarten girls. *Developmental Psychology, 11,* 405–406.

Milne, A., Myers, D., Rosenthal, A., & Ginsburg, A. (1986). Single parents, working mothers, and the educational achievement of school children. *Sociology of Education, 59,* 125–139.

Moen, P., & Dempster-McClain, D. I. (1987). Employed parents: Role strain, work time, and preferences for working less. *Journal of Marriage and the Family, 49,* 579–590.

Moynihan, D. P. (1965). *The Negro family: The case for national action.* (Office of Policy Planning and Research, Department of Labor). Washington, DC: U.S. Government Printing Office.

Myers, L. W. (1975). Black women and self-esteem. In M. Millman & R. M. Kanter (Eds.), *Another voice* (pp. 240–250). Garden City, NY: Anchor Books.

Padavic, I. (1991). Attractions of male blue-collar jobs for black and white women: Economic need, exposure, and attitudes. *Social Science Quarterly, 72,* 33–49.

Parish, W. L., Hao, L., & Hogan, D. P. (1991). Family support networks, welfare, and work among young mothers. *Journal of Marriage and the Family, 53,* 203–215.

Perrucci, C., & Targ, D. (1988). Effects of a plant closing on marriage and family life. In P. Voydanoff & L. Majka (Eds.), *Families and economic distress* (pp. 55–71). Newbury Park, CA: Sage.

Peters, J. M., & Haldeman, V. A. (1987). Time used for household work. *Journal of Family Issues, 8,* 212–225.

Pleck, E. H. (1978). A mother's wages: Income earning among married Italian and black women, 1896–1911. In M. Gordon (Ed.), *American family in social historical perspective* (pp. 490–510). New York: St. Martin's Press.

Presser, H. B. (1987). Work shifts of full-time dual-earner couples: Patterns and contrasts by sex of spouse. *Demography, 24,* 99–112.

Presser, H. B. (1988). Shift work and child care among young dual-earner American parents. *Journal of Marriage and the Family, 50,* 133–148.

Ratcliff, K. S., & Bogdan, J. (1988). Unemployed women: When "social support" is not supportive. *Social Problems, 35,* 54–63.

Reid, P. T. (1982). Socialization of black female children. In P. W. Berman & E. R. Ramey (Eds.), *Women: A developmental perspective* (137–155). Bethesda, MD: U.S. Department of Health and Human Services, National Institutes of Health.

Reid, P. T., & Robinson, W. L. V. (1985). Professional black men and women: Attainment of terminal academic degrees. *Psychological Reports, 56,* 547–555.

Reskin, B. F., & Coverman, S. (1985). Sex and race in the determinants of psychophysical distress: A reappraisal of the sex-role hypothesis. *Social Forces, 63,* 1038–1059.

Retherford, P. S., Hildreth, G. J., & Goldsmith, E. B. (1989). Social support and resource management of unemployed women. In E. Goldsmith (Ed.), *Work and family: Theory, research, and applications,* (pp. 191–204). Newbury Park, CA: Sage.

Rieber, M., & Womack, M. (1967). The intelligence of preschool children as related to ethnic and demographic variables. *Exceptional Children, 34,* 604–615.

Romer, N., & Cherry, D. (1980). Ethnic and social class differences in children's sex-role concepts. *Sex Roles, 6,* 245–263.

Romero, G. J., Castro, F. G., & Cervantes, R. C. (1988). Latinas without work: Family, occupational and economic stress following unemployment. *Psychology of Women Quarterly, 12,* 281–297.

Rosen, E. I. (1987). *Bitter choices: Blue-collar women in and out of work.* Chicago: University of Chicago Press.

Ross, C. E. (1987). The division of labor at home. *Social Forces, 65,* 816–833.

Scanzoni, J. (1975). Sex roles, economic factors, and marital solidarity in black and white marriages. *Journal of Marriage and the Family, 37,* 130–144.

Schlozman, K. (1979). Women and unemployment: Assessing the biggest myths. In J. Freeman (Ed.), *Women: A feminist perspective* (pp. 290–312). Palo Alto, CA: Mayfield Publishing.

Schulz, D. (1969). *Coming up black: Patterns of ghetto socialization.* Englewood Cliffs, NJ: Prentice-Hall.

Shamir, B. (1985). Sex differences in psychological adjustment to unemployment and reemployment: A question of commitment, alternatives or finance? *Social Problems, 33,* 67–79.

Spitze, G. (1988). Women's employment and family relations: A review. *Journal of Marriage and the Family, 50*, 595–618.

Staples, R. (1970). The myth of the black matriarch. *The Black Scholar,1*, 8–16.

Stevans, L. K., Register, C., & Grimes, P. (1985). Race and the discouraged female worker: A question of labor force attachment. *Review of Black Political Economy, 15*, 89–97.

Stinson, J. F., Jr. (1990). Multiple jobholding up sharply in the 1980's. *Monthly Labor Review, 113*, 3–10.

Sweet, J. A. (1973). *Women in the labor force.* New York: Academic Press.

Sweet, J., & Bumpass, L. (1987). *American families and households.* New York: Russell Sage Foundation.

Taylor, M. (1988). A gender-based analysis of the consequences of employment reductions on well-being: Plant workers in two Newfoundland fishing outports. *Canadian Journal of Community Mental Health, 7*, 67–79.

Taylor, R. J., Chatters, L. M., Tucker, M. B., & Lewis, E. (1990). Developments in research on black families: A decade review.*Journal of Marriage and the Family, 52*, 993–1014.

Thomas, V. G. (1986). Career aspirations, parental support, and work values among black female adolescents. *Journal of Multicultural Counseling and Development, 14*, 177–185.

Thomas, V. G. (1990). Problems of dual-career black couples: Identification and implications for family interventions. *Journal of Multicultural Counseling and Development, 18*, 58–67.

Thompson, L., & Walker, A. J. (1989). Gender in families: Women and men in marriage, work, and parenthood. *Journal of Marriage and the Family, 51*, 845–871.

Thompson, M. S., & Ensminger, M. E. (1989). Psychological well-being among mothers with school age children: Evolving family structures. *Social Forces, 67* 715–730.

Tienda, M., & Glass, J. (1985). Household structure and labor force participation of black, Hispanic, and white mothers. *Demography, 22*, 22, 381–394.

Tienda, M., & Jensen, L. (1988). Poverty and minorities: A quarter-century profile of color and socioeconomic disadvantage. In G. D. Sandefur & M. Tienda (Eds.), *Divided opportunities* (pp. 23–61). New York: Plenum Press.

Turner, C. B., & Turner, B. F. (1982). Gender, race, social class, and self-evaluations among college students. *Sociological Quarterly, 23*, 491–507.

U.S. Bureau of the Census. (1991a). The black population in the United States: March 1990 and 1989. *Current population reports*, Ser. P-20, No. 448. Washington, DC: U.S. Government Printing Office.

U.S. Bureau of the Census. (1991b). *Statistical abstract of the United States: 1991.* Washington, DC: U.S. Government Printing Office.

U.S. Bureau of Labor Statistics. (1992). *Current population survey: March 1991.* Washington, DC: U.S. Government Printing Office.

Vandell, D. L. (1991). Belsky and Eggebeen's analysis of the NLSY: Meaningful results or statistical illusions? *Journal of Marriage and the Family, 53*, 1100–1103.

Vandell, D. L., & Ramanan, J. (1990, April). *Effects of early and concurrent maternal employment on children from economically disadvantaged families.* Paper presented at the International Conference on Infant Studies, Montreal.

Warr, P., & Parry, G. (1982). Paid employment and women's psychological well-being. *Psychological Bulletin, 91,* 498–516.

White, L., & Keith, B. (1990). The effect of shift work on the quality and stability of marital relations. *Journal of Marriage and the Family, 52,* 453–462.

Wilson, M. (1989). Child development in the context of the black extended family. *American Psychologist, 44,* 380–383.

Woods, M. B. (1972). The unsupervised child of the working mother. *Developmental Psychology, 1,* 14–25.

Zill, N., & Peterson, J. (1982). Learning to do things without help. In L. Laosa & I. Sigel (Eds.), *Families as learning environments for children* (pp. 343–374). New York: Plenum Press.

■ Part 4
Issues Facing Families of Employed Mothers

■ 11
Child Care Concerns of Employed Mothers

Mary Benin and Yinong Chong

Finding quality, affordable, reliable child care is one of the most serious problems faced by employed mothers. Child care concerns not only increase a mother's level of stress (Googins, 1991) but make her less productive at work (Fernandez, 1986; Googins, 1991). The severity of child care problems faced by employed mothers is perhaps most vividly indicated by Fernandez's (1986) finding that 47% of female employees with children aged 5 years and under have considered quitting because of child care problems.

Child care concerns are primarily an issue for employed mothers and for single-parent fathers. Married men seem to be relatively immune from child care problems whether or not their spouse is employed. For example, Fernandez (1986) reports that 72% of employed mothers but only 28% of employed fathers with children aged 2 to 5 have missed work to care for a sick child. The tendency for mothers, and not fathers, to be responsible for child care is an issue not only for family equity but for corporate family policies as well. Married men make up the majority of upper-level management, and it is at this level that personnel policies are determined. If men have not experienced the problems of finding quality child care or substitute care for sick children, they tend to be less sensitive to the need for child care benefits for employees. In Fernandez's study, 45% of men but only 7% of women in upper-level management rejected all six company-supported child care benefits proposed in the survey.

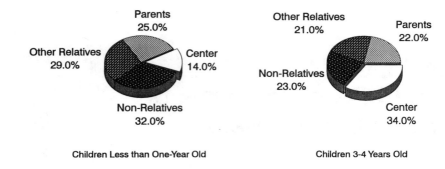

Children Less than One-Year Old   Children 3-4 Years Old

In percentages

FIGURE 11.1   **Child care arrangements, of employed women (in percentages), U. S. Bureau of the Census Data (1987).**

CHILD CARE USAGE

Figure 11.1 displays the U. S. Bureau of the Census (1987) data on child care arrangements for children of employed mothers. The majority of babies were cared for in homes other than their own, usually by nonrelatives and or relatives other than the parents. Approximately one quarter of children under age 1 with employed mothers used parental care arrangements in 1984–85. Only 14% of babies were in organized child care facilities. As for children aged 3 and 4, with employed mothers, the majority were in organized child care centers, with the rest almost equally divided between parental, other relative, and nonrelative care. Thus, as children grow older, the use of organized child care facilities rises substantially, and care by relatives and nonrelatives drops.

The percentages in Figure 11.1 are based on the general population. However, when one controls for race, differences in usage are apparent. Figure 11.2 shows the primary modes of child care by race of the parents, based on 1988 data from the National Survey of Families and Households (NSFH)[1], (see Sweet, Bumpass, & Call, 1988, for a description). Several differences are striking. Centers are used by 23% of Anglos and blacks but by only 7% of Mexican-American families with young children. Grandparents are used by 29% of black and 30% of Mexican-American families but by only 12% of Anglo families. Anglos are twice as likely as blacks and four times as likely as Mexican-Americans to use in-home sitters. Some of these differences may result from cultural differences in preferences for

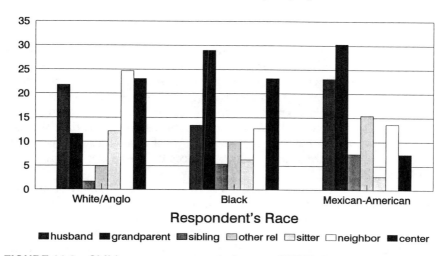

FIGURE 11.2 Child care arrangements by race (NSFH data, 1988).

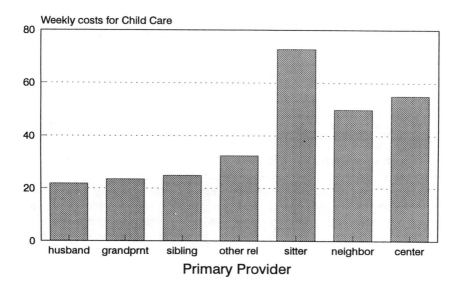

FIGURE 11.3 Child care costs by provider (NSFH data, 1988).

and availability of certain types of care. However, cost may also be a factor.

Figure 11.3 shows the costs of various types of child care, based on the 1988 NSFH data. It is clear that all types of nonfamily child care, portrayed in the last three bars of the figure, are more expensive than child care provided by family members. Not surprisingly, having a sitter come to the child's home is the most expensive type of child care. Taking one's child to an organized child care center costs more than taking the child to a non-family-member's home. However, in most cases these "family day care homes" are unregulated, which reduces the costs, but the quality is quite variable.

Combining the information in Figures 11.1 and 11.2, it is not surprising that Mexican Americans spend less, on the average, for child care than do whites or blacks, as they are least likely to use the more expensive nonfamily day care. Based on NSFH data, Mexican-American families with employed mothers and young children spend an average of $29 per week on child care, compared to $33 for black families and $46 for Anglo families. However, controlling for type of child care, these racial differences are not significant.

CHILD CARE PREFERENCES

Parental Care

Studies show that many parents consider parental care the ideal form of care for young children, even when the other forms of care are actually used. For example, in a recent *USA Today* poll of 439 employed parents with children under age 13, 77% of fathers and 70% of mothers responded affirmatively to the following hypothetical question: "If money was not a factor, would you or your spouse stay home to care for your child?" (cited in Sonenstein, 1991). Findings of Mason and Kuhlthau (1989), based on mothers in the greater Detroit metropolitan area, also show parental care to be the child care method of choice of employed mothers.

Moen and Dempster-McClain (1987) report that over half of employed mothers in the 1977 Quality of Employment Study, with children aged 12 and under, would prefer to spend less time working so that they could spend more time with their husbands and children. However, under most current company pay structures, few mothers have the option of working part-time, as part-time work pays much less per hour than full-time work and provides no benefits.

As Harriman (1982) points out, it is not engraved in stone that the work week is 40 hours, but that standard has been unquestioningly accepted. Feminist leaders have not ardently reproached employers for offering only the lowest-skill and lowest-paid jobs on a part-time basis. However, the authors believe that alternative work schedules that would allow the parents to be the primary child care providers should be prominent in the discussion of providing quality care for children of employed mothers.

Although research has not shown that nonparental child care is harmful, if parents prefer caring for their own children, the work force should be more flexible in providing work schedules that permit more parental care. Permanent part-time work with decent wages and prorated benefits would help many mothers to spend more time at home, as would job sharing with shared benefits. Most married-couple families with school-age children could benefit from staggered work schedules, for example, 7–3 and 9–5, which would allow one parent to be home before school and the other after school. Flexible work hours would help parents to meet doctors appointments and go to school functions. Parents of preschool-age children could benefit from home-based work and shift work.

However, even with more permanent part-time work and more staggered and flexible work schedules, many children will have to spend several hours a day in the care of someone other than the parents. Children whose mothers need or choose to work full-time will spend typically more than 8 hours a day in some form of child care. Thus, it is essential that mothers have high-quality options available to them and the type of care that meets their children's age and personality needs.

Nonparental Care

Sonenstein (1991) points out that child care choices are often made under conditions of limited supply of available and affordable options. When choices are restricted, the arrangements that parents use may not necessarily reflect their preferences. Thus, the use patterns in Figures 11.1 and 11.2 partially may reflect choice and partially may reflect compromises that parents have to make to find and afford child care.

Several factors have been found to influence what type of nonparental care is selected for children of employed mothers. These include age of child; the family's income, size, and composition; its members' socioeconomic characteristics and personal tastes; and exogenous phenomenon, such as the availability of institutional day care centers or nursery schools (Duncan & Hill, 1975, 1977; Lehrer, 1983). Most studies conducted in the 1970s found that the availability of older children, friends, and relatives and the lower perceived price and perceived higher quality of such modes led mothers to choose these informal arrangements rather than formal ones (cf. Heckman, 1974). However, in the 1980s there was a phenomenal increase in the availability and popularity of formal child care. In a recent survey of Detroit-area mothers of preschool-age children, Mason and Kuhlthau (1989) found that although care by the father and other relatives is overwhelmingly the most popular choice of child care for children under the age of 3, day care centers and other formal care arrangements are the most popular choice for 4- and 5-year olds.

Nonemployed Mother's Preferences

One of the major barriers to employment for mothers of young children is the lack of available and affordable child care. When asked if they would seek employment were reliable care available at reasonable cost, 26% of nonemployed mothers of children under the age of 5 indicated they would look for work (U. S. Bureau of the Census, 1983). O'Connell and Bloom (1987) found that the proportions responding affirmatively in the census survey were higher among women who were never married, black, low-educated, and low-income. Further evidence of the link between child care and employment comes from studies in which such care has been provided. Campbell et al. (Campbell, Breitmayer, & Ramey, 1986) found that providing free child care to teenage mothers increased the percentages who were self-sufficient and who completed high school. Robins (1988) found that the availability of child care on the premises of public housing increased the percentage of mothers who were employed and decreased the percentage who were dependent on welfare. Political conservatives have long desired to reduce welfare funding. One economical way to accomplish this is to subsidize convenient, reliable care for low-income mothers of young children.

QUALITY OF CHILD CARE

There is extreme variation in the quality of child care available in this country. Unfortunately, excellent child care centers are rare. As part of the National Child Care Staffing Study, 227 day care centers in five metropolitan areas of the United States were examined, and only 12% of the sample classrooms received a rating of good (Whitebook, Howes, & Phillips, 1989). The same study found that small group size and high teacher qualifications increased children's language development, whereas high staff turnover rates decreased children's language development. Zaslow (1991) reports on several studies showing that the quality of child care, as measured by teacher training, teacher's interaction style, child-staff ratios, and class size, not only affect the child's academic and social development in the preschool years but continue to do so into the early school years.

Unfortunately, all employed mothers do not have equal access to quality care. Zaslow (1991) notes several studies that have found that families with high socioeconomic status receive the highest-quality child care. In the National Child Care Staffing Study, it was found that middle-income families receive the lowest-quality care relative to either high- or low-income families (Whitebook et al., 1989).

Clearly, the whole country benefits if all children have access to quality early childhood education. A child's chances for such an education are affected not only by his or her parents' socioeconomic status but also by the state in which he or she resides. One disadvantage of not having strong federal standards for child care facilities or staff training is that the state regulations vary greatly. For example, most private child care centers operate with child-to-staff ratios very near the minimum for their state, and those ratios vary from 3:1 to 7:1 for children aged 1 and under and from 6:1 to 16:1 for 3-year-old children (U. S. Department of Labor, 1988). Clearly, the children who live in states with low ratios have a much greater chance of having a quality child care experience than do those who live in states with deplorably high ratios.

EMPLOYER-ASSISTED CHILD CARE

Although few employers provide any form of child care assistance, some recent trends are encouraging. According to data from the Employee Benefits Survey, between 1984 and 1989 the percentage of full-time employees in medium and large private establishments who were offered child care assistance grew from 1% to 5% (Hyland, 1990). Professional and technical employees are more likely to be offered a child care benefit than are service or production employees. Furthermore, government employees and employees of large private firms are more likely than employees of small firms to be offered a child care benefit (Hayghe, 1988). The most frequent forms of child care benefits are information and referral services and counseling services. Five percent of firms offer such services to at least some of their employees. Only 3% offer employees assistance with child care expenses, and only 2% sponsor day care, either on- or off-site. The few employers who are sponsoring day care are those in service areas that have a shortage of trained female workers, such as hospitals and banks.

The major reason that more employers don't get involved in providing child care benefits is cost. However, when employers do provide some form of child care, the benefits are substantial, including improved employee morale, recruitment advantage, lower absentee rates, less turnover, greater employee work satisfaction, better public relations, less tardiness, and increased productivity (Friedman, 1986). One well-designed study matched employees using a near-site child care center with two groups of other employees from the same firm: mothers using other child care arrangements and employees with no or grown children. Not only was the absenteeism rate for the day care users lower than that for participants in the two control groups, the average monthly turnover rate for the program users was over three times lower than that of the control groups (Friedman, 1986).

Employees want their employers to provide child care. A White House poll in 1981 found that 85% of respondents felt that employers should provide child care at the place of employment or arrange part-time schedules with full job benefits (Rappaport, 1984).

CARE OF SICK CHILDREN

Fernandez (1986) found that providing care for sick children was the number-one problem (of a list of 15) for female employees with children. Most formal child care centers and many informal family day care homes do not accept sick children. Parents often have satisfactory everyday arrangements for young children but find it difficult to arrange for substitute care for sick children, especially on short notice.

The most frequent arrangement to care for sick children is that the mother stays home. In Googins' (1991) study, he found that 66% of married female respondents stayed home with their sick children, compared to only 21.3% of married male parents. There are probably several reasons that mothers are more likely than fathers to miss work: (1) unless they are salaried workers, the loss of a day's pay for the wife will usually cost the family less than the loss of the husband's wage because women typically earn less than their husbands; (2) because of sex-role stereotyping, the mother is perceived to be the more nurturing parent, and thus some families may believe that the mother is the more appropriate parent to care for sick children; (3) because of sex-role stereotyping, it may be more acceptable to the wife's employer for her to miss work to care for a sick child than it is for the husband to miss for that reason. Few companies officially condone time off to care for sick children. Informally, supervisors may be more accepting of mothers taking such time off than of fathers. Findings from Googins (1991) support the notion that it may be difficult for fathers to take time off to care for sick children. In his study, only 30% of single-parent fathers, compared to 65% of single-parent mothers, reported staying home to care for sick children. It seems unlikely that single-parent fathers have twice as easy a time finding care for sick children as do single-parent mothers. Lack of opportunity to stay home may drive fathers to more desperate or expensive options than mothers use.

TABLE 11.1 **Employed Mothers' Arrangements for Care of Sick Children (NSFH Data, 1988)**

Type of Care	Children Aged 0–4	Children Aged 5–11
Mother stays home	59%	54
Regular child care	26%	—
Husband or partner	3%	17%
Other relatives	10%	25%
Neighbor or babysitter	1%	8%
Child stays alone		1%
Older sibling		4%
Day care		1%
Other arrangement		1%
Total	99%	112%[a]

[a]Total greater than 100% because multiple responses allowed.

Table 11.1 gives the current modes of care for sick children used by employed mothers in the NSFH data. It is clear that the mother is overwhelmingly responsible for sick children. When children are of school age, grandparents and other relatives are the second most frequent choice. For young children, regular child care arrangements are the second choice, but that also may be relative care. Husbands or partners are the third most likely choice for care for sick school-age children, but in only 3% of the cases are they the most likely choice for preschool-age children.

Clearly, employers would prefer that parents use other arrangements that do not involve their missing work. But what do parents prefer? Landis and Earp (1987) surveyed mothers whose children went to day care centers and asked them what forms of child care they preferred for sick children. For their first and second choices, 30% of the respondents preferred in-home options only. Those choices were usually care by parents, followed by care by relatives, friends, or baby-sitters in the home. However, 26% chose only out-of-home care for their mildly ill children. The first choice for out-of-home care was a sick room at the regular day care center, and the second choice was a supervised room for sick children at the parents' workplace. Forty-four percent of parents chose a combination of in-home and out-of-home care. Thus, some 74% of families would be interested in out-of-home care for their mildly ill children, were it available.

Currently, few day care centers and even fewer workplaces have a special room dedicated to meet the needs of sick children, and these are by far the most popular out-of-home options with parents. Parents were not enthusiastic about the hypothetical choice of having a sick-child-care worker come to their home or having a community center for sick children. Perhaps these options were seen as less familiar and thus less comfortable for children than going to their regular child care center or to their parents' workplace, where they know Mom or Dad is nearby.

The employees who were most interested in out-of-home care were minority, single, and low-income parents. This result is not surprising, as they are most likely to be hourly rather than salaried workers and thus most likely to suffer economic loss resulting from staying home with sick children.

BEFORE- AND AFTER-SCHOOL CARE

According to government estimates, in the 1990s, 75% of women with school-age children will be in the work force (U. S. Bureau of labor Statistics, 1987), and in 1984 approximately 2.1 million children aged 5 to 13 cared for themselves when not in school (Bruno, 1987). Although most families are able to have at least one parent home before the children go to school, according to the NSFH data, in 20.6% of families with employed mothers, the parents are home sometimes, rarely, or never before their 5–11-year-old children go to school. Of those families in which neither parent is home, in 16.5% the child is home alone, and in 26.7% the child is home with an older sibling.

It is even harder for working parents to be home after school. Only 26% of working parents in the NSFH were able always or usually to be home after school with their 5–11-year-old schoolchildren. When the parents are not home, in 11.3% of cases the child is home alone, and in 27.7% of cases the child is home with an older sibling. Many parents worry about the care their children are getting after school. In fact, in the business world a new term is being widely used—the "three o'clock syndrome"—which "refers to reduced productivity and higher error and accident rates as employees' minds turn to their children around the time when school lets out" (Friedman, 1986, p. 28).

In a few cases, the child who is left home alone is a kindergartner or a first- or second-grader. However, Cain and Hofferth (1989) estimate that less than 1.3% of 7-year-olds and even fewer 6- and 5-year-olds are left alone, and only about 3% of 7-year-olds are left in the care of someone under the age of 14. Few people would argue that it is appropriate for children of this young age to be left alone; however, the majority of children in self-care are older.

Currently, there is much debate in the literature regarding the advantages and disadvantages of self-care for older children. Robinson, Rowland, and Coleman (1986) argue that the case against self-care is mainly based on flawed scientific data and isolated events made sensational by the popular press. Scientific review of the effects of self-care on children has concluded "that there are few or no differences in the social and cognitive development of self-care children when compared to children in adult care" (Flynn & Rodman, 1989, p. 663; see also Robinson et al., 1986).

Presently, not enough after-school programs are available for the employed mothers who wish to use them. Because child care advocates are interested in having more after-school programs, they often do not argue with the negative image of "latchkey children" presented by the media. The advocates of after-school programs feel that a stronger case can be made for rapidly expanding after-school programs at schools and community centers if the politicians believe that self-care leads to negative consequences such as alcoholism, drug abuse, teenage pregnancy, and becoming crime victims. Unfortunately, as Flynn and Rodman (1989) point out, there may be some unintended negative consequences, such as the general public's being misled into believing that after-school self-care is dangerous and detrimental to children. Women who cannot find satisfactory after-school care for children may drop out of the work force rather than leave their children in self-care. Other women may unnecessarily delay their reentry into the work force for fear of leaving their preadolescents in self-care.

Knowledge of the effects of self-care for older children[2] is limited because few rigorous studies have been conducted. The results show that whether or not self-care is advisable depends on the neighborhood and the self-care arrangement. Urban children seem to fare worse than suburban and rural children. They are more likely to be afraid and to suffer from boredom and loneliness. Fortunately, research has shown that children living in central cities are less likely than suburban or rural children to be in self-care (Cain & Hofferth, 1989). Further, children who have rules and a routine to follow while at home, such as not watching TV unless all of their homework is done, fare much better than children who are left unsupervised without such rules and routines (Steinberg, 1986).

THE ROLE OF RESEARCH

Silverstein (1991) points out that research on child care has focused on trying to detect any negative impacts of other than mother care. Although 20 years of research on this topic has not reliably found problems of any magnitude, researchers continue to refine measures in attempts to document the existence of problems. This research agenda seems unproductive given that current economic conditions and the large number of single-parent homes dictate that most children will be cared for many hours by someone other than their mothers. It would be far more useful for researchers to focus on the impact of quality care no matter who provides it and to "tie research on child care to the negative consequences of the lack of affordable, government-subsidized, high-quality programs" (Silverstein, 1991, p. 1030).

PUBLIC POLICY

As has been pointed out repeatedly by Kahn and Kamerman (1987), Zigler (1990), and others, our country is the only one of the modern industrialized countries not to have formal family and child care policies. At issue is not only determining what the child care policies of the United States should be but how they can be obtained.

Kamerman (1985) argues that "feminists and feminist organizations (the National Organization for Women, for example), or the various professional women's organizations, have been conspicuously absent from the leadership group on the child care issue" (p. 260). She believes that there are two major reasons why it has not been on the agenda of women's organizations: (1) it is not seen as central to all women because child care affects only some women and even then for just a part of their lives, and (2) acknowledging that child care is of particular salience to women reinforces traditional stereotypes that child care is women's responsibility.

Kamerman (1985) counters the first argument by pointing out that repeated surveys of employed women have shown that child care needs and concerns are the number-one problem faced by employed women. She notes that because of the large number of divorces and the high employment rate of single mothers, over half of the employed women have minor children (Kamerman, 1985). We have also seen that the lack of available and affordable child care is the main reason nonworking mothers of young children give for not working. (O'Connell & Bloom, 1987). Further, given that the poverty rate for working mothers of young children is only one tenth that of unemployed mothers, it should be a high priority for everyone interested in reducing the number of women in poverty to promote more widely available, quality, affordable child care (Kamerman, 1985).

Kamerman (1985) counters the argument that feminists should ignore the child care issue to avoid reinforcing the stereotype that child care is a women's job by noting that child care is salient to more employed women than men. Only 38% of employed men, compared to 55% of employed women, have minor children, primarily because of the high divorce rate and the much greater likelihood that children live with their mother following divorce. The voices of child care professionals and children's advocacy groups, such as the Children's Defense Fund, have not been adequate to promote national policies to establish safe, affordable child care for all children whose parents work. If women's groups ignore the issue, it is unlikely that child care will become a national concern; only a minority of employed men are fathers of young children, and those who are fathers are unlikely to be responsible for finding child care. Kamerman argues that the dangers of ignoring the child care issue should be of greater concern to feminists than the dangers of reinforcing the stereotype of women as primary caretakers.

Zigler (1990) argues that the main reason we have not had a family policy passed is that it has been considered a women's issue, and women's issues are not high-priority issues on Capitol Hill. He reminds us that after the summer drought in the late 1980s, the farming lobby had a relief package passed, and similarly, after a flag-burning spree, veterans quickly got Congress to pass a anti–flag burning bill. As a 20-year lobbyist for a child care policy, he states: "I can only conclude that as a woman's issue, child care can go nowhere" (p. 186).

Unfortunately, although the need for quality child care should be an issue for all citizens, men have not yet found this to be a high-priority issue. In a 1988 survey of human resources vice presidents and union leaders, Martin et al. found that women in these positions were much more likely than their male counterparts to believe that family policies would benefit workers. As reported earlier, Fernandez (1986) found that female employees were much more likely than males to experience child care problems and to identify child care benefits as high priorities. Thus, although a lobby other than a feminist one might be more effective, at this time it seems that it is mainly women who are concerned with the issue.

Zigler (1990) recommends recouching the argument for child care in terms of the need to establish quality early childhood education for all children in order to regain our competitiveness in the world industrial market. Regaining industrial competitiveness has become part of the political agenda in this country. Perhaps the argument for better regulation of and subsidies for quality preschool care would have a broader appeal if they were linked to increasing our competitiveness rather than to reducing women's family/work conflicts or making it possible for poor women to work. It is a sad comment on our politicians' priorities that making it easier for women to support themselves and their families is not a vital issue.

NOTES

1. The NSFH was funded by a grant (HD21009) from the Center of Population Research of the National Institute of Child Health and Human Development. The survey was designed and carried out at the Center for Demography and Ecology at the University of Wisconsin-Madison under the direction of Larry Bumpass and James Sweet. The fieldwork was done by the Institute for Survey Research at Temple University.
2. The age at which it is appropriate to allow children to be home alone after school is itself an issue. Robinson, Rowland, and Coleman (1986) report that fifth grade is the most common time for children to begin self-care.

REFERENCES

Bruno, R. (1987). After-school care of school-age children: December 1984. *Current population reports*, Ser. P–23, No. 149. Washington, DC: U. S. Government Printing Office.

Cain, V. S., & Hofferth, S. L. (1989). Parental choice of self-care for school-age children. *Journal of Marriage and the Family, 51,* 65–77.

Campbell, F. A., Breitmayer, B., & Ramey, C. T. (1986). Disadvantaged single teenage mothers and their children: Consequences of free educational day care. *Family Relations, 35,* 63–68.

Duncan, G. J., & Hill, C. R. (1975). Modal choice in child care arrangements." In G. J. Duncan & J. N. Morgan (Eds.), *Five thousand American families:—patterns of economic progress* (Vol. 3, Chap. 7). Ann Arbor, MI: Survey Research Center, Institute for Social Research.

Duncan, G. J., & Hill, C. R. (1977). The child care mode of working mothers. In G. J. Duncan & J. N. Morgan (Eds.), *Five thousand American families:—Patterns of economic progress* (Vol. 5, Chap. 14). Ann Arbor, MI: Survey Research Center, Institute for Social Research.

Fernandez, J. P. (1986). *Child care and corporate productivity.* Lexington, MA: Lexington Books.

Flynn, C. P., & Rodman, H. (1989). Latchkey children and after-school care: A feminist dilemma? *Policy Studies Review, 8,* 663–673.

Friedman, D. E. (1986). Child care for emplyees' kids. *Harvard Business Review, 65,* 28–34.

Googins, B. K. (1991). *Work/family conflicts.* New York: Auburn House.

Harriman, A. (1982). *The work/leisure trade-off.* New York: Praeger.

Hayghe, H. V. (1988, September). Employers and child care: What roles do they play? *Monthly Labor Review,* pp. 38–44.

Heckman, J. J. (1974). Effects of child-care programs on women's work effort. *Journal of Political Economy, 82*(2, Suppl.), 136–163.

Hyland, S. L. (1990, September). Helping employees with family care. *Monthly Labor Review,* pp. 22–26.

Kahn, A. J., & Kamerman, S. B. (1987). *Child care: Facing the hard choices*. Dover, MA: Auburn House.

Kamerman, S. B. (1985). Child care services: An issue for gender equity and women's solidarity. *Child Welfare, 3*, 259–271.

Landis, S. & Earp, J. A. (1987). Sick child care options: What do working mothers prefer? *Women and Health, 12*, 61–77.

Lehrer, E. (1983). Determinants of child care mode choice: An economic perspective. *Social Science Research, 12*, 69–80.

Mason, K. O., & Kuhlthau, K. (1989). Determinants of child care ideals among the mothers of preschool children. *Journal of Marriage and the Family, 51*, 593–603.

Martin, P. Seymour, S. Courage, M., Godbey, K., & Tate., R. (1988). Work-family policies: Corporate, union, feminist, and pro-family leaders' views. *Gender and Society, 3*, 385–400.

Moen, P. & Dempster-McClain, D. I. (1987). Employed parents: Role strain, work time, and preferences for working less. *Journal of Marriage and the Family, 49*, 579–590.

O'Connell, M., & Bloom, D. (1987). *Juggling jobs and babies: America's child care challenge* (Population Trends and Public Policy, No. 12). Washington, DC: Population Reference Bureau.

Presser, H. B. (1989). Can we make time for children? The economy, work, schedules and child care. *Demography, 26*, 523–543.

Rappaport, M. (1984). Childcare comes of age. *Management World, 13*, 30–32.

Robins, P. K. (1988). Child care and convenience: The effects of labor market entry costs on economic self-sufficiency among public housing residents. *Social Science Quarterly, 69*, 122–136.

Robinson, B. E., Rowland, B. H., & Coleman, M. (1986). *Latchkey kids*. Lexington, MA: Lexington Books.

Silverstein, L. B. (1991). Transforming the debate about child care and maternal employment. *American Psychologist, 46*, 1025–1032.

Sonenstein, F. L. (1991). The child care preferences of parents with young children: how little is known. In J. S. Hyde & M. J. Essex (Eds.), *Parental leave and child care: Setting a research and policy agenda* (chap. 20). Philadelphia: Temple University Press.

Steinberg, L. (1986). Latchkey children and susceptibility to peer pressure: An ecological analysis. *Developmental Psychology, 22*, 1–7.

Sweet, J., Bumpass, L., & Call, V. (1988). The design and content of the National Survey of Families and Households (Working Paper NSFH–1). Center for Demography and Ecology. Madison: University of Wisconsin.

U. S. Bureau of the Census. (1983). Child care arrangements of working mothers: June, 1982. *Current popula;tion reports*, Ser. P–23, No. 129. Washington, DC: U. S. Government Printing Office.

U. S. Bureau of the Census (1987). Who's minding the kids? Child care arrangements: Winter 1984–85. *Current population reports*, Ser. P–70, No. 9. Washington, DC: U. S. Government Printing Office.

U. S. Bureau of Labor Statistics. (1987). *Statistical abstract of the United States* (107th ed.) Washington, DC: U. S. Department of Commerce.

U. S. Department of Labor. (1988). *Child care: A workforce issue* (Report of the Secretary's Task Force). Washington, DC: U. S. Government Printing Office.

U. S. Department of Labor, Women's Bureau. (1982). Employers and child care: Establishing services through the workplace (Pamphlet No. 23). Washington, DC: U. S. Government Printing Office.

Whitebook, M., Howes, C., & Phillips, D. (1989). *Who cares? Child care teachers and the quality of care in America.* Berkeley, CA: Child Care Employee Project.

Zaslow, M. J. (1991). Variation in child care quality and its implications for children. *Journal of Social Issues, 47,* 125–138.

Zigler, E. (1990). Shaping child care policies and programs in America. *American Journal of Community Psychology, 18,* 183–215.

■ 12
Family Roles and Responsibilities: What Has Changed and What Has Remained the Same?

Maureen Perry-Jenkins

A common theme that arises when examining the literature on the family over the past two decades is the focus on changing family structure. A plethora of books and articles on family life open their discussion by citing the impact of women's increased labor force participation on the family. A major postulate in this literature is that as women take on new roles outside the family, family members, especially husbands, will have to adjust their work and family roles in a complementary fashion. For example, Hood (1986) suggests that "underlying much of this research is the assumption that the provider role is the reciprocal of the housewife/mother role and that, therefore, changes in the allocation of provider-role responsibilities are closely related to changes in the allocation of other household responsibilities" (p. 349). However, the research that has tested this assumption is fairly consistent in its conclusion. Men do not take on significantly more household work when their wives are employed (Ferber, 1982). The literature does suggest that husbands of employed wives may take on slightly more childcare responsibilities (Pleck, 1985); however, their increased involvement in this area does not match their wives' shift in work load (Pleck, 1977).

A goal of this chapter is to examine why we have not witnessed the expected reallocation of work and family role responsibilities among husbands and wives when they are in dual-earner situations. It will be proposed that we must look beyond changes in role behaviors, such as women's increased employment hours or the amount of time men spend doing household chores, and pay closer attention to the meaning that men and women attach to their roles. Role theory and feminist theory will be examined in an effort to place the concept of family roles in a larger theoretical perspective, as well as to lend support to alternative explanations for why the inequity in the division of labor persists in dual-earner families. A second aim of this chapter will be to review some of the relevant research that looks beyond simple role behaviors to examine the implications of men's and women's attachment to the provider and housewife/mother roles for the division of labor in the home. Finally, the discussion will close with a look at how family role definitions and behaviors may vary when we look beyond the white, middle-class population; the group upon which the majority of research in this area rests. An ecological perspective stresses the importance of examining how differing family contexts, such as low-income families, single-parent families, and families of different racial and cultural backgrounds, may lead individuals to define and act out their roles in different ways. It is through examining diversity in family contexts that we will come to better understand how roles are constructed and maintained in families.

ROLE THEORY AND FAMILY ROLES

Before launching into a discussion of family roles it is important to place the concept of roles within the theoretical perspective from which it sprang. As Nye and Gecas (1976) clearly demonstrate in their review of the role concept, scholars have not reached consensus on the specific meaning of the concept or the means to measure it. In its most simplistic sense the term *role* refers to a part or character played by an individual, such as mother, brother, housewife, or breadwinner. The literature on roles, however, points to quite varied interpretations of the concept. The structural tradition, introduced by Linton in 1936, defines *role* as "an element of culture (normative) associated with a given social status position" (Nye & Gecas, 1976, p. 4). In contrast, the interactionist tradition (Mead, 1934) "lays major emphasis on the emergent quality of roles" (Nye & Gecas, 1976, p. 5).

More specifically, a structural perspective would lead one to focus on cultural and normative prescriptions and proscriptions that dictate the "appropriate" behavior of husbands, wives, fathers, mothers, and children in families. Structuralists would examine societal definitions of specific roles and examine how well individuals behaved within the criteria for that role.

In contrast, the interactionist perspective would emphasize the developmental and creative aspects of roles. A well-known scholar in this tradition, Ralph Turner (1970), not only defined roles that could be reasonably defined from cultural expectations such as the breadwinner role and the housewife role but also identified family roles such as the encourager, the mediator, and the harmonizer. A basic tenet of Turner's conceptualization of roles is that humans are created through a social system and through social interaction. Individuals create their own reality through roles. The organization of the family provides an arena for both structuralist and interactionist interpretations of roles because families usually subscribe to both formal roles (e.g., provider, caregiver) and informal roles (e.g., nurturer, martyr). The challenge comes in reconciling these two alternative perspectives on roles.

Nye and Gecas (1976) offered some guidance in merging the two different conceptions of roles:

> It would be possible to resolve the conflicting definitions by assigning the single term "role" to a set of cultural expectations of behavior, attitudes, and values while employing dynamic concepts such as role enactment or role behavior to the actual behaviors performed. While any individual scholar is likely to be more interested in one or the other the awareness of the other and some common role language would greatly increase the value of the concept. (p. 7)

Thus, it appears that there may be utility in examining family roles, not only as they are defined culturally but also as family members perceive and enact their respective roles.

Work by Goffman (1961) in the area of role theory offers insight into some key concepts included in this theoretical approach. Goffman suggests that roles are the basic unit of socialization in society and that it is by understanding these roles that individuals come to organize their behavior in accordance with expectations. Goffman distinguishes between two important concepts in role theory that are hypothesized to be related to why individuals take on certain roles: the concepts are *role attachment* and *role commitment*. According to Goffman, in individual becomes committed to a role when, because of the "fixed and independent character of institutional arrangements," he or she is forced to take on a certain course of action. Basically, an individual becomes locked into a position and is required to live up to the promises and sacrifices built into that role. Goffman argues that a person only becomes deeply committed to a role she or he performs routinely.

Role attachment, on the other hand, refers to one's becoming affectively and cognitively enamored with a role but not necessarily being committed to it. It is expected, however, that an individual will become attached to a role if she or he is a committed and regular performer of it.

UNDERSTANDING THE PROVIDER AND HOUSEWIFE/MOTHER ROLES

It is my contention that the distinction between role commitment and attachment has implications for understanding men's sense of responsibility and connection to the provide role and women's connection to the housewife/mother role. As is evidenced by Hood's (1986) work with dual-earner couples, employed women often do not experience the commitment to the provider role that men do. In general, women do not feel locked into the position to provide. Moreover, it is not their *duty* to provide (Haas, 1986; Hood, 1986). As long as women have that sense of freedom from providing, they can be attached to the provider role but not necessarily committed to it. Similarly, it can be argued that men do not experience commitment to the homemaker/parent role as women do; they are not locked into this role. Goffman (1961) proposed that the social and institutional arrangements in our society require that men be committed to the provider role and women to the housewife/mother role. Additionally, he argues that commitment to these roles will usually come to represent a major part of the self.

Turner (1970), writing along these same lines, suggested that the reason men continue to invest in the male occupational role is simply that a man's occupation identifies him. The provider role is intimately linked with a man's sense of self and self-esteem. The importance of earned income and a view of oneself as a capable provider has been demonstrated in a number of empirical studies to be related to men's self-esteem. Komarovsky (1940) found that men unable to fulfill their roles as economic providers to the family became more unstable emotionally. More recently, Kessler (1982) found that income was the most important predictor of men's psychological distress. Similarly, Staines, Pottick, and Fudge (1986) showed that the most important indicator of low job and life satisfaction was a sense of inadequacy as a provider. It appears, therefore, that men have a lot to lose if they "give up" their provider role. These findings offer some explanation for why men may not relinquish their provider role responsibilities even when their wives are employed and also point to possible reasons for men's lack of participation in household work.

The links between role responsibility and well-being are less clear when examining women. A large body of research points to the small but positive effects of employment on women's well-being (Freudiger, 1983; Gove & Geerken, 1977; Spitze, 1988), suggesting that enacting the provider role is related to women's sense of self. Research on women's roles as gatekeepers to their husbands' involvement in family work, however, points to the importance of women's commitment to their home caretaker role as well. For women, although employment is usually positively linked to their well-being, they may remain reluctant to relinquish responsibility for their housewife/mother role because, traditionally, it has been this role that has offered women their greatest sense of worth. Here too there is evidence to suggest that women have something to lose by relinquishing housewife/mother responsibilities and assuming provider responsibilities.

To conclude, roles are much more than the role behaviors one performs. The preceding discussion suggests that as role behaviors of women change in one arena we should not necessarily expect to see reciprocal changes in men's role behaviors. The emphasis must shift from examining the enactment of behaviors to understanding the meanings these roles hold for both men and women. Simply looking at a person's behavior or the role she or he enacts is a far cry from understanding the value of that role for a person's sense of self. At a macro level, we must also recognize the role of society in dictating more structural definitions of roles, which plays into individual's conceptions of their roles. Thus, role theory offers a useful approach to understanding the division of family responsibilities in dual-earner families by pointing to the importance of examining and distinguishing among concepts such as role enactment, role attachment, and role commitment. It should be noted, however that feminist scholars have critiqued much of role theory as being deterministic and inflexible. The following discussion reviews some of the feminist arguments against role theory and goes on to describe ways in which differences in the two theoretical positions may be reconciled.

A FEMINIST PERSPECTIVE ON FAMILY ROLES

The feminist reaction to role theory has been, in large part, a response to Parsons' (1970) classic depiction of the family in which the man takes on the instrumental tasks and women are in charge of the expressive roles.

Feminist theorists have rejected the notion of a nuclear household in which a working social order is fixed and specialized and instead have proposed further questioning and theorizing about the nature of sex and gender outside this rigid model. Thorne (1982) has argues that the language of roles suggests a sense of the fixed and dichotomous, with the result that the concept of roles has restricted women's and men's abilities to experience alternative roles. Role theory, particularly the concept of gender roles, isolates gender issues into one discrete category and fails to recognize gender as a "master identity" that cuts across many roles and situations (West & Zimmerman, 1987). Further, Thorne (1982) argues that the conceptualization of gender as a role makes it difficult to examine its influence on other roles.

There is little doubt that as a society we have rigidly prescribed roles for men and women; yet I would propose that it is in understanding men's and women's interpretation of their worker, parent, or spouse roles that we begin to see how gender is incorporated into the construction of each role. It is the master identity of gender that leads men and women to develop different meanings and attachments to what objectively and behaviorally appear to be the same role. In Ferree's (1990) words, "While the sex role model assumes a certain packaging of structures, behaviors, and attitudes, the gender model analyses the construction of such packages" (p. 868). Thus, although the feminist debate over the usefulness of role theory is far from settled, for the purposes of this discussion it is proposed that aspects of role theory are useful in understanding the specialization of men's and women's roles that persist in American society. In addition, it is proposed that the construction of gender and family roles cannot be understood independently of each other.

West and Zimmerman (1987) have proposed that gender not be conceptualized as a role not as a set of traits or variables: "gender is the product of social doings of some sort" (p. 129). Other researchers have also highlighted the importance of social interaction and interdependence between roles, especially when examining family role relationships (Peplau, 1983). In particular, the roles of provider and homemaker require that each partner share a mutual set of expectations regarding the other's responsibilities. In keeping with the idea of the interactive nature of roles, the definition of roles used in this chapter is based on Hood's (1986) conceptualization. Roles are "mutual expectations negotiated by the actors that define each actors responsibility to other family members in a given situation" (p. 354). Moreover, intricately woven into these role expectations is the production of gender as well. In understanding roles within families, it is important to recognize that gender permeates all levels of the establishment of roles. Consequently, it is women's and men's notions about gender that ultimately define and give meaning to their roles as providers and home caretakers. It is this symbolic construction of roles that holds implications for how a role is enacted within the family.

A feminist discussion of family roles and the division of labor would be remiss if it failed to address the importance of power in the negotiation of role responsibilities. The construct of power arises in most discussions of men's and women's roles in our culture; and a number of authors have noted that males exert power over females (Henley, 1977; Thorne, 1982; Unger, 1979). Power is usually defined as the control of resources and core social institutions that enables a person to get another person to behave differently than he or she would otherwise (French & Raven, 1959; Sherif, 1982). The issue of power becomes especially important when attempting to understand husbands' and wives' day-to-day processes of social exchange. In short, couples bargain with each other in terms of the relative power they possess, and they arrive at certain decisions. One domain of interaction for couples surrounds the division of family labor. It has been shown that men's perceptions of power and resources stem from their fulfillment of the provider role, regardless of whether their wives are employed or not. It may be that it is not necessarily the objective resources the husband brings to the bargaining table but his perception of power and resources that plays a part in his willingness to compromise or concede to his wife.

Ferree (1988) proposed that a wife's employment status alone indicates very little about how family roles are negotiated. She suggested that to understand power relations in a marriage we need to know how both spouses conceptualize provider-role and homemaker-role responsibilities and to examine the entitlements implicit in certain roles. Only then will be be able to assess "under what circumstances paid jobs can create the conditions that empower women to attempt to change the household division of labor, and sometimes succeed"(p. 5).

The literature reviewed above points to the importance of distinguishing between role behaviors that spouses enact and husbands' and wives' conceptualizations of their roles. It was proposed that role theory and feminist theory are not in direct opposition if one accepts the idea that gender is not a role but a master identity that influences the development of all other roles in families and in society. It was also posited that just as roles are created through social interaction, so too is gender. Thus, as we turn to the empirical literature on family roles in the next section, it will be critical to bear in mind the distinction between actual role enactment versus one's perception of role responsibility, as well as considering how social interaction and gender influence the construction of roles.

FAMILY ROLES: WHY SO LITTLE HAS CHANGED

If we look strictly at role behaviors, women are "behaving" more as providers, whereas men have modified their home caretaker behaviors very little (Spitze, 1988). Equitable shifts in behavior have not occurred, and the question becomes; why not? One answer to that question rests with a closer examination of men's and women's sense of duty and responsibility to their provider and home caretaker roles. The scant amount of research on the topic of role responsibility indicates that even women employed full-time outside the home rarely feel a "duty" to provide financially for the family (Haas, 1986; Hood, 1986). An interesting question that follows from this line of inquiry is, how does variation in commitment and attachment to provider and hometaker roles relate to men's and women's involvement in household work?

A number of studies have attempted to assess the importance of the provider role as it relates to the housewife/mother role. For example, Slocum and Nye (1976) found that even though the majority of wives and nearly half of the husbands did not think the husband should have to provide for his family by himself, only 6% of husbands and 10% of wives thought it was a wife's duty to work if children were in school, but not in preschool. Lopata (1971) found that in ranking roles in order of importance, 64% of housewives and 54% of working wives ranked the provider role as most important for men. Hood (1986) concludes from her review of the literature on the provider role that

> At present, working couples are willing to relieve the husband of some of his provider responsibility and acknowledge that the wife's contribution is important and perhaps even necessary. However, only a minority will agree that the duty to provide should be shared equally. Perhaps this inequity is the transitional double standard of the 1980's. (p. 354)

It is clear that a number of scholars have begun to recognize the provider role as important, especially when attempting to understand husbands' and wives' division of work and family responsibilities. What has been less clear in this literature is how to measure the provider role in a way that taps all of its complexity. Despite what Hood (1986) refers to as the pivotal nature of the provider role, most researchers fail to measure directly either women's responsibility for providing or men's views on relinquishing the provider role. Often proxy measures for provider responsibility have been utilized, such as number of hours in the labor force, absolute and relative income of wife, and at times the husbands' and the wife's attitudes toward her work role. In the following discussion, two studies are reviewed that attempted to measure directly both men's and women's provider-role attitudes in an effort to examine whether beliefs about one's role as a provider were differentially related to individual well-being, family relationships, and the division of labor in families.

Men's Provider-Role Attitudes, the Division of Labor, and Family Relationships

In the first study to be reviewed, a sample of 43 men in dual-earner families were interviewed, and their feelings of attachment to their provider role were examined (Perry-Jenkins & Crouter, 1990). Two main hypotheses were examined. First, it was hypothesized that men's attitudes about their provider role would be related to their involvement in family work. Second, it was hypothesized that discrepancies between provider attitudes and actual behavior in household work would be related to lower marital satisfaction. For example, it was expected that men who reported main/secondary ideas about providing (i.e., man is the main provider and the wife's income is seen as secondary) but were involved in a high number of household tasks would report low marital satisfaction because their attitudes and behavior were not in sync. In turn it was expected that men whose attitudes matched their level of involvement in household tasks would report relatively high marital satisfaction.

Based on work by Hood (1986), an attempt was made to measure men's provider role attitudes directly by assessing a number of dimensions elucidated by Hood that related to attitudes about providing. Four different dimensions of the construct were examined: they include (1) the husband/wife wage ratio, (2) beliefs about who should provide for families in general, (3) preferences regarding who should provide in one's own family, and (4) assessment of who actually provided in one's own family. Respondents answered a number of multiple-choice questions that tapped attitudes about the importance of each spouse's income, who should provide for families, and perceptions about who *does* provide in one's own family. In addition, two open-ended questions assessed (1) respondents' views about wives' employment and under what circumstances wives should work and (2) respondents' reports on who handles family finances and how both incomes are used (e.g., separate or joint accounts, wife's money used for extras or for key expenses). Subsequently, responses were coded independently and men were classified into one of three categories: (1) *main/secondary providers*, defined their provider role as primary and their wives' contributions as secondary, (2) *ambivalent coproviders* acknowledged the importance of their wives' incomes but were ambivalent about sharing the provider role, and (3) *coproviders* acknowledged the importance of their wives' work and reported sharing provider responsibilities.

Hood's results indicated that men's reports of provider-role responsibility were related to the division of labor in the home and to men's marital satisfaction. To summarize, men who reported their primary role was provider and who rated their wives' employment as less important to the family performed significantly fewer household tasks than did men who reported sharing provider-role responsibility with their wives. In the second part of this study the author proceeds to examine how Hood's congruence between provider-role beliefs and actual role behaviors were related to marital satisfaction. It was found that the men reported higher marital satisfaction in two situations: (1) when men were strongly attached to the provider role and performed few household tasks and (2) when men reported sharing provider role responsibilities with their wives and performed a high number of household tasks. Thus, it was not simply attitudes or behaviors alone that were important but rather the match between role attitudes and role behaviors that related to marital satisfaction. It is important to recognize that objectively all of the men in this study were part of a dual-earner couple where the wife was employed full-time; however, the important factor related to men's involvement in household work was not wives' employment status but *their* attitudes about their role as providers.

Linkages Between Women's Provider Attitudes and Family Life

With a slight twist on the theme, a similar study was conducted that examined linkages between wives' provider attitudes and wives' well-being, the quality of family relationships, and the division of labor (Perry-Jenkins, Seery, & Crouter, in press). Again, the rationale guiding this study was that simply enacting provider-role behaviors (e.g., working outside the home) was not the critical factor in understanding how women's work related to their own well-being and family life. What was important was how women interpreted their provider role and the importance of their jobs. It was hypothesized that variability in the way women conceptualized their provider role would be linked to differences in their psychological well-being, family relationships, and the division of labor in the home. In fact, a very different picture of individual well-being and family dynamics emerged for women with different provider orientations.

Women answered the identical provider-role questions that men completed in the first study. Based on their coded responses, wives were placed in one of three categories: (1) main/secondary providers, (2) ambivalent coproviders, and (3) coproviders. Discriminant function analyses were then performed to examine how aspects of women's well-being, marital and parent-child relationships, and the division of labor discriminated between women in the provider groups. A brief summary of the results follows.

With regard to psychological well-being, the main/secondary and ambivalent coprovider wives were the most depressed and reported the highest levels of role overload; coprovider wives were less depressed and relatively less overloaded. Looking at the data on the division of labor helps to explain some of these findings. The husbands of main/secondary wives performed approximately half as many tasks as did husbands of ambivalent coprovider and coprovider wives; it is not surprising that the main/secondary wives were overloaded. Interpreting ambivalent coprovider wives' low levels of well-being is less straightforward because their husbands performed almost twice as many tasks as do main/secondary husbands. What may be more important to the ambivalent wives' well-being, as the findings of Ross, Mirowsky, and Huber (1983) would suggest, is not what their husbands are doing in terms of housework but the women's ambivalent feelings about what *they* are doing, namely, paid work outside the home. Interestingly, it was the ambivalent coprovider wives who reported the lowest levels of marital satisfaction among the three groups. It may be that women who are supporting the family financially but feel ambivalent about doing so "vent" their depression and feelings of overload on their husbands.

Clearly, these two studies lack generalizability because of the small sample size. However, the fact that hypotheses were supported suggests that this avenue of research is an important one to pursue with larger and more diverse samples. Taken together, these two studies suggest that it is the meaning that men and women attach to their provider role that holds implications for the division of labor in families, individuals' psychological well-being, and family relationships. It was shown that it is not simply enacting the role behaviors, such as being employed, that relates to family outcomes but the interpretation of those behaviors as they relate to spouses' conceptualization of their provider roles that is the critical factor.

A flaw in the two studies just reviewed and in the majority of research on dual-earner families is the almost exclusive focus on white, middle-class families. This bias limits the generalizations we can make to other types of families, such as single-parent and low-income families, families of color, and families of different ethnic backgrounds. In the final section, issues that arise when examining different family contexts will be discussed, and directions for future research will be proposed.

FAMILY ROLES BEYOND THE WHITE, MIDDLE-CLASS MOLD

As was mentioned at the outset of this chapter, despite a growing interest in blue-collar and low-income families, as well as families of different racial and ethnic backgrounds, the majority of research on family roles in employed families has been narrowly focused on middle- and upper-middle-class white populations. An issue that arises when examining provider role responsibilities in financially secure families is that often couples have the luxury of not needing to rely on a second income. In such cases, a woman's work is often viewed as discretionary because her income is not vital to the family's economic security. Interesting questions arise regarding men's and women's notions about their provider roles when focusing our inquiry on blue-collar or low-income families as well as looking at single-parent families.

Ferree (1987) is one of the few researchers to examine work and family roles with a working-class population. She suggests that family scholars have assumed that women in the working class work only out of necessity; and therefore researchers have paid little attention to the meaning of work in these women's lives. Ferree's research with working-class women looked beyond that assumption to examine women's experiences of their jobs. She concludes: "Though financial necessity admittedly compels many women to work, they, like their husbands, receive much more than merely financial rewards from the job, rewards that are not as available in housework" (p. 439)—rewards such as feelings of competence, social contacts and interaction with other adults, and independence. In addition, unlike the research reviewed earlier, in which the majority of white, middle-class women *did not* endorse the idea that it was their duty to help provide for the family, in Ferree's working-class sample the women *did* endorse work as their duty. The question remains as to the implications of working-class women's commitment to the provider role for the division of labor in the home and for family relationships. Ferree's work suggests that women who take on provider role responsibilities empower themselves within the family, leading them to expect, and perhaps even demand, more equal participation from their husbands. Clearly, this hypothesis calls for more empirical work to examine the relationship between women's provider attitudes and the division of labor at home.

Mother-only families offer another context to examine how women define their provider role responsibilities. In mother-only families, mothers take on full responsibility for both providing financially for the family and being the homemaker and mother. In this context, should we expect to see women reporting the same positive outcomes in terms of psychological well-being that men who are sole providers have consistently reported (Kessler, 1982; Staines et al., 1986)? A partial answer to this question lies in some preliminary data from a sample of 55 mother-only families (Perry-Jenkins & Gilman-Hanz, 1991), in which all of the single-mothers were employed full-time in working-class jobs; and all had at least one child between the ages of 8 and 12. Fifty-four of the 55 mothers interviewed expressed feelings of freedom, independence, and control as being the most positive aspect of their provider roles. As one single-mother concluded, "It is my life, my decision, and my choice." In another's voice, "Knowing I don't need a husband to survive is the best part of providing." The dramatic consistency in single mothers' responses to the positive aspects of being sole provider point to the importance of this role in their lives. Again, future work is called for to examine linkages between single mothers' provider attitudes, their psychological well-being, and family relationships.

Finally, to address fully how family roles are designated and played out within families we must begin to look at all family members, including children. Thus far, little research exists with regard to children's roles and behaviors in families. For example, does children's involvement in household chores vary across family contexts such as in dual-earner, single-earner, or single-parent families? Does involvement in household tasks within these different family contexts mean the same thing to children as they interpret their behavior in terms of a family role? Goodnow (1988) has begun to explore this issue and suggests that chores may be interpreted differently depending on the purpose and usefulness they serve in the family. Goodnow also suggests that the meaning that children assign to their work may hold implications for a number of developmental outcomes for children. Clearly, the role behaviors that children undertake in families have implications for mothers' and fathers' role behaviors. A complete examination of family roles must examine the role behaviors taken on by all members of the family system as well as assess the meaning that each member attaches to his or her behavior.

In closing, family researchers must begin to study family roles in all of their complexity, which includes assessing not only role behaviors but attitudes, commitments, and attachments to roles. The theory and research reviewed in the preceding discussion indicates that the same objective reality can be construed in a variety of ways, and it is each individual's construction of reality that is the critical element to assess when trying to understand work and family role behavior. The significance of the research discussed in these pages can be summed up quite eloquently in the (slightly modified) words of the Thomases (1928): "If [women and] men define their situation as real, they are real in their consequences" (p. 572).

REFERENCES

Ferber, M. A. (1982). Labor market participation of young, maried women: Causes and effects. *Journal of Marriage and the Family, 44*, 457–468.

Ferree, M. M. (1987). Family and job for working-class women: Gender and class systems seen from below. In N. Gerstel and H. E. Gross (Eds.), *Families and work*. Philadelphia: Temple University Press.

Ferree, M. M. (1988, November). *Negotiating household roles and responsibilities: Resistance, conflict, and change*. Paper presented at the annual meeting of the National Council on Family Relations, Philadelphia.

Ferree, M. M. (1990). Beyond separate spheres: Feminism and family research. *Journal of Marriage and the Family, 52*, 866–884.

French, J. R. P., Jr., & Raven, B. (1959). The bases of social power. In D. Cartwright (Ed.), *Studies in social power* (pp. 150–167). Ann Arbor: University of Michigan Institute for Social Research.

Freudiger, P. (1983). Life satisfaction among three categories of married women. *Journal of Marriage and the Family, 45*, 213–219.

Goffman, I. (1961). *Encounters: Two studies in the sociology of interaction*. New York: Bobbs-Merrill.

Goodnow, J. (1988). Children's household work: Its nature and functions. *Psychological Bulletin, 103*, 5–26.

Gove, W. R., & Geerken, M. (1977). The effect of children and employment on the mental health of married men and women. *Social Forces, 56*, 66–76.

Haas, L. (1986). Wives' orientation toward breadwinning: Sweden and the United States. *Journal of Family Issues, 7*(4), 358–381.

Henley, N. M. (1977). *Body politics: Power, sex, and nonverbal communication*. Englewood Cliffs, NJ: Prentice-Hall.

Hood, J. C. (1986). The provider role: Its meaning and measurement. *Journal of Marriage and the Family, 48*, 349–359.

Kessler, R. C. (1982). A disaggregation of the relationship between socioeconomic status and psychological distress. *American Sociological Review, 47*, 752–763.

Komarovsky, M. (1940). *The unemployed man and his family*. New York: Random House.

Linton, R. (1936). *The study of man*. New York: Appleton-Century-Crofts.

Lopata, H. Z. (1971). *Occupation: Housewife*. New York: Oxford University Press.

Mead, G. H. (1934). *Mind, self, and society*. Chicago: University of Chicago Press.

Nye, F. I., & Gecas, V. (1976). The role concept: Review and delineation. In F. I. Nye (Ed.), *Role structure and the analysis of the family* (pp. 3–14). Beverly Hills, CA: Sage.

Parsons, T. (1970). *Social structure and personality*. New York: Free Press.

Peplau, L. A. (1983). Roles and gender. In H. H. Kelley, E. Berscheid, A. Christensen, J. H. Harvey, T. L. Huston, G. Levinger, E. McClintock, L. A. Peplau, & D. R. Peterson (Eds.), *Close relationships* (pp. 220–264). New York: Freeman.

Perry-Jenkins, M., & Crouter, A. C. (1990). Men's provider-role attitudes: Implications for household work and marital satisfaction. *Journal of Family Issues, 11*(2), 136–156.

Perry-Jenkins, M., & Gilman-Hanz, S. (1991, November). *Life on the edge: Work and family strain in mother-only families.* Paper presented at the annual meeting of the National Council on Family Relations, Philadelphia.

Perry-Jenkins, M., Seery, B., & Crouter, A. C. (in press). Linkages between women's provider-role attitudes, women's psychological well-being and family relationships. *Psychology of Women Quarterly.*

Pleck, J. H. (1977). The work-family role system. *Social Problems, 24,* 417–427.

Pleck, J. H. (1985). *Working wives/working husbands.* Beverly Hills, CA: Sage.

Ross, C. E., Mirowsky, J., & Huber, J. (1983). Dividing work, sharing work, and in-between: Marriage patterns and depression. *American Sociological Review, 48,* 809–823.

Sherif, C. W. (1982). Needed concepts in the study of gender identity. *Psychology of Women Quarterly, 6,* 375–398.

Slocum, W. L., & Nye, F. I. (1976). Provider and housekeeper roles. In F. I. Nye (Ed.), *Role structure and analysis of the family* (pp. 81–100). Beverly Hills, CA: Sage.

Spitze, G. (1988). Women's employment and family relations: A review. *Journal of Marriage and the Family, 50,* 595–618.

Staines, G. L., Pottick, K. J., & Fudge, D. A. (1986). Wives' employment and husbands' attitudes toward work and life. *Journal of Applied Psychology, 71,*(1), 3–20.

Thomas, W. I., & Thomas, D. S. (1928). *The child in America.* New York: Alfred A. Knopf.

Thorne, B. (1982). Feminist rethinking of the family: An overview. In B. Thorne & M. Yalom (Eds.), *Rethinking the family* (pp. 1–24). New York: Longman.

Turner, R. H. (1970). *Family interaction.* New York: John Wiley.

Unger, R. K. (1979). *Female and male: Psychological perspectives.* New York: Harper and Row.

West, C., & Zimmerman, D. H. (1987). Doing gender. *Gender and Society, 1*(2), 125–151.

■ 13
Social Support for Working Families

Patricia O'Reilly and Felecia M. Briscoe

During most of this century the typical family has been portrayed as consisting of a father who was the breadwinner and left home each day for his job in the workplace and a mother who stayed home and took care of the children and managed the household responsibilities. Today, more than ever, the family does not fit this stereotype, with less than 7% of American families resembling this image (Braverman, 1989). By 1989, 56% of mothers with children under the age of 6 years and 64% of mothers with children under the age of 18 were in the paid labor force (U. S. Department of Labor, 1989a).

It is highly unlikely that women will decrease their participation in the work force. In fact, projections from the U. S. Department of Labor (1989a) indicate that even more women will enter the labor force and that two thirds of the new entries in the labor force between 1986 and the year 2000 will be women. Despite the pervasive myth that women in the workplace are taking jobs away from men, most women who are mothers work outside the home, as do fathers, out of the necessity to provide their families with a quality standard of living. As the U. S. economy has changed from one based in heavy industry to a service economy, salaries have dropped, relative to the cost of living, and both parents have had to work to increase the family income in order to maintain their standard of living. Additionally, the number of single-parent families are increasing and by far more likely to be headed by single women than by single men (Weitzman, 1985). The reality that began in the 1980s and is evident in the 1990s is that most children in this country will be reared in household in which their single parent or both parents work outside the home.

According to statistics provided by the U. S. Department of Labor (1989a), in 1985 nearly 30.6 million children under the age of 18 lived either in a single-parent household in which the parent worked outside the home or in a two-parent home in which both parents were employed outside the home. A total of 8.7 million of these children were under 6 years of age. Most recently, the fastest-growing group of women in the labor force has been mothers with children under the age of 1 year. During the 1990s the predictions are that 75% of women with school-age children will be in the labor force, compared with 40% in 1970 (U. S. Department of Labor, 1988). In addition, one in every two marriages ends in divorce, and the rate of married mothers heading families increased 356% between 1970 and 1983 (Sidel, 1986). Given the above statistics, societal support for parents, particularly mothers working outside the home, seems inperative.

In this chapter we examine the types of societal support available to parents who work outside the home. Governmental policies, business and corporate policies, and culturally sanctioned family practices are examined and found to provide little or no support for parents who work outside the family. The effects this lack of societal support has on the family and on working parents is discussed. Finally, the authors suggest some changes in today's societal policies regarding families that are needed by American families.

GOVERNMENTAL POLICIES CONCERNING EMPLOYED PARENTS

During the administrations of Presidents Reagan and Bush in the 1980s and early 1990s, there has been much political rhetoric about the sacredness of the American family. During this same period the number of American families with both parents or the single parent employed in the labor force has greatly increased. However, despite the political profamily rhetoric, it is clear that there has been little evidence of the legislative support required by families as a result of these societal changes. Kamerman (1980) has indicated that unlike 75 other industrialized nations, the United States does not have a government-sponsored family policy that provides some form of paid maternity benefits, parental leave, and subsidized child care.

Steiner (1981) suggests that, despite the wealth of profamily rhetoric, a national family policy is impossible in the United States because "the meaning of profamily cannot be agreed upon"(p. 26), and consequently "our intangible sentiments that are the foundations of strong family relations can neither be legislated nor set forth in executive order or court decree" (p. 215). A case in point is the most recent attempts by Congress to legislate a parental leave bill. President Bush vetoed the first bill in 1989 and the second one in 1991. One of the reasons President Bush gave for not signing the bill was that it would be too expensive for small businesses.

President Bush's rationale for vetoing the parental leave bill is unconvincing. Seventy-five other, much smaller industrialized nations with small businesses have federal policies that provide for parental leave (Kamerman, 1980). Furthermore, Kamerman and Kahn (1978) write: "there is a rich tradition of state programs and laws which may certainly be described as embodying relatively extensive and quite explicit family policy" (p. 432). Gerstel and Gross (1987) suggest that "many government initiatives bearing on economic well-being—including tax and social security plans, welfare and work-incentive programs, childcare and child support systems—are part of this 'family policy'" (p. 458).

An examination of federal family policies leads quickly to the conclusion that it is contradictory and inconsistent and is interpreted differently from administration to administration. Folbre (1987) trace the history of Aid to Families with Dependent Children (AFDC), which was initiated during the Depression of the 1930s to keep single mothers (mostly widows) with children out of the work force. Through subsequent administrations the federal government has vacillated on its eligibility requirements for AFDC. Currently, AFDC has been transformed into a vehicle that forces single mothers into the labor force, where they have had to work in the lowest-paying jobs. Since 1971, in order to receive AFDC, single mothers with children under the age of 6, ironically, have had to be in the labor force. The question who will watch the children or who will pay for the child care necessary for the single parent to find and keep a job has not been addressed.

A women's ability to become pregnant is still a barrier for her in the workplace, but at least discrimination based on pregnancy is illegal. Title VII of the 1964 Civil Rights Act, as amended in 1978, specifically states that women cannot be denied employment nor be terminated or forced to go on leave at some arbitrary point because of pregnancy. A woman cannot be penalized because of pregnancy in reinstatement rights, which include credit for previous service, accrued retirement benefits, and accumulated seniority (U. S. Department of Labor, 1988).

On March 21, 1991, the Supreme Court unanimously forbade employers from excluding fertile women from toxic workplaces in order to protect any children they *might* have in the future (*UAW v. Johnson Controls*, 89–1215). Approximately 25,000 women who worked in lead-contaminated workplaces had been threatened with unemployment prior to that decision (Moseley, 1991). Feminists hailed it as a victory for women in the workplace because, had the Supreme Court not ruled against the proposed policy—and the others that would be sure to follow—there would have been another barrier to women's access to and achieving upward mobility in the workplace. Interestingly enough, no such proposal was offered for men, who could also need protection for any children they might father in the future.

State parental leave policies vary widely. Only 8 of the 50 states have parental leave laws for people who do not work for the state (U. S. Department of labor, 1990). Furthermore, even the states that have parental leave laws allow only for a duration of less than 3 months.

An examination of U. S. governmental policies that support the working parent leads swiftly to the conclusion that there is little or no societal support for patents in the paid labor force despite the vigorous profamily rhetoric of the 1980s and 1990s.

CORPORATE AND BUSINESS FAMILY POLICIES

The discussion of employers' responsibilities to provide on-site child care, parental leave, job sharing, and flextime have been part of the rhetoric surrounding the entry of women into the workplace since the 1970s. Although there are companies that provide child care at the work site, subsidize employees' child care expenses, provide parental leave, or offer flextime work scheduling, the percentage of such companies is small. In 1987 there were only 700 businesses (200 companies and 500 hospitals) that offered on-site child care or subsidized employees' child care expenses (U. S. Department of Labor, 1989a). In 1987 only 25% of U. S. companies offered some paid personal leave time for patents to take care of sick children (U. S. Department of Labor, 1989b). Although there still is a lot of talk in the federal government and business, most of the outcomes fall short of meeting the needs of working parents.

Gerstel and Gross (1987) indicate that although the number of corporations with maternity policies have increased since the 1970s, most offer only short leave periods—less than 3 months—mostly unpaid. Paternity leaves sound supportive of family life, but in actuality the number of companies that have policies permitting fathers to take time off to parent a newborn or a newly adopted child are far fewer than those that offer paid maternity leave.

Rothman and Marks (1987), in their discussion of flextime work policies, make it clear that flextime has become a way of helping parents meet their dual obligations of work and family. In 1987, 37% of workers had a flextime option. Businesses that have flextime policies require workers to organize their work schedules around a core of hours during which they must be on the job, but they allow flexibility around starting or finishing times. At first feminists applauded the flextime policies, believing that they were supportive of the needs of working women. Now many feminists, such as Susan Faludi (1991), are reexamining flextime policies within a contest of their possibly being just another way to keep women responsible for both job and family.

Other options offered by U. S. companies to aid with child care include personal leave time, voluntary reduction of work time from 5% to 50% (with an accompanying reduction in pay and a loss of fringe benefits), and a flexiplace work program (U. S. Labor Department, 1989b). The companies that provide personal leave time grant their employees time off for personal reasons besides their own illness. Women are the paid workers who use personal leave time to take care of sick children (U. S. Labor Department, 1989b). Men who use personal leave time use it for personal development rather than as a means of juggling the responsibilities of job and family (U. S. Labor Department, 1989b). In 1987, 18% of workers (mostly female) had part-time work, with none of the fringe benefits including personal leave time (U. S. Labor Department, 1989b).

The workplace has changed little in response to the large numbers of mothers who have entered it. Employers have remained largely insensitive to the needs of the family and working parents. A review of the social policies available to support working parents indicates that, according to United States policymakers in the 1990s, the worlds of work and the family are separate and disparate. Most companies and businesses still maintain rigid work schedules, and both parents are forced to behave as though their family ceases to exist during work hours.

Although it would be erroneous to say that we have no family policy in this country, Gerstel and Gross (1987) pose the relevant question of whom it supports. They suggest that public policy actually reinforces the man's role as head of household and breadwinner while supporting woman's roles as homemaker and parent. Dorris (1991) also notes that the man's role as parent is actively discouraged. Gerstel and Gross (1987) report that some feminists believe that through public policy men's power in the family has been transferred to the state, thus allowing husbands and fathers to continue to have the ultimate financial power over women and children, whereas employed women continue to bear the responsibilities of caring for the children and managing the household.

Faludi (1991), in her discussion of the backlash against women's rights in this country points out that this backlash has created a terrible climate for women in the workplace: "Reaganomics, the recession, and the expansion of a minimum-wage service economy also helped, in no small measure, to slow and even undermine women's momentum in the job market" (p. 363). In the 1980s, the administrations of Presidents Reagan and Bush chose to ignore reports of the declining status of women in the workplace, and the media reinforced the issue by reporting "that women's only problem at work was that they would rather be home" (Faludi, 1991, p. 363). According to Faludi, during the Reagan administrations women who were single heads of households lost billions of dollars in child care assistance, medical aid, legal services, nutritional supplements, and subsidized housing (Faludi, 1991).

BEYOND POLICY

It is clear that it is no longer relevant to ask, should mothers work outside the home? They are doing to and will continue. It is unfortunate that most of the research in child development and psychology continue to support the oppressive myth of the centrality of motherhood. This myth implies that the presence or absence of the mother is the primary factor in a child's development. It is difficult to find literature in which the focus is on the father as having a central role in either the family system or the development of his children (Silverstein, 1991).

For nearly 20 years studies have been conducted that have searched for possible negative consequences of the employment of mothers and of substitute child care. In fact, many positive outcomes of maternal employment have emerged (Silverstein, 1991). For example, women who work outside the home report better physical and emotional health than do women who are full-time homemakers (Barnett & Baruch, 1987). And Hoffman (1986) found that positive effects for children of working mothers included less restrictive views of sex roles and more independence in taking care of their personal needs.

STRESSES EXPERIENCED BY WORKING PARENTS

Kamerman (1980) has addressed the stress that working parents experience in a society that is unresponsive to the needs of families. She found that in the absence of widely available government-sponsored family policy, families are forced to "package" (p. 36) child care. This packaging can include multiple kinds of arrangements, such as school, a relative's home, a spouse, and baby-sitters. The stress involved in keeping these arrangements going usually falls on women, who have the major responsibility for child care and household management.

Employed mothers most often suffer from multiple role stress. Even though more mothers are now employed outside the home, fathers have not significantly increased their participation in child care and household responsibilities (Hochschild, 1989, Kamerman, 1980). Hochschild (1989), in her study of 50 families, reported that this unequal sharing of family management was the single most important cause of marital conflict. In contrast, Ross and Mirowsky (1987) found that accessible child care and a husband's willingness to share responsibilities were directly related to decreasing role stress for working mothers.

The single most pervasive stress factor in the lives of women and children in this country is poverty. Weitzman (1985) predicts that during the 1990s the majority of children in the United States will experience life in a single-parent household, 90% of which are headed by women. The correlation between economic adversity and single-parent families has been well articulated (Sidel, 1986; Stipek & McCroskey, 1989).

Hochschild (1989) contends that U. S. society has responded to the mass entrance of women into the work force with the cultural myth of the "supermom" rather than with changes that would support the needs of children with working parents. Hochschild and others (Pogrebin, 1983; Silverstein, 1987) are clear about the reality behind this romantic image of the svelte, attractively dressed young woman holding baby in one hand and briefcase in the other. According to these authors, this reality includes the stress that comes with working two jobs, the resentment that may be directed toward a husband who does not share child care and household responsibilities, and the overall fact that it is impossible to achieve super-human goals. The image of the supermom implies that success or failure is dependent on personal competence rather than on the absence of a social network that would require public support (Silverstein, 1991).

WHERE DO WE GO FROM HERE?

It's simple to suggest that the workplace has to change and that fathers have to share responsibilities in child care and household management. However, the issues are more complicated when one begins to examine them within a societal context.

The gap between men's and women's wages is far from a thing of the past. In 1986 the gap seemed to be narrowing. Popular media reported that women were making 70 cents to a man's dollar, but this statistic was based on weekly rather than yearly salaries and was improperly inflated (Faludi, 1991) . Faludi (1991) reports that at the end of 1986, when the U. S. Census Bureau calculated the gender pay gap based on yearly wages, women earned 64 cents, rather than 70 cents, to a man's dollar. However, by 1988 even this small gain was lost by many women. In 1988 a college-educated white woman as well as black women were still making the same 1950s 59 cents to a male counterpart's dollar (Faludi, 1991). According to Faludi, older working women, who had actually made 61 cents to a man's dollar in 1968, were down to 58 cents in 1986. Additionally, by 1988, Hispanic women found their wages backsliding: they were making only 54 cents to a white man's dollar (Faludi, 1991).

The pay gap has been getting worse for women in managerial positions; by 1989, when the average male manager receive a 4% pay increase, his female counterpart received none. The gap was also increasing in the very occupations that had attracted large numbers of women in the 1980s, including the service industry: food preparation, waiting tables, and cleaning services (Faludi, 1991).

Faludi (1991) also reports that although occupational gender segregation declined in the 1970s, it stalled in the 1980s. A gender-segregated work force was one of the main reasons that in 1986 more women were taking home poverty wages than in 1973. During this same period, large numbers of women were pouring into female ghetto jobs, which included, in addition to the jobs listed above, typing, secretarial, and receptionist positions. Black women have been increasingly segregated into traditional female jobs, including teaching, nursing, social work, and secretarial positions (Faludi, 1991). From 1976 to 1986 the lowest rungs on the federal civil service ladder went from 67% female to 71% female (Faludi, 1991). Women breaking into the blue-collar job ranks also made no progress during the 1980s. By 1988 the few women who had made it into the trades were shrinking in the job categories of carpenters, electricians, plumbers, large-equipment operators, and automobile mechanics (Faludi, 1991).

These statistics are in themselves depressing, but it is also important to note that the workplace and the environment it provides for women is basically hostile. Despite all of the legislation concerning sex equity in the workplace, reported sex discrimination and sexual harassment reached all-time highs during the years of President Reagan's administration. Faludi (1991) reports that "annual charges of sexual harassment climbed 70 percent between 1981 and 1989" (p. 368). Perhaps the number of sexual discrimination cases increased because women felt they had some legal recourse, but nevertheless the increasing numbers indicate that sexual harassment is one of the biggest stressors with which working women have to cope, and currently there is nothing to suggest that it is lessening in the 90s.

The workplace remains basically the same as it always has been: an environment developed by and for competitive men that incorporates their values of the battlefield and continue to be an environment in which family issues are invisible. Currently, there is nothing in this society to make us believe that employers will drastically change the workplace into one more cognizant of the needs of working parents of both genders. As indicated earlier, the business policies and practices that do support women and men as parents with family concerns are few and vanishing.

In the overall picture it is difficult to see how so many American government officials and corporations can continue to give lip service to their support of the family. Seventy-five percent of American businesses by their antifamily work policies, are in the forefront of destroying the family, the very institution many say they are supporting. Only 25% of companies actively enact workplace policies that are profamily (U. S. Department of Labor, 1989b). One example is the shoe company Stride Rite, which has provided on-site day care for workers' children since the 1960s. Until government, business, and industry in the United States begin to view women as fully competent workers and welcome their contributions and skills, the workplace will remain hostile to women. Until American business and industry see both men and women as parents, both of whom have family responsibilities, workplace policies that support families will continue to be limited, and workplace scheduling will remain rigid and inflexible.

Silverstein (1991) rightly recommends that research in psychology and child development be done with different assumptions. These assumptions should include the importance of the father's role in child rearing and acknowledgment that his parenting role is central to the functioning of the family system. She also suggests that much more research needs to be done in examining the outcomes of substitute child care. Further research, she predicts, will help to dispel the oppressive myth of the mother who is on call for her family 24 hours a day and without whose presence the family will disintegrate and children's development will not flourish. Pogrebin (1980) makes a strong case for "parity parenthood" (p. 118). She insists that what is necessary for parity parenting is an overhaul of the power structure in the marriage and "the distribution of housework and child care duties, the job-family priorities of both partners, and eventually, the social system and labor market in which the family functions" (pp. 120–121).

It is clear that the dominant culture has much to lose *and* much to gain with these changes. Those with power have been successful for generations in having women rear the children and manage family responsibilities thereby leaving them free to pursue their interests on the battlefield or in the corporation. At the same time this power to abnegate their responsibilities as a parents has resulted in a loss in feeling connected with the former generation (a missing father) and the future generation (their own children) (Chodorow, 1978; Rubin, 1983). Such a loss of human connection with other human beings by those in power has resulted in a value system in our society that is primarily hierarchical, individualistic, and viciously competitive. This value system is evident in the workplace and in the government's reluctance to sponsor laws that create a working environment that is hospitable to parents.

Female and male union members who believe that their family responsibilities are as important as their work responsibilities need to enjoin their unions to provide family benefits such as parental leave and paid parental leave and child care in contract negotiations. Women and men also need to join with groups like the National Organization for Women (NOW) that are actively lobbying at the federal and state levels for paid parental leave. Legislators need to hear from the people whose lives are negatively affected by the lack of supportive family policies and other social support systems for families. We are a nation whose administration constantly speaks about the family and family values. The Bush administration and those that follow must become aware of real family needs rather than the mythical , mother-at-home types of families portrayed by the media. Government needs to begin developing legislation to support rather than to deprive and mistreat one of our society's most important institutions, the family. Families are endangered because legislators and corporate policymakers are so out of touch with the reality of the American family and how it functions in the 1990s.

REFERENCES

Barnett, R. C., & Baruch, G. K. (1987). Social roles, gender and psychological distress. In R. C. Barnett, L. Biener, & G. K. Baruch (Eds.), *Gender and stress* (pp. 122–143). New York: Free Press.

Barverman, L. B. (1989). Beyond the myth of motherhood. In M. McGoldrick, C. M. Anderson, & F. Walsh (Eds.), *Women and families* (pp. 227–243). New York: Free Press.

Chodorow, N. (1978). *The reproduction of mothering: Psychoanalysis and the sociology of gender.* Berkeley: University of California Press.

Dorris, M. (1991, September). What men are missing. *Vogue*, p. 510.

Faludi, S. (1991). *Backlash: The undeclared war against American women.* New York: Crown.

Folbre, N. (1987). The pauperization of motherhood: patriarchy and public policy in the United States. In N. Gerstel & H. Gross (Eds.), *Family and work* (pp. 491–511). Philadelphia: Temple University Press.

Gerstel, N., & Gross, H. (1987). *Families and work.* Philadelphia: Temple University Press.

Hochschild, A. (1989). *The second shift.* New York: Viking.

Hoffman, L. W. (1986). Work, family, and the child. In M. S. Pollak & R. O. Perloff (Eds.), *Psychology and work: Productive change and employment* (pp. 173–220). Washington, DC: American Psychological Association.

Hoffman, L. W. (1989) Effects of maternal employment in the two-parent family. *American Psychologist, 44,* 283–292.

Kamerman, J. B. (1980). *Maternity and parental benefits and leaves: An international review* (Impact on Policy Series, Monograph No. 1). New York: Columbia University, Center for the Social Sciences.

Kamerman, S. B., & Kahn, A. J. (Eds.). (1978). *Family policy, government and families in fourteen countries*. New York: Columbia University Press.

Moseley, G. (1991, June). Our babies ourselves. *Business and Health*, pp. 31–34.

Pogrebin, L. C. (1980). *Growing up free*. New York: McGraw-Hill.

Pogrebin, L. C. (1983). *Family polities: Love and power on an intimate frontier*. New York: McGraw-Hill.

Ross, C. E., & Mirowsky, J. (1987). Child care and emotional adjustment to wives' employment. *Journal of Health and Social Behavior, 29*, 127–138.

Rothman, S. M., & Marks, E. M. (1987). Adjusting work and family policy. In N. Gerstel & H. Gross (Eds.), *Family and work* (pp. 469–477). Philadelphia: Temple University Press.

Rubin, L. (1983). *Intimate strangers*. New York: Harper & Row.

Sidel, R. (1986). *Women and children last*. New York: Penguin Books.

Silverstein, L. (1987, February). *Balancing babies and briefcases: The dilemma of working parents*. Paper presented at the Continuing Education Seminar of the Brooklyn Friends School, Brooklyn, NY.

Silverstein, L. (1991). Transforming the debate about child care and maternal employment. *American Psychologist, 46*, 1025–1103.

Steiner, G. (1981). *The futility of family policy*. Washington, DC: Brookings Institution.

Stipek, D., & McCroskey, J. (1989). Government and workplace policy for parents. *American Psychologist, 44*, 416–423.

U. S. Department of Labor, Women's Bureau. (1988). *A working woman's guide to her job rights*. Washington, DC: U. S. Government Printing Office.

U. S. Department of Labor, Women's Bureau. (1989a). *Employers and child care: Benefiting work and family*. Washington, DC: U. S. Government Printing Office.

U. S. Department of Labor, Women's Bureau. (1989b). *Work and family resource kit*. Washington, DC: U. S. government Printing Office.

U. S. Department of Labor, Women's Bureau. (1990). *State maternity/parental leave laws*. Washington, DC: U. S. Government Printing Office.

Weitzman, L. (1985). *The divorce revolution*. New York: Free Press.

■ Concluding Thoughts

Judith Frankel

The purpose of this book is to establish the ground rules for a new tradition of American motherhood. Women today are exercising their options to experience different life-styles—some through choice, some through necessity. The major shift in their lives has been the increase in the number of employed women. Describing the consequences of this change over the past 30 years was the form used by this book to evaluate the present situation of families of employed mothers.

The different chapters in the book describe the extent of maternal employment, its effect on various family members, the theoretical and practical implications of this situation for a variety of families from different walks of life, and the support families receive (or do not receive) from society and government.

Three major themes emerged from this extensive examination of the literature on the subject. The first theme is the variety of family structures under which employed mothers live. There are as many different ways of being a family of an employed mother as one can imagine. And although each form is unique, with its own aura, its own structure and style of living out that structure, there are commonalities for all the families.

The second theme encompasses the overriding commonality for all families of employed mothers: the necessity for child care arrangements and the difficulties most families experience in pursuing this goal. A sub-issue under this theme is the manner in which daily living chores are handled, still most often by the mothers and still with difficulty. Although this situation may be slowly changing, the changes are small.

The third theme springs from the second. The social supports for families of employed mothers are slim. Child care and housework are a challenge for these families, a challenge they are not getting much assistance in meeting.

These themes lead me into a personal conclusion, one that has so aptly been stated by Jean Baker Miller (1986):

> If we as a human community want children, how does the total society propose to provide for them in such a way that women do not have to suffer or forfeit other forms of participation and power? How does society propose to organize so that men can benefit from equal participation in child care? (p. 128)

Legislation, government intervention, and the support of industry, although necessary, are not sufficient to make maternal employment a truly workable situation. For the new tradition of motherhood to obtain and reach fulfillment, a total redefinition of family and family roles must be integrated into societal consciousness. All members of the family must be responsible for all family functions. Women must no longer be the respository of all domestic and nurturing responsibilities. Fathers, living with their children or in separate arrangements, must take their place as responsible parents. In order for them to do so, all of the rules of industry and society must change to reward both male and female workers for pursuing the interests and responsibilities of family.

I am aware that this conclusion is much more far-reaching in continuing to suggest changes that have thus far turned out to be sporadic at best and cosmetic at worst. The material presented in this book demands major change in order to progress into the 21st century. I foresee these changes coming.

REFERENCE

Miller, J. B. (1986). *Toward a new psychology of women.* Boston: Beacon Press.

Index

⑤ *Springer Publishing Company*

ADOLESCENT ASSERTIVENESS AND SOCIAL SKILLS: A CLINICAL HANDBOOK

Iris G. Fodor, PhD, Editor

A comprehensive new book highlighting relevant areas of this type of work with adolescents. Actually spanning both clinical and theoretical concerns, Dr. Fodor and her contributors begin with an introductory overview of social skills training and assertiveness, followed by a section focusing on Latin-, Afro-, and Asian-American adolescents. Subsequent sections address special populations such as the physically disabled, as well as special programs in schools.

Contents

1992   296pp   0-8261-7490-6   *hardcover*

$] *Springer Publishing Company*

FATHERHOOD AND FAMILIES IN CULTURAL CONTEXT

Frederick W. Bozett, RN, DNS, and
Shirley M.H. Hanson, RN, PhD, Editors

Defining "culture" in its broadest sense, this multidisciplinary volume synthesizes contemporary research and theories about males as parents—and the multiple cultural factors influencing their socialization and enactment of the family role. Foreword by Michael E. Lamb.

Contents

(Volume 6 in the Springer Series: Focus on Men)
1991 290pp 0-8261-6570-2 hardcover